K

WORKING TOGETHER

WORKING TOGETHER

How Workplace Bonds Strengthen a Diverse Democracy

CYNTHIA ESTLUND

UNIVERSITY PRESS

2003

OXFORD
UNIVERSITY PRESS

Oxford   New York
Auckland   Bangkok   Buenos Aires   Cape Town   Chennai
Dar es Salaam   Delhi   Hong Kong   Istanbul   Karachi   Kolkata
Kuala Lumpur   Madrid   Melbourne   Mexico City   Mumbai   Nairobi
São Paulo   Shanghai   Taipei   Tokyo   Toronto

Copyright © 2003 by Oxford University Press, Inc.

Published by Oxford University Press, Inc.,
198 Madison Avenue, New York, New York 10016

www.oup.com

Oxford is a registered trademark of Oxford University Press

Library of Congress Cataloging-in-Publication Data
Estlund, Cynthia.
Working together: how workplace bonds strengthen a diverse democracy
/ by Cynthia Estlund.
p. cm.
Includes bibliographical references and index.
ISBN 0-19-515828-8
1. Diversity in the workplace—United States.   2. Discrimination in
employment—United States.   3. Discrimination in employment—Law and
legislation—United States.   4. Industrial relations—United States.   5.
Organizational behavior—United States.   6. Personnel management—United
States.   7. Labor laws and legislation—United States.   I. Title.
HF5549.5.M5 E845 2003
331.11'43'0973—dc21   2002156305

1   3   5   7   9   8   6   4   2

Printed in the United States of America
on acid-free paper

FOR SAM, JESSICA, AND LUCAS

PREFACE

This book is about the significance of ordinary workplace conversations and interactions—especially conversations and interactions among heterogeneous groups of co-workers—to democratic life. Drawing on an eclectic mix of empirical research and social and political theory, I aim to elucidate the central and distinctive role of workplace relations and of the law regulating the workplace, within what is often called "civil society."

The germ of this book was planted several years ago when I took on the vexing problem of discriminatory workplace harassment and freedom of expression. I saw a great deal at stake on both sides of what was at that point a rather polarized debate. On one side, it was clear that harassment—including some purely verbal harassment by co-workers with no supervisory authority over the target—is a potent mechanism for maintaining inequality and segregation in the workplace. The ban on discriminatory harassment is a crucial and necessary part of the law's commitment to workplace equality on the basis of race and sex in particular. On the other side, however, the law's tendency to induce employers to censor and monitor employees' informal interactions raised serious concerns not only about employees' freedom of speech but about their freedom of interaction more generally.

In the heated face-off in the law reviews between the partisans of workplace equality and the libertarian partisans of free speech, something was missing. I had explored elsewhere the importance of employee speech in and about the workplace and the value of workplace conversations in democratic society. Coming to the problem, as I did, from a labor law background made me especially wary of a doctrine that effectively compelled employers to use their economic power over employees to regulate co-worker interactions. Especially striking to me was the contrast between the vision underlying this doctrine, in which employers were required to regulate and discipline some employees in the interest of others, and the New Deal vision of labor relations, in which employers were to be constrained from regulating co-worker interactions in the interest of employees' freedom to discuss shared interests and undertake collective action in support of those interests.

Working through that problem led me to an initial account of the distinctive nature of the workplace community in the post–Civil Rights Act era and the special significance of workplace conversations and sociability. That led me to the concept of "public discourse" and from there to modern ideas about civil society, social capital, and associational life generally. All these constructs seek to capture dimensions of social life outside of formal politics that crucially shape political discourse and governance in modern democratic society. My continuing dissatisfaction with the treatment—or, more often, the neglect—of the workplace in these accounts led eventually to this book.

One more autobiographical influence on this project bears noting. During my time at the University of Texas School of Law, the Hopwood litigation challenging the legality of our affirmative action program was an absorbing topic of discussion (especially in my house, as my husband and colleague Sam Issacharoff was centrally involved in the legal defense of the Law School). The litigation focused our attention on precisely what had been achieved through affirmative action, and on what was going to be lost when the courts' invalidation of the program led initially to a virtual bleaching of the student body. What seemed most important to me was missing in the conventional understandings of what was at stake in the survival of affirmative action. It was not just about making up for past injustice (though there was plenty of that to make up for in Texas); nor was it just about the diversity of views and experiences that the affirmative action program had brought into the classroom (though there was plenty of that, too). What we had gained through affirmative action, and were losing with its demise, was a racially and ethnically *integrated* student body, even integrated study groups and groups of friends, which had produced an integrated body of young alumni and the germ of an integrated legal profession in Texas. What was mostly missing from the leading legal arguments in favor of affirmative action— both in higher education and in the workplace—was the importance of forming common experiences, amicable relationships, ties of familiarity and shared loyalty across racial lines that still divide the society.

I first explored some of the themes and claims developed here in a series of law review articles. Several of those articles contain more than glimmers of these themes: *Freedom of Speech in the Workplace and the Problem of Discriminatory Harassment*, 75 TEXAS LAW REVIEW 687 (1997), *The Workplace in a Racially Diverse Society: Preliminary Thoughts on the Role of Labor and Employment Law*, 1 UNIVERSITY OF PENNSYLVANIA JOURNAL OF LABOR & EMPLOYMENT LAW 49 (1998), *The Changing Workplace as a Locus of Integration in a Diverse Society*, 2000 COLUMBIA BUSINESS LAW REVIEW 331 (2000), and especially *Working Together: The Workplace, Civil Society, and the Law*, 89 GEORGETOWN LAW JOURNAL 1 (2000). But I have found that one virtue, perhaps the sole virtue, of the slow emergence of this book is that my understanding of what happens in the workplace—and how it relates to other arenas of social life—has continued to evolve. As a result, there is much that is new (and improved) in this book. In fact, I believe that not a single paragraph survives untouched from those earlier publications.

In part that is due to the exceptional editorial guidance of Dedi Felman at Oxford University Press. She brought the idea of doing this book to me before I brought it to her. Since then she has been an extraordinarily perceptive and engaged editor, keeping the big picture in focus even when I suffered from the myopia of authorship, and consistently pushing me in productive directions. Her clearheaded perception of what was distinctive about my argument and her commitment to its reaching a broader audience happily prevailed over my own impatience to be done with it and helped to produce a much better book.

During the long gestation period of this book I have accumulated many other debts as well. When I began working through these ideas, I was happily ensconced at the University of Texas School of Law, from which I received valuable research support. I owe a great deal to my colleagues there and miss them still. In connection with this particular project, I acknowledge especially the insightful contributions of my Texas colleagues Willy Forbath, Jack Getman, Doug Laycock, and Sandy Levinson. Among them, I owe a special debt to Jack Getman. As my labor law teacher at Yale Law School twenty-two years ago, he first encouraged my interest in the intersection of free speech and labor law. As my colleague, running companion, co-teacher, and constant interlocutor at Texas, he pushed me to reckon with the implications of harassment law for worker solidarity and to recognize the capacity of workers to work through conflicts among themselves through daily interactions and collective institutions.

I completed the *Working Together* article and wrote the book after moving to Columbia Law School. There I found a stimulating and generous group of colleagues, many of them with interests, ideas, and prodigious knowledge that intersected with this project. My work on this book benefited especially from conversations with Mark Barenberg, Vince Blasi, Mike Dorf, Ariela Dubler, Jack Greenberg, Chuck Sabel, Carol Sanger, Susan Sturm, Kendall Thomas, and John Witt.

At Columbia I also found terrific research assistants. For their help on the *Working Together* article, much of which has been incorporated into this book, I would like to thank Xi Chen, Laurence Denny, Latrice Geory, Jay Hewlin, Jason Karlinski, Tiffany Martin, Brian Nagatani, Lianne Pinchuk, and Alexander Roth. For their help with the additional research that went into this book, I would like to thank Emma Dewald, Daniel Suleiman, Pankaj Venugopal, and especially David Ryan.

Some of the most helpful criticisms, comments, and suggestions have come from outside my home institutions (and my home). Over the years I presented pieces of this work at several law schools, including Boston University, Cornell, Minnesota, Notre Dame, NYU, Roger Williams, UCLA, and USC. The responses were encouraging, engaging, skeptical, and invariably helpful. Over the years I have also prevailed upon the generosity of many other readers, sometimes trading on the diffuse currency of friendship (or family), sometimes with no claim but common participation in the scholarly enterprise. I would especially like to acknowledge the thoughtful comments of Regina Austin, Harry Boyte, Xavier de Souza Briggs, Jim Brudney, the late David Charny, Dave Estlund, Mitu Gulati, Larry Kramer, Deborah Malamud, Jason Mazzone, Rick Pildes, William Julius Wilson, and Mark Yudof.

From the very beginning, I have had the good fortune of living with a particularly thoughtful and supportive colleague, Sam Issacharoff. No one is happier than he is to have this book out of my hands and into the world, and few have done more to help bring that about. Finally, I would like to thank our wonderful children Jessica and Lucas. During my labors on this project, they have moved from Austin, Texas, to New York City, grown from children to teenagers, and acquired a sometimes startling wisdom and wit about the world without driving me crazy or pushing me away. No parent could ask for more.

CONTENTS

WORKING TOGETHER

INTRODUCTION

Working Together

Marvlieu Hall, a college-educated African-American woman in her thirties, lives with her family in a nearly all-black neighborhood of Queens in New York City. She attends an all-black church at which her husband is the pastor, and she is active in Jack & Jill, an African-American social organization. Joan Dauria, a white woman of Greek descent, lived until recently in Westport, Connecticut, an overwhelmingly white suburb. Her family, her neighborhood, her church congregation, and her social circle in Westport is entirely white. It is hard to see how the daily lives of Marvlieu and Joan would ever intersect. But they did. Marvlieu and Joan met several years ago at work and became good friends. Their friendship began in the hours they spent together each working day. But it did not end there. Although both have changed jobs and Joan has moved across the country, she and Marvlieu still visit each other and talk regularly.

The experiences of Marvlieu and her friend Joan are not quite typical, but they are not altogether exceptional, either. In discussions about the workplace, one generally finds ready and widespread assent to two heartening propositions: First, the typical workplace is a veritable hotbed of sociability and cooperation, of constructive and mostly friendly interactions among co-workers day after day, and often year after year. Second, of all the places where adults interact with others, the workplace is likely to be the most demographically diverse. In a society that is still largely segregated, the workplace is where working adults are most likely to associate regularly with someone of another race.

What happens inside the workplace, and what *can* happen there, responds simultaneously to two powerful but usually separate strains of contemporary social criticism in the United States. American society is suffering both from declining levels of social and civic engagement, and from the lasting legacy of slavery in the form of racial division and segregation. We are less connected to our neighbors than we were fifty years ago, while our neighborhoods—as well as our families, schools, congregations, and voluntary associations—continue to be largely segregated along racial lines, at least along the black–white divide. We enjoy less trust, cooperation, sociability, and sense of community overall; yet whatever sense of community we do experience is still racially skewed and divided.

There is, to be sure, debate over these claims: Has there really been a significant decline in civic and social engagement, or just in particular traditional forms of engagement? Has progress toward racial equality and integration been steady and significant, or has it been discouragingly slow and halting? But if these questions themselves are important to the vitality of democratic life, then we should be looking for answers in the workplace. For workplaces are, generally speaking, both more sociable and cooperative and more integrated than most places where adults spend time.

Together, these two propositions—the convergence of regular and constructive interaction and a degree of demographic diversity—suggest that what happens in the workplace is extraordinarily important in a diverse democratic society, and should be explored and cultivated. But these two propositions are especially striking when juxtaposed to some other widely accepted propositions about human interaction at work: The workplace is hardly a domain of freedom, equality, or democracy. Most people have little choice about whether to work and, once on the job, little choice about with whom they work on a daily basis. Interaction among co-workers is often compelled by managers; it is constrained by rules and job duties and the threat of discipline or discharge; and it all takes place within a context of economic power and necessity if not coercion. Moreover, the workplace is subject to a staggering array of governmental regulations governing many aspects of the composition, organization, and treatment of the workforce.

The involuntariness of workplace associations—the economic compulsion to work, the compulsion of managerial authority within the workplace, and the external compulsion of law—seems to cast a shadow over the relations that form there and is widely held to disqualify the workplace from the celebrated domain of civil society. The boundaries of civil society are rather indistinct, but they are generally drawn to encompass those aspects of social life that are outside of formal political structures of governance but that are crucial to the vitality of democratic politics. And those boundaries are generally drawn to exclude the instrumentalities of both the state and the market; both public sector and private sector workplaces fall outside most modern maps of civil society. The workplace is perhaps the antithesis of the "voluntary associations" that are at the center of those accounts.

But the very involuntariness of interactions within the workplace turns out to play a curiously constructive role in making possible the extraordinary convergence of close and regular interaction and a relatively high degree of demographic diversity. Both the external law governing workplaces and the constraints that operate within workplaces help to make the often-troubled project of racial integration work relatively well there. People can be forced to get along—not without friction, but with surprising success.

One would not wish for all of society to be run on such principles. There are many arenas—the family, religious congregations, many voluntary groups—in which we cannot or do not want to force people to associate with others whom they prefer to avoid. There are other arenas—especially neighborhoods—in which the law faces severe practical limits on its capacity to combat discriminatory decisions and preferences. In all these areas, there is ambivalence on both—or all—sides of the color line about the project of integration. But we can and do compel racial integration in the workplace, and we do so with relatively little social upheaval or "white flight." That is partly because the process of "working together" both depends on and helps to produce relatively constructive intergroup relations. In other words, to the extent that racial and ethnic diversity becomes an inescapable fact of life for employers—and the law can help to make it so—then workers and managers, and the psychology and economics of workplace relationships, will do much of the work of making those relationships constructive and even amicable.

This book explores the paradoxical nature and the paramount importance of workplace bonds in a diverse democratic society. It stakes a claim for the public and political value of the millions of conversations that take place every day among co-workers. And it argues that the law of the workplace has played a crucial part, and could play an even more effective part in the future, in realizing the good that can come out of the experience of working together. For it may be in those places where we are forced to get along and get things done together, and not where we choose to do so, that we have the best chance of meeting some of the most profound challenges facing American society.

Bowling Alone But Working Together: Connectedness in the Workplace

The importance of cooperative social bonds among citizens is underscored by recent debates over America's "declining social capital."[1] For Professor Robert Putnam, the forlorn image of the solitary bowler is emblematic of a disturbing erosion of civic engagement. Echoing Tocqueville, Putnam argues that the vitality and efficacy of democratic political institutions depends crucially upon the society's store of "social capital"—"networks, norms, and trust . . . that enable participants to act together more effectively to pursue shared objectives."[2] And it is said to be largely through participation in voluntary clubs, associations such as the PTA, fraternal and professional organizations, and even bowling leagues that citizens develop these social ties. As Americans are devoting progressively less time and energy to these civic associations, as well as to informal socializing, the store of social capital in American society is eroding.

The "bowling alone" thesis has fueled a vigorous debate among scholars and social commentators about the state of civil society, the role of associational life in a democracy, and the prescription for civic renewal.[3] Much in the debate turns on which social networks count as sources of social capital. In particular, it matters a great deal whether the workplace, which is demanding more rather than less of people's time, is viewed as an important source of connectedness. Putnam's leading account of social capital building offers a qualified "yes," but his misgivings about the quality and changing nature of workplace ties (along with the paucity of longitudinal data about those ties) place them at the margins of the social capital map.[4] The workplace is more marginalized in—even excluded from—contemporary accounts of the domain of public discourse. When they take up at all the question of where public discourse occurs, those accounts identify voluntary associations, the communications media, and the "public forum" where citizens debate the issues of the day. "The workplace is for work," it is said, not for public debate and deliberation.

The marginalization or omission of the workplace in these accounts is not a simple oversight. It reflects a widespread conception of the boundaries of "civil society." The concept of civil society has had several incarnations.[5] But most contemporary definitions exclude not only the state but also the market and its constituent institutions, pervaded as they are by instrumental and economic motives and organizing principles.[6] Both public sector and private sector workplaces—as creatures of the state and the market, respectively—are thereby left out of the picture. In these accounts, voluntary associations are at the center of civil society and ordinary workplaces are at best peripheral.[7]

Yet something seems amiss with this account. For we may be bowling alone, but we are working together. Indeed, by some reckonings, we are working together more than ever before.[8] Most adults spend a good part of their waking hours at work—much more time than they spend in voluntary clubs and organizations.[9] They spend a great deal of that time interacting with co-workers. Co-workers routinely interact and cooperate closely in carrying out their jobs. They socialize at the beginning and end of the workday, during breaks, in locker rooms and restrooms, and at the proverbial water cooler. Some of what they talk about is work, and some of it is about the terms and conditions of work that they share with each other—the stingy health plan, the anticipated bonuses, the speed-up of production, rumored layoffs. But co-workers also talk about current events, sports and popular culture, family, and other stuff of daily life. They talk about things that are important to them more often with co-workers than with anyone else outside of their families.[10]

Over weeks, months, or years of working together, co-workers learn about each others' lives and develop feelings of affection, empathy, sympathy, and loyalty for each other. They often become friends. They also experience friction and conflict, even anger and resentment. But, with a paycheck and everything else that is at stake in a job, they often find ways to work through or around conflicts and to get the job done in spite of personal differences. The bottom line is that more people say they get "a real sense of belonging" among their co-workers than among any group other than family or friends—more than among neighbors, more than among fellow members of religious congregations or clubs.[11]

To speak of the "workplace" obviously glosses over enormous differences among workplaces. Workplaces come in many shapes and sizes, and they vary enormously along precisely the dimensions that matter here. Nonetheless, this can surely be said: The workplace is the single most important site of cooperative interaction and sociability among adult citizens outside the family. The sheer amount of sociability and cooperation that takes place every day in workplaces should place them at the center of any account of what holds a complex, modern democratic society together. Workplace associations, and the cooperation, sociability, and solidarity that they foster, do not take the place of the voluntary associations celebrated by Putnam and other proponents of civil society. The connections made there are shaped by distinctive features of the workplace, and they play a distinctive role in a democratic society. But no account of civil society or of associational life is complete without a thorough reckoning with the nature and significance of ties among co workers.

Living Apart But Working Together: Integration in the Workplace

The significance of those ties begins to take further shape if we put faces on the co-workers who cooperate and communicate and commiserate with each other. They are not the same people we meet in our homes, in our neighborhoods, or, often, in our religious congregations and voluntary associations. Co-workers come not only from different families and different neighborhoods but often from different cultural, religious, racial, and ethnic backgrounds. For the workplace, in part as a result of the civil rights laws, is *comparatively* integrated; it is the single most significant site of regular and ongoing interaction among adult citizens of different racial and ethnic identities, and especially among black and white citizens.

There is a good deal of controversy over how sharply race divides American society.[12] On the one hand, since the 1960s, formal segregation has been banished, and major social institutions have been at least partially integrated. During that period, social surveys chronicle dramatic progress in black and especially white attitudes toward each other and toward integration. Expressed opposition toward interracial romance and marriage—a bellwether of conscious racial attitudes—has dramatically declined.[13] Self-reported friendships between black and white Americans are far more common than they were a few decades ago. In one survey, for example, the percentage of respondents who reported having a "friend" of the other race rose from 62 percent to 82 percent among blacks from

1964 to 1989, and from 18 percent to 66 percent among whites.[14] Yet one wonders where those friendships originate; for, in spite of the dismantling of official barriers to integration, American society is still, to a considerable degree, spatially divided along racial lines, particularly between black and white citizens. I focus initially on this particular divide because it tends to be both the most troubled and the best documented in American society.

Let us begin where people live. Perhaps least surprisingly, racially mixed families, though far more common than they once were, are still the exception.[15] The increasing numbers of progeny of racially mixed marriages are shaking up our ideas and our policies regarding racial identity, but they are not yet breaking down racial divisions altogether. Neighborhoods are more racially mixed than they were thirty years ago; yet even in metropolitan areas that are racially heterogeneous, most citizens still live in neighborhoods occupied predominantly, if not overwhelmingly, by people of their own race.[16] The persistence of residential segregation clearly limits the development of interracial social ties.[17] Moreover, even people who live in racially mixed neighborhoods tend to have little contact with their different-race neighbors.[18]

Things do not look much different in the public schools—the first large-scale laboratory of legal desegregation. Nearly fifty years after *Brown v. Board of Education*, and after a tumultuous generation of court-ordered busing, the demographic makeup of public schools—where parents as well as children form social networks—still tends to track that of their neighborhoods.[19] Most public schools, even in metropolitan areas with substantial black populations, are still attended predominantly by children of one race, and it seems likely that school segregation will increase as the courts withdraw from the business of school desegregation.[20]

What about the voluntary associations that figure so prominently in most accounts of civil society? Religious congregations—one important kind of association—are generally quite homogeneous: the vast majority of black and white church- and synagogue-goers report that all or nearly all of their congregation is of their own race.[21] Other voluntary associations appear to be somewhat more diverse. In one large recent study, 27 percent of both white and black respondents reported that their primary "group," or voluntary association, was entirely of their own race; an additional 48 percent of whites and 28 percent of blacks reported that the association was mostly of their own race; the remaining respondents—25 percent of whites and 46 percent of blacks—reported that "some," "only a few," or "none" of the other members of the group were of their own race.[22] Of course that means that a rather high percentage of these associations are quite homogeneous in terms of race. Individuals who prefer to associate with others of the same race may choose to join homogeneous groups or even no groups. Indeed, it appears that individuals in more heterogeneous communities have a lower rate of participation in civic associations than do individuals in more homogeneous communities.[23] That fact raises serious questions to which we will return. Racially integrated voluntary associations and religious congregations, at their best, can foster almost uniquely egalitarian bonds based on common beliefs, moral commitments, and interests. But they are too rare and too easily avoided in today's world to function as leading vehicles of societal integration.

In other arenas, recent decades have brought greater progress toward integration. One is higher education, in which legal pressures and voluntary affirmative action efforts have dramatically changed the demographics of many campuses.[24] Unfortunately, racial integration in higher education may be seriously threatened by recent rollbacks of affirmative action. Moreover, higher education occupies just a few years in the lives of most of those who enjoy its privileges. Those years, and the connections that form during those years, can help bring about a more integrated future. But higher education cannot bear the primary burden of promoting integration in the society at large.

Another much-celebrated story of progress is the military, and particularly the Army. The military is not an oasis of interracial harmony; there are tensions and complaints of discrimination.[25] Yet an official commitment to equal opportunity and African-American progress has yielded the most racially integrated of all the nation's basic institutions.[26] The military touches a relatively small portion of the population for what is usually only a limited period of their lives; its impact on the society as a whole is accordingly limited. Still, the military is an instructive example of racial integration to which I will return. For now, it is simply worth noting that military institutions are workplaces. They are distinctive workplaces in many ways. But the military's comparative success in carrying out the project of integration is often traced to features that it shares, in exaggerated form, with workplaces in general: People are compelled by their organization, and by the governing rules and authority structures, to trust and cooperate with others—others whom they might not choose as associates in a voluntary setting—in the intensive and concerted pursuit of concrete, shared objectives.

That brings us to the main point of this brief survey of the state of racial integration in American society: The single most promising arena of racial integration—at least for adults—is the workplace. This is not to say that the typical workplace is genuinely integrated, but that even the partial demographic integration that does exist in the workplace yields far more *social* integration—actual interracial interaction and friendship—than any other domain of American society. The fact that this has been brought about partly by the deliberate operation of law suggests something further about the potentialities of the workplace as a site of integration and intergroup connectedness, and about the ability of the society to realize those potentialities. I will turn to the role of law shortly. Let us first look at the state of integration within workplaces.

Workplaces are in fact only moderately integrated, especially as between white and black employees. Most white workers report having co-workers of another race, though most still have few or no black co-workers.[27] One recent survey asked respondents to "think about the people [they] immediately work with." Over two-thirds of all respondents reported having at least one black co-worker; 24 percent reported that between 10 and 50 percent of their co-workers were black. The numbers were lower among white respondents; 63 percent reported one or more black co-workers. But the numbers were much higher among those working in larger companies: Over 90 percent of those in companies with 250 or more employees, and over 75 percent in companies with 100 to 249 employees, reported working directly with at least one black co-worker.[28]

These numbers by no means depict a thoroughly integrated workforce. But given the high levels of segregation elsewhere in society, the workplace is where working adults are most likely to have genuine interaction across racial lines; in particular, it is the most frequent (and often the only) source of significant contact between black and white citizens.[29] For example, when Memphis residents were asked to "think of places where you associate most often with people of different racial or ethnic backgrounds, which of the following places comes to mind first?," about half of both black and white respondents answered "work"; none of the other options—casual occasions, sporting events, community events, church, or other—was chosen by more than 19 percent.[30] In a 1995 St. Louis survey, both black and white respondents, when asked where they had contact with people of the other race, mentioned the workplace more often than any place else.[31] African Americans, in particular, have much more contact with whites at work than in their neighborhoods or their churches. In a recent New York Times poll, for example, in which 17 percent of black respondents reported that almost all of their co-workers were black, 73 percent reported that almost all of their religious congregation was black, and 45 percent reported that almost all of their close neighbors were black.[32]

So the picture is decidedly mixed, and I do not pretend otherwise. But even given the incomplete and troubled state of workplace integration, the interracial contacts that do occur at work appear to generate most of the real social interaction and most of the reported friendships that arise across racial and ethnic lines. Simple local polling data are suggestive. For example, among the black and white St. Louis residents who reported having co-workers of the other race, about three-quarters of them reported having close friendships among those co-workers.[33] More systematic studies confirm that working in a racially mixed workplace is associated with more significant interracial interactions—and, in particular, more interracial friendships—than is, for example, living in a racially mixed neighborhood.[34] A recent analysis of national data by Xavier de Souza Briggs confirmed that, after accounting for other factors, white respondents' "socializing with co-workers" was strongly associated with having at least one friend of another race.[35]

So there is reason to believe that the dramatically increased incidence of reported friendships between black and white citizens stems largely from increased integration and interaction in the workplace. But this is not primarily a story about friendship. It is about the more widely shared but diffuse sense of connectedness that arises out of daily cooperation, informal sociability, and shared interests, grievances, successes, and failures among co-workers. Those connections may often be quite weak, and they may often be troubled and fractious. But their potential strength is suggested by the frequency with which they develop into real friendships across even the most stubborn lines of social division.

Consider William Kornblum's account of relationships within one South Chicago steel mill, where he worked as a "participant-observer," in the early 1970s.[36] As a general matter, race relations at this time and place were tense at best, and the neighborhoods surrounding the plant were sharply segregated by race and ethnicity. For workers in these neighborhoods,

> the steel plant is the milieu which presents the greatest opportunity as well as the necessity to form personal attachments transcending the moral and physical boundaries of neighborhoods. Seniority and skill are the main criteria in making work assignments, and attachments formed over a lifetime in the mills often cut across the racial, ethnic, and territorial groupings which may divide men in the outside community.[37]

Opportunities for these sorts of attachments varied from one work group to another, depending in part on the degree to which the work itself required cooperation and trust. The attachments that did form, however, spilled beyond the mill:

> When white and black steelworkers labor together over long careers in the mill, they no longer must rely in their dealings with each other on the stereotypes which govern relations between whites and blacks outside the mill. Men from interracial work groups routinely share wakes, funerals, retirement parties, weddings, and a host of family activities over the course of their lives in the mill.[38]

Racial tensions and prejudice did not vanish. But they inevitably were softened and mixed with feelings of solidarity, respect, friendship, and affinity.

A significant body of empirical research on intergroup relations confirms that cooperative interaction of the sort that often happens at work tends to produce more positive attitudes and relations across ethnic and racial lines. This is the burden of the "contact hypothesis," one of the most venerable and widely tested hypotheses in modern social psychology. More than a half-century of empirical research has illuminated the complexity, as well as the asymmetry, of intergroup relations: Biases and stereotypes persist, and their burdens fall heavily on those groups that are underrepresented in good jobs and desirable workplaces, and especially in management. Still, it is widely recognized that sustained cooperative interaction across group lines tends to produce more positive intergroup relations and attitudes.

In the real world, that sort of sustained and cooperative interaction is most likely to happen, if at all, in the workplace. In the workplace, and often only there, citizens must find ways of cooperating on an ongoing basis, over weeks or years, outside of and often counter to traditional racial, ethnic, or sexual hierarchies. So Americans of different racial and ethnic groups may be mostly living in separate families and separate neighborhoods and joining separate associations and religious congregations; but often, and increasingly, they are working together.

These claims have their greatest force, and are most developed here, in the context of black–white relations. They extend in more or less analogous ways to other lines of social division as well. The analogy is most direct in the case of other racial or ethnic divisions that are marked by skin color or appearance. Workplace diversity, interaction, and cooperation across visible lines of ethnicity can be expected to produce greater tolerance and affinity and less hostility and stereotyping between groups. The analogy is less direct in the case of gender, which is a basis for stereotyping, discrimination, and social conflict, but not usually of spatial separation outside the workplace. There is, in short, plenty of intimate and cooperative contact between men and women outside of the workplace. Even so, what happens in the contemporary workplace—where the law prohibits the assignment of positions, tasks, status, and working conditions on the basis of sex, and where women increasingly find themselves working together as peers with men, or with authority over men—is different and ripe with implications for gender relations outside the workplace, and even in the family. The workplace—even while it has been plagued by gender conflict and stratification—has been a crucial arena for women's progress toward full and equal citizenship in the society at large.

Compulsion and Connectedness: The Paradoxical Role of Law and Hierarchy in Workplace Relations

Like the data on interracial friendship, the intergroup relations research suggests but does not quite capture the importance of workplace cooperation and sociability in a diverse democratic society like ours. The citizens of a complex and heterogeneous democratic society share the project of self-governance with other citizens of different beliefs, backgrounds, life circumstances, and values. Each member of the society has some small voice—through voting (or not voting), opinion polls, and engagement in other social and political undertakings—in innumerable decisions that affect the lives and livelihoods of those others. Personal connections among individuals from different backgrounds and communities provide a medium for the exchange of experiences and opinions, and for the discovery of commonalities and of differences in those experiences and opinions. Those connections form a concrete foundation for more diffuse qualities of empathy and broad-mindedness that shape political preferences, enable compromise, and enrich public discourse. The special value of connectedness across lines of social division such as race is captured by the concept of "bridging social capital."[39]

If it is indeed important to have *some* significant domain of regular, close interpersonal contact and cooperation across group lines—and I hope to persuade doubters that it is—then the workplace is the society's single best hope.[40] As compared to other arenas of social life, there is more intergroup interaction taking place in the workplace now, and there are greater institutional capabilities, broader constitutional power, and a stronger political will to promote constructive intergroup interaction there in the future. The workplace is thus an especially promising incubator of the bonds of social solidarity and empathy that link the individual citizen to the broader diverse citizenry.

Paradoxically, the unique potential of workplace ties stems partly from the very features of the workplace that, for many observers, place the workplace outside the boundaries of "civil society": The regulability of the workplace and its lack of autonomy from the state; and the unfree, undemocratic, and economically driven nature of workplace organizations and relationships. Reckoning with those objections will take us to the heart of the distinctive role I am claiming for the workplace in civil society. For the crucial convergence of diversity and intense sociability and cooperation among co-workers is possible partly *because* of the economic hold that the workplace has on individuals, and *because* of the hold that the law has on the workplace.

Unlike the classic voluntary associations, the workplace, including its composition and its internal organization, is properly subject to extensive regulation by the state. That may undermine its ability to perform what I call the "sword and shield" functions of civil society and of the voluntary associations at its core: the creation of a buffer against the state and an autonomous domain in which dissidence, difference, and liberty can flourish and individual voices can be aggregated and amplified and can eventually challenge the prevailing political order. But civil society, and associational life in particular, perform other crucial functions that depend not on separating and shielding individuals from the society at large but on linking them to each other and to the society. Associations help to foster connectedness among citizens, to build the skills and social networks that enable collective undertakings, and to enable the exchange of experiences and ideas and the shaping of opinions and preferences. None of these "linking" functions requires the sort of autonomy from the state that the "sword and shield" functions do. Indeed, the workplace can *better* foster connectedness among individuals from different racial and ethnic groups precisely *because* it is subject to state regulation in the form of the employment discrimination laws.

The second objection to the inclusion of the workplace in civil society points to the hierarchy, coercion, and compulsion that pervade workplace relations. It may seem paradoxical to celebrate and seek to amplify the role of the workplace—undemocratic, unequal, and unfree as it typically is—in a democratic society committed in principle to political equality and liberty. It is important to recognize, first, that workplaces are complex, varied, and changing. They exhibit more than traces of solidarity, egalitarianism, cooperation, and self-rule. Some of those traces arise from the law's rudimentary and incomplete framework for democracy in the workplace, embodied in the New Deal's National Labor Relations Act (NLRA); some are emerging out of managerial practices that ignore or even defy that legal framework. But neither aging law nor emerging practices can be said to establish freedom and democracy in most workplaces. Hierarchy and power, and thus the paradox, remain.

It turns out, however, that the role of the workplace in democratic society is not simply a function of the extent of democracy in the workplace. Indeed, the instrumental and even the hierarchical dimensions of workplace relations help to bring individuals together across lines of social division that they would not otherwise choose to cross, and to make those potentially conflict-ridden interactions relatively constructive. That is not to say that a more authoritarian workplace regime is more likely to foster productive social ties across group lines. What seems crucial is not hierarchy as such, but rather the fact that, one way or another in any productive workplace, workers must be motivated to get a job done together. Workers who are motivated by reciprocal loyalty and a fair reward structure, and are free to associate with each other and communicate shared concerns, have more opportunity to form constructive and egalitarian social ties than workers who are ruled by strict hierarchical authority. At the extreme, where workers are ruled by threats and fear, management may fear that sociability will lead to solidarity, and may suppress both. In those workplaces especially, the law should do more to enable employees to discuss and pursue their shared interests at work. But that is precisely the point: The law can do more. The law has traction in the workplace and could be turned to the cause of promoting sociability, cooperation, and collective voice among employees if we were persuaded of the importance of that cause.

These two complicating features of the workplace—its regulability by the state and its saturation with economic power and necessity—are related. For the hold that the law has on the workplace stems partly from the hold that the workplace has on individuals. Most adults have to work—and usually have to work with and for others—in order to make a living for themselves and their dependents. The work one does in the world is also a primary source of self-worth, identity, and social connections. So people are highly motivated to meet the demands that are made upon them at work—the rules, sanctions, and social norms of the workplace—and to find ways of dealing with conflict and dissatisfaction at the workplace rather than simply quitting. The very involuntariness of work, and the primarily instrumental motives that operate there, help to draw people to a workplace and to keep them there even as workplace demographics change. We are thus familiar with the phenomenon of "white flight" from newly integrated schools and neighborhoods; but one hears rather little of "white flight" from increasingly diverse workplaces. The law has a greater capacity to alter workplace demographics and behaviors and effectively to engage individuals across lines of group identity that they would not ordinarily choose to cross.

Some Implications for Citizens and Policymakers

For those who are persuaded of the civic value of workplace bonds, the question is how to propagate and strengthen those bonds. Workplace organizations and managers are in a good position to do this—to hire and maintain integrated workforces and to cultivate egalitarian and cooperative relations within those workforces. That is not a simple project, but it is one as to which managers can draw on a wealth of knowledge and advice. Scholars from a variety of disciplines have greatly advanced the state of the art of improving intergroup cooperation and equity within organizations. What I aim to do here is different. I ask how law and public policy can be deployed to build up the possibilities of working together. Of course, law can do this only by compelling, persuading, or inducing those within organizations to create more cooperative, integrated, and egalitarian workplaces. But rather than add to the burgeoning literature on how firms can do that, this book seeks ways to motivate firms to mine that literature and to figure out how to improve their own organizations. Public spirited firms and managers may be motivated by the sheer moral force of the argument; others will need the additional motivating force of legal compulsion or inducement.

So when I ask what the law can do to build up the public resources of workplace integration and connectedness, I focus on the general legal principles, rules, procedures, and sanctions that all organizations have to take into account as they go about their daily business. The law thus operates on the internal organization of workplaces by indirect means—by inducing firms to organize themselves and conduct their business in such a way as to both avoid legal sanctions and accomplish their own economic objectives.[41] The question addressed here is not how organizations can best improve intergroup relations, but rather how the levers of public policy can be employed to induce organizations to find better ways of promoting intergroup equality and cooperation. How can the law harness the powerful resources within organizations and steer them toward the goal of fostering egalitarian intergroup cooperation? This book offers only a broad-brush sketch of the possibilities, for a detailed analysis would severely test the patience and attention of the general reader.

Perhaps the single most important thing the law can do to promote constructive intergroup ties in the workplace would be to make demographic diversity a fact of organizational life. That alone would go a long way toward motivating firms to figure out for themselves how to make this demographically diverse organization function productively—how to overcome intergroup tensions and inequities that interfere with getting the work done (and that may threaten to erupt into litigation). So we will consider how successful antidiscrimination law is at making organizational diversity a fact of life, and how it might be made a more effective engine of workplace equity and integration.

In some organizations and some jobs, simple nondiscrimination may not be enough to bring about demographic diversity. Surely, in light of the societal value of "working together," the law should permit organizations to construct an integrated workforce, if necessary, by race- and gender-conscious means. That brings us, of course, to the law of affirmative action in employment. Demographic heterogeneity is crucial to the ability of the workplace to serve its distinctive mediating role. The argument advanced here thus supports the use of race-conscious or gender-conscious efforts to achieve workplace integration, and it does so in ways and in contexts in which neither of the more familiar diversity or remedial arguments provides solid support. On the other hand, some forms of race- and gender-conscious affirmative action may heighten the salience of and tension around group differences and may undermine the potential for fruitful, constructive interaction across those lines of social division. The mediating role of the workplace thus casts new light on the controversy over affirmative action in employment. It does not, however, dissolve the conflict, for it does not cut in only one direction.

Consider, too, the law of discriminatory harassment. That law seeks to prevent supervisors and co-workers from imposing discriminatory conditions of employment, or reinforcing workplace segregation, by creating a hostile environment on the basis of race, sex, or other traits. The law of discriminatory harassment is an essential pillar of the law's support for constructive and egalitarian interaction in a setting of compulsory integration—close, personal, and not entirely voluntary interaction across lines of social division. Yet when the law of discriminatory harassment is translated by risk-averse employers into workplace policies, it often takes on a highly censorious cast. A workplace that is purged of all mention of sexuality, gender, race, ethnicity, nationality, and religion would be a rather sterile place. It would not be the locus of sociability and connectedness that the workplace can and should be for individuals and for the society as a whole.

The implications of the "working together" thesis extend beyond the law of employment discrimination. For it is not only the demographics of the workplace or the structure of intergroup relations that affect the capacity of the workplace to foster connectedness and communication among workers. The experience of working together is shaped as well by the freedom that workers have to share their concerns with each other and to take action together, by the extent of collaborative and cooperative mechanisms within the organization of work, and by the sheer sociability of the workplace.

The law has a well-established (if not a well-executed or successful) role in supporting the freedom of workers to discuss and act on shared work-related concerns. The National Labor Relations Act, enacted in 1935, is the historic core of the legal constitution of the American private sector workplace. When it actually enables workers in a diverse workplace to form a union and bargain collectively with their employer over issues of shared concern, the NLRA stands as the law's most impressive contribution to the mediating potential of workplace relations. For unions at their best do much of what workplaces do by way of promoting social integration, intergroup solidarity, and democratic deliberation; yet they also do much more, for they are more voluntary, more egalitarian, more autonomous, and more deeply animated by common interests and goals, and by an ethos of commonality, than are workplace relations themselves. Unfortunately, unions have not always been at their best in this respect; some unions stubbornly resisted desegregation. Unions have largely overcome their history of racial exclusion, and some have become leading vehicles of multiracial coalition politics. At the same time, however, unions have declined in size and power, and now reach a small and diminishing share of the labor force.

The decline of organized labor reflects in part the decline of labor law. Even the negative rights established by the law—the basic legal norms of freedom of association and expression among workers and freedom from employer reprisals on that basis—are underenforced and incompletely realized. The thesis advanced here thus adds a new and important dimension to contemporary discussions about what the law does and what it should do to protect employees' freedom to communicate and associate with each other and to promote employees' ability to participate in the governance of the workplace.

The law also has a longstanding role in enforcing minimum material terms and conditions of employment. One element of the New Deal's "constitution" of the workplace was the principle that material conditions of work, though largely left to the reconstructed market regime of collective bargaining, were subject to a minimum federal standard of decency. At first blush these laws may seem to have no particular relevance here. But in those workplaces in which the material conditions are most appalling—because of either the law's limited reach or its underenforcement—the potential that lies in "working together" is among the many casualties. These workplaces are occupied disproportionately by nonwhite and immigrant workers and are often highly segregated. The grueling pace of work, the intense supervision, the ever-present threat of injury or of discharge, and the paucity of time and space for informal interaction all conspire to defeat the possibility of constructive intergroup cooperation and communication.

The law's mission in establishing minimally decent terms and conditions of employment—now pursued under the banner of economic justice—still meets resistance both from recalcitrant employers and from market-oriented academics. But the argument of this book shows that more than efficiency and profits, and even more than economic justice, is at stake in this debate. If we were to find more effective ways of regulating low-wage workplaces—of enforcing a decent floor on working conditions and of realizing workers' legal right to associate, communicate, and press collectively for improved working conditions—we would at the same time realize a rich societal payoff in connectedness and social integration.

A Roadmap

The book is organized as follows: Part I draws on a range of sources to develop an account of the workplace as a center of sociability, cooperation, and communication within relatively diverse groups of working adults. Chapter 2 paints with a broad brush a portrait of social relations at work—how much time working adults spend there; how they relate to co-workers, supervisors, and subordinates; what they talk about; and what kinds of relationships form as a result. Chapter 2 also begins to explore the social spillover from workplace interactions. Chapter 3 moves from that rather undifferentiated depiction of "the workplace" to a more nuanced typology of modern workplaces. In emerging trends toward fluidity, flexibility, contingency, and cooperation, I find ambiguous and divergent implications for relations among co-workers and the integrative role of workplace relations. Some of these trends promise to enhance that role while others threaten to undermine it. But some of the trends that seem most destructive of workplace connectedness collide with and are constrained by features of human psychology and imperatives of production that together produce powerful impulses toward sociability, cooperation, and solidarity among co-workers.

Chapter 4 turns from the organization of workplaces, and the general state of sociability, cooperation, and connectedness found there, to the significance of workplace demographics and the extent and the importance of diversity at the workplace. In part, it draws on a large body of research on the social psychology of intergroup relations to illuminate the societal consequences of intergroup cooperation, particularly in the context of race and ethnicity. It also poses the question of why integration works comparatively well in the workplace, and suggests that answers may lie in those very features of workplace associations that for many social theorists render them suspect forms of associational life—in the fact that workers are essentially compelled, by their organizations and indirectly by the law, to get along.

Chapter 5 moves to the distinctive arena of gender integration at work. Workplaces and occupations are much more integrated along gender lines than they were thirty years ago; yet they are still much more segregated than many other spheres of social life. What is distinctive about relations between men and women at work is not that they are closer or more common there than elsewhere, but that they develop under the formal mandate of gender equality. That mandate's realization, however partial, means that men and women increasingly find themselves working together as peers or in roles that reverse the traditional gender hierarchy. That experience is bound to spill over into gender relations in the society and even within the family. The dynamics in some ways parallel and in other ways diverge from the dynamics that attend interracial interaction at work.

Part II takes a more theoretical turn and sets out to give some depth and specificity to the link between the nature of workplace relations and the needs of a complex and heterogeneous democratic society. Chapter 6 draws on and challenges some leading accounts of civil society and civic engagement to argue that workplace interaction does many of the things that associational life is said to do in a democratic society; and that the fact that it does these things in a setting that often is, and that the law can help to make, comparatively integrated is of particular moment. Chapter 7 turns squarely to the issue of compulsion and the significance of legal regulation and of hierarchy and authority in workplace governance. I argue that the distinctive contribution of workplace relations to democracy rests in part upon the very features that, on some accounts, are said to disqualify the workplace from a leading role in civil society: its amenability to regulation and its suffusion with power and authority. But that contribution also depends on the rudiments of liberty and equality that the law has imposed on the workplace.

In short, the regulability of the workplace—what the law has done and what it could do to promote the democracy-enhancing role of workplace associations—enables us to transcend a troubling tension between, on the one hand, the importance of associational autonomy and, on the other hand, the virtues of "congruence" between liberal democratic principles and the internal organizing principles of associations. In the workplace we can do more through law to promote the democracy-enhancing qualities of workplace associations without thereby eroding some essential feature of autonomy.

Part III offers a preview of some of the critical and prescriptive implications of the thesis for the management and especially the regulation of the workplace. Chapter 8 takes up some important aspects of the law governing group status and intergroup relations—what I call the equal protection clause of the workplace. Chapter 9 turns to other aspects of the law of the workplace—in particular, some aspects of "labor law"—that bear upon workplace sociability, cooperation, solidarity, and freedom of association.

Chapter 10 concludes by posing a troubling question: If workplace ties are so good at bringing citizens together and building connectedness, then why has there been an erosion of "generalized social trust" and other conventional measures of civic engagement? The answer that I offer is neither simple nor itself untroubling, but it underscores the importance of what happens at work.

As compared to past generations, we live in an increasingly mobile, diverse, and integrated society in which more of the people we see around us are not only strangers but are visibly different from ourselves. We have less opportunity to form the kinds of thick and multistrand bonds that are based partly on sameness, and more opportunity to form bonds across lines of social difference. But the latter sort of bonds are harder to build. They may not form at all without some degree of compulsion. And when they do form, they are likely to be thinner and more fractious than bonds built on a foundation of sameness. "Bridging bonds" of the kind that form among co-workers may link individuals more weakly to a more diverse group of people, and through them to a broader segment of the community. Those bonds may not generate as strong a sense that "most people can be trusted"; but they help to generate a crucial sense of "being in this together." Perhaps with time, and with progress toward equality and integration within the workplace and beyond, trust will grow as well.

Part One

CONNECTEDNESS AND DIVERSITY

IN THE CONTEMPORARY WORKPLACE

Americans appear to be devoting less time to informal socializing, joining fewer clubs and organizations, engaging in less political activity, and expressing less trust in their fellow citizens in recent decades.[1] Connectedness in the workplace stands as an important exception to this pattern. Unlike nearly every other form of associational life, the workplace is holding steady as a place where people "get a real sense of belonging." Co-workers are ranked right after family and friends, and ahead of neighbors, church or synagogue members, or any other groups, as giving that "sense of belonging."[2] Notably, co-workers are ranked equally highly by those born before 1946 and by those born after 1964, while every other kind of associational tie, other than family and friends, has dropped off sharply for the younger cohort. Of course, that is largely because most people need to work. They may watch television rather than attend club meetings—television is indeed one of the primary culprits Putnam identifies in the decline of associational life—but they would be hard pressed to choose television over work. People do not exactly choose to go to work, and they do not choose much of what they do there. Yet people often find a "real sense of belonging" there.

The importance of this fact will come into sharper focus when we consider the identity of the co-workers among whom so many people feel that "sense of belonging." For one's co-workers come not only from different families and different neighborhoods from one's own, but often from different cultural, religious, racial, and ethnic backgrounds. In particular, the workplace is the single most significant site of regular interaction among adult citizens of different racial and ethnic identities, and especially among black and white adults. I will return to the question of the extent and the significance of demographic, and especially racial, diversity at work in chapter 4. But let us first look at what happens among co-workers at the workplace that might explain the "real sense of belonging" that so many people say they find there.

CONNECTEDNESS IN THE WORKPLACE

A Sketch

Admittedly, it is perilous at best to generalize about work and "the workplace." My workplace experience as a law professor, for example, would seem to have little in common with that of the fast-food server, the automobile assembly worker, the hospital orderly, or the file clerk. My experience shares little even with that of the urban public school teacher across Morningside Park or of the maintenance worker at my own law school. There are vast differences in pay, working conditions, status, authority, autonomy, and satisfaction from one job to another—differences that matter here, and to which chapter 3 is largely devoted. But it is necessary, as well as possible, to begin this account by considering some common features of workplace interaction.

Cooperation, Sociability, and Solidarity among Co-Workers

The workplace is, to begin with, one site of social connectedness that is claiming somewhat more rather than less of people's time. To be more specific: While adult men's work week and age of retirement have both declined slightly, women's commitment to the workforce—both their hours of work and the number of years they spend in the workforce—have increased dramatically over the past several decades.[1] I will have more to say in chapter 5 about the increasingly similar, though still distinct, commitments and trajectories of men and women in the workplace. But for the moment it is enough to observe that paid work, and even full-time work, is becoming a nearly universal experience of adult life, not a "separate sphere" dominated by men.

We have already taken note of the sheer amount of time that most adults spend at work. Moreover, even amidst talk of "free agency" and the demise of lifetime employment, employees often remain with the same organization and work with the same people day after day, over many years. Years of almost daily interactions inevitably give rise to social ties, and often friendships, among co-workers.

Working adults have more meaningful conversations—conversations about things that they consider important—with co-workers than with anyone outside of their families.[2] A 1985 survey found that, among full-time workers who talk about "important matters" with anyone, nearly half do so with one or more co-workers. And among full-time workers who report having at least one "close friend," half report having a close friend who is a current co-worker; 29 percent report having two or more close friends at work. Twenty percent draw half or more of their close friends from among current co-workers. For about 1 in 20 full-time workers, sadly, their only "close friends" and the only people with whom they discuss important matters are co-workers.[3]

It is more than the sheer amount and duration of contact among co-workers that tend to promote these relationships. It is the process of working together. Relations among co-workers form under the imperative of getting work done. Getting the work done typically requires at least minimally cooperative and constructive relations. Workplaces thus tend to be governed by explicit and implicit norms of civility. Professor Stephen Carter recognizes this in his introductory rendition of a daily life awash in incivility. The hypothetical protagonist is bombarded on the way to work by rude fellow drivers, sales clerks, and radio commentators; but "you at last arrive at your job, where you are expected to be polite."[4]

Of course, what it means to "be polite" at work is a complicated matter. Clearly, civility norms vary greatly from one workplace to another. They may also prescribe strikingly different manners for different levels of a workplace hierarchy and *between* different levels of the hierarchy. What counts as civil behavior by managers toward mailroom workers, maintenance personnel, or secretaries may bear little resemblance to the behavior expected of the latter toward the former. Civility norms, or adherence to them, may also depend upon the sex and the ethnicity of the actors. And unfortunately, lines of sex and ethnicity may correspond to different levels of the workplace hierarchy.

The problem of discriminatory harassment signals the more-than-occasional breach or breakdown of civility norms, or sometimes the clash of competing civility norms. That problem also reminds us that, in today's workplace, the fact that one is "expected to be polite," and what it means to "be polite," is shaped not only by the need to get a job done and by the way work is organized; it is shaped as well by the law of discriminatory harassment and employer fears of liability. This rather remarkable legal effort to reform co-worker relationships gives a glimpse of the larger role that law does and can play in shaping the experience of working together. It seems nonetheless clear that, whatever the impact of the law of discriminatory harassment, some sort of civility must prevail most of the time in any functioning workplace. Whatever the state of civility norms is (or should be) in the society at large, most working adults spend much of their lives in a place where, in the words of Professor Carter, "you are expected to be polite."

The cooperative and social nature of much work itself also tends to depend upon and to engender trust.[5] Co-workers, including subordinates, supervisors, and managers, routinely depend on each other in carrying out their jobs. In some jobs, workers entrust each other with their lives and physical safety. Levels of trust vary dramatically from one organization to another, as well as from one job to another within the same organization. In most organizations, levels of trust between management and employees vary greatly between levels of the organization. Management may confer upon some categories of employees—especially managers and professionals—wide discretion and freedom from direct monitoring. Others—especially those who do the most routine work—may enjoy little discretion and little freedom in how they perform their jobs. These variations are important and will bear a closer look in the next chapter. But most employees—and many more today than 20 years ago—report that they enjoy considerable autonomy in deciding how to do their jobs.[6] Indeed, some degree of trust is necessary to any organization and any work relationship, for it appears to be virtually impossible to monitor human labor closely enough to rely exclusively on tangible carrots and sticks to motivate performance.[7]

So the need to get the job done tends to promote reasonably civil and constructive relations, and some degree of mutual trust, even among co-workers who initially have little mutual affinity and little in common. At the same time, being part of the same organization and getting the job done together tend to *create* common ground and to cultivate mutual affinity. That common ground may be found in a shared commitment to the goals of the organization. That is especially common for those who work in education or health care or some other service-oriented nonprofit organization. But it is not uncommon in the private sector. An employee of a real estate development firm speaks proudly of the company's "mission . . . of finding ways . . . to redevelop and to rejuvenate cities." A software engineer tells of being part of "something bigger than myself" at work.[8] Employees commonly assert at least a superficial sense of shared commitment to their organization and a belief that they and their co-workers are doing good in the world through their work.

But whether or not organizations manage to engender that kind of shared commitment—indeed, perhaps especially in those organizations that do not— common conditions of employment often give rise to shared interests and feelings of solidarity among similarly situated workers. However little individuals share when they join a firm, as co-workers they immediately begin to share some of the most important features of their economic and social existence: a basic wage structure, health and retirement benefits (or none), physical surroundings with all their dangers or amenities, a corps of supervisors and managers, and a shared social network—in short, basic elements, tangible and intangible, of their livelihoods and social lives. Dissatisfaction with those shared conditions can readily coalesce into at least incipient collective dissent.

Not all organizations foster a lot of trust and cooperation, and not all foster strong solidarity among co-workers; but it is hard for an organization to get by without creating one or the other, and at least some of each. So, for example, it is possible for management to structure an organization on the basis of minimal trust and cooperation between rank-and-file workers and management, and to rely largely on close monitoring and sanctions to induce performance. But in doing so, management may only succeed in promoting greater solidarity, or at least shared resentment, among similarly mistrusted co-workers.[9] One might say that firms get the kind of connectedness in their workforce that they deserve— either organizational connectedness or oppositional connectedness.

The phenomenon of unionization is a particularly dramatic expression of the solidarity that sometimes arises out of working together. Unionization requires workers to give up the possible advantages of going it alone, to court the ire of management, and often to risk their jobs and their livelihoods, all to advance the good of the group. As we will discuss below, unionization not only demonstrates the solidarity that can arise out of shared workplace experiences, grievances, and aspirations; it also actively cultivates solidarity. Unions' ability to advance workers' interests depends on workers' sharing common aims; their interests are served by seeking terms of employment that quell divisions, minimize competition, and expand common ground and mutual interdependence among the workforce.[10]

Unions are not the only sort of voluntary association or the only organizational expression of solidarity that can arise out of the experience of shared discontentment at work. At least where workers perceive discrimination and disadvantage on the basis of group membership, solidarity and the impulse to seek a collective voice may also arise within racial, ethnic, or sexual minority groups within the workplace.[11] The rise of identity-based "caucuses" has the potential to divide co-workers (not just from managers but from peers) as well as to advance their members' interests. But at a minimum it is further evidence of the associational energies that arise out of shared work and working conditions.

Solidarity among co-workers need not, however, take the form of collective dissent. It may coexist with trust between workers and management, for example, in a unionized workforce with a history of stable collective bargaining and co-operative labor–management relations.[12] Or it may happen spontaneously and informally as a product of social interaction among human beings who come to care about each other. This occurred among the ethnically mixed but sex-segregated work groups in the pre–New Deal factories out of which the industrial unions grew. Lizabeth Cohen cites "many examples of female solidarity . . . , of women secretly doing hard jobs assigned to older ones, taking turns staying home to avoid layoffs, or restricting output . . ."[13] That these alliances arose among ethnically mixed groups of workers at a time of rampant ethnic divisions and tensions is a fact of enormous importance to which we will return. That these alliances arose in a sex-segregated environment is a noteworthy and in some ways troubling fact to which we will also return.

But we need not reach back to some golden age of workplace solidarity to find stories of workers helping each other out with no immediate prospect of a tangible reward. Consider the experience of journalist Barbara Ehrenreich, who went "undercover" in the world of low-wage employment to find out how workers made ends meet (or didn't) in near-minimum wage jobs. In her jobs as a waitress, a hotel maid, a nursing home aide, and a Wal-Mart clerk, she often found co-workers helping each other out, picking up slack, and passing on invaluable advice without any discernible instrumental motive.[14] Among the waitresses at a large chain restaurant, for example, she says:

> All in all, we form a reliable mutual-support group: if one of us is feeling sick or overwhelmed, another will "bev" [i.e., take and fill beverage orders for] a table or even carry trays for her. If one of us is off sneaking a cigarette or a pee, the others will do their best to conceal her absence from the enforcers of corporate rationality.[15]

Of course, there is nothing very mysterious about people helping out others with whom they spend hours each day in conditions of shared adversity. We might even attribute this impulse to self-interest by positing an expectation of reciprocity. But that reductionist characterization should take nothing away from the recognition that shared work often creates conditions under which mutual support makes sense to people who have little but their shared work in common. Something in the experience of working together, even for a few days, can bring out a sense of "being in this together" and a willingness to make small sacrifices for each other.

Economist George Akerlof sought to cast theoretical light on this phenomenon by examining the puzzling behavior of some very hardworking clerical workers who consistently performed well above minimum production standards without getting higher wages than their co-workers who performed close to the minimum. Akerlof invoked the anthropological concept of gift-giving to explain what neoclassical economic theory could not. He posited that the superworkers gave a "gift" of extra effort to their employer with an expectation of reciprocity in the form of a "fair" uniform wage *and* leniency toward marginal co-workers. But why would they do this? Akerlof hypothesized:

> Persons who work for an institution (a firm in this case) tend to develop sentiment for their co-workers and for that institution. . . . [I]f workers have an interest in the welfare of their co-workers, they gain utility if the firm relaxes pressure on the workers who are hard pressed; in return for reducing such pressure, better workers are often willing to work harder.[16]

For some readers, the story may have a fairy-tale quality. Its moral is at odds with the standard economist's assumption that workers respond chiefly to individual economic incentives and with managers' attachment to merit-based and performance-based pay structures. Such incentive structures, as well as the implicit threat of discharge or other carrots and sticks that employers use to spur individual or team performance, may strain solidarity among co-workers. At the same time, the increasing fluidity and instability of workplace relations, the increasing reliance on outsourcing and other contingent sources of labor, and the reputed demise of internal labor markets all seem to threaten the foundations of trust and solidarity among co-workers. These market forces and managerial practices remain to be reckoned with in chapter 3.

Still, it is widely understood that workers care about each other and that they hold to, and hold their employers to, norms of fairness toward both individuals and the group. Indeed, the workplace has been described as a "hotbed" of social norms. Employers' compliance with those norms meets with trust and reciprocity in the form of zealous job performance; violations may be met with shirking or collective resistance, overt or covert.[17]

So working adults spend much of their time in a social environment that, to varying degrees, is governed by norms of civility and reciprocity, that fosters experiences of mutual trust, cooperation, and sociability, and that engenders common concerns and communication about those concerns. Working together in this environment generates personal feelings of affection, sympathy, empathy, and friendship among co-workers. Not surprisingly, relationships that form in the workplace often spill beyond it and make up much of our social circles.[18]

The workplace serves not only as a source of potential friends; it serves as a kind of community within which many individuals experience "a real sense of belonging." As one software programmer explained to an interviewer, it was among her co-workers that she gained a "sense of community":

> Those are the people whose lives I follow. . . . [where I have] some sense of belonging to something bigger than myself, or bigger than myself and my husband, as a family. . . . I haven't joined civic groups [in my home community] and I don't go to church regularly, that's pretty much where I find my sense of community. Is at work.[19]

Companies vary greatly in the extent to which they actively cultivate social ties, trust, and community among their employees; we will return to these variations. But it is increasingly true that, "for many people, the neighbors they know best may be those across the cubicle wall."[20] As other forms of social engagement decline, people increasingly find that crucial "sense of belonging" more among their co-workers than in their neighborhood, their local community, churches or synagogues, or clubs or other groups—more than in any group other than family or friends.

Some firms actively pursue the idea of the workplace as the "new American neighborhood." They have brought into the workplace "neighborhood" banks, general stores, cafes, libraries, health clubs, gift shops, ball fields, along with the conventional cafeterias and the increasingly popular child care facilities. It is no wonder, then, to find stories like that of Becky O'Grady:

> She joined [the company] in 1990, one of 30 MBAs recruited by the company—six of whom—including O'Grady—ended up marrying each other. Today, she does her dry cleaning, car tune-ups, film developing, exercising, and much more at the shops tucked along the company's labyrinthian corridors. When she's not at work, where she's the marketing manager for cereals, O'Grady socializes almost entirely with workmates.[21]

There is something undeniably creepy about the all-encompassing "workplace as neighborhood"; it evokes the old "company town" in the pastel tones of Celebration, U.S.A.[22] It is a vivid reminder that the workplace can, and perhaps has, become *too* central to our identities and social lives.[23] On this dystopian note in what may otherwise seem to be an overly utopian account of the workplace community, let us begin to consider the consequences of workplace social ties for the rest of social and civic life.

A Preliminary Look at the Social Spillover from Workplace Ties

Work absorbs not just an increasing share of our time but an increasing share of our emotional and social energies. Even domestic life has suffered. The "time bind"—the expansion of work time and the reduced time at the home with family and children—has become a well-publicized source of stress for two-career and single-parent families. But Professor Arlie Hochschild discovered a paradoxical result of the "time bind": many stressed-out parents in her study found the workplace to be a more relaxed and supportive environment, and work relationships a more reliable source of personal satisfaction, than home and family, where time pressures contributed to conflict and to feelings of anxiety, failure, and inadequacy.[24]

All this suggests that, whether or not the growing importance of the workplace as a site of social connectedness is something to celebrate, it is certainly something to investigate. The question on the table—and one to which much of this book is devoted—is how sociability, cooperation, and solidarity at work affect the society at large. But let us begin to investigate that question by asking whether increasing demands of the workplace have contributed to the erosion of other forms of social and associational life. That possibility would certainly cast a shadow over our conception of the role of workplace connectedness in the society at large.

One might reasonably suspect that longer hours of work, and the steady flow of women into the full-time labor force, are themselves culprits in the decline of other forms of civic life. But some data contradict this hypothesis. Professor Putnam found that "[e]mployed people are *more* active civically and socially than those outside the paid labor force, and among workers, longer hours are often linked to *more* civic engagement, not less."[25] For women the picture is more complex: the most civically active group consists of women who work part-time "by choice," not out of economic necessity; full-time work, especially when it is motivated by economic necessity, is associated with less social involvement. But for single mothers in particular, as for most groups, "work outside the home has a positive effect on virtually all forms of civic engagement, from club membership to political interest."[26]

The link between employment and social engagement should not be too surprising. It is the mirror image of the now-familiar dynamic by which the long-term unemployed often sink into anomie and lethargy.[27] This may be a product of financial worry, loss of self-esteem, or many other factors; involuntary unemployment disrupts virtually every aspect of daily life. But it is also the case that unemployment deprives individuals of their most regular and intensive occasions for purposeful, cooperative social interaction. So the positive association between employment and civic engagement makes sense.

Even so, the positive association for most groups between *hours of work* and other forms of civic engagement is quite remarkable, for the sheer competition for time seems to point inexorably in the opposite direction. This evidence suggests the possibility that something quite powerful happens at work that counteracts the negative impact on time available and actually promotes other forms of civic engagement. Putnam notes one such mechanism: "work outside the home means exposure to a wider array of social and community networks."[28] Indeed, for many people the workplace has become the primary locus of their community, civic, and charitable involvements. But it is not just that working brings people into contact with *other* opportunities for social engagement and social capital formation. Work itself involves intense social engagement, cooperation, and trust.

Another mechanism by which work may contribute to civic engagement lies in the formation of "civic skills," or the skills of communication, persuasion, decisionmaking, and compromise that are useful in civic and political activity. Sidney Verba and his collaborators have shown that the workplace is a leading source of civic skills.[29] At the workplace, individuals—some obviously more than others—practice skills of communication, cooperation, compromise, and decision-making. For professionals and managers, the workplace is the single most important source of civic skills; for other employees, who have less opportunity to practice those skills at work, other associations are more important. But as more collaborative and participatory workplace structures become widespread, more workers gain access to civic skills at work. Workers who learn "interpersonal and conflict-resolution skills" and problem-solving skills at work report finding those skills useful in their churches, community organizations, and even at home.[30] That is true even in workplaces that can by no means be described as "democratic" in their internal organization.

Again, the point is not simply that workplace interaction builds skills that are useful in *other* arenas of social and civic life; workplace interaction *is itself* an important arena of social and civic life. I will explain this point with some care below. But for the moment I want to emphasize three points that I have made so far: First, cooperation, sociability, and fellowship—whatever their incidence in other social domains—are positively rampant in the workplace. Second, the claim that Americans' work lives are significantly detracting from other forms of civic engagement and civil society is at least unproven. Third, there is some evidence that workplace interactions and relationships make a positive contribution to civic life—that constructive and satisfying interactions among co-workers create positive spillover into the society as a whole.

Let us dwell a bit longer on this last and most difficult question about the consequences of cooperation and sociability at work. At a minimum, workplace interactions generate social contacts and civic skills that carry over into the rest of civic life. But what about the less tangible qualities of trust, generosity, solidarity, and willingness to cooperate? These qualities are often found and often cultivated in the workplace; but do they carry over into life outside the workplace?

Robert Lane, in his book *The Market Experience*, summarizes a number of studies showing that a great deal of what is learned at work—cognitive skills, habits of discipline, a sense of personal control or efficacy, and self-esteem—becomes generalized and woven into individuals' very makeup and social existence.[31] In particular, "[p]eople in cooperative jobs at work thought of the world as more of a cooperative place than those who were rewarded for competitive behavior at work."[32] Similarly, a major longitudinal study, which followed 785 male workers employed in a variety of occupations for ten years, found that "self-directed work (substantively complex, loosely supervised, and nonroutine) . . . promotes . . . attitudes of tolerance, respect, and trust."[33] Of course the question remains whether most work is either cooperative or "self-directed"; we will return to that question below. But insofar as some degree of both cooperation and self-direction is very common at work, it does appear to generalize to life and the world beyond.

In fact, it is not just idealized "self-directed" jobs that produce positive social spillover. One study found that factory work, as compared to rural agricultural work, "increases both the tendency to hold opinions and the tendency to tolerate or even value the opinions of others, even 'weaker' others such as (in these underdeveloped countries) a man's wife or son.'"[34] This is fascinating, first, because these two tendencies—to hold opinions and to respect the opinions of others—seem potentially at odds, yet together they capture much of what it means to be a citizen in a liberal democratic society. It is also fascinating because factory work is conventionally regarded as quintessentially degraded and alienated. But as compared to the solitary business of farming, the experience of group production and interdependency, even on the assembly line, appears to lay a firmer psychological foundation for democratic citizenship.

This claim finds further, though more inferential, support in the voluminous experimental data on the prevalence of and the conditions associated with social cooperation. Social scientists have run hundreds of so-called "social dilemma" experiments in which individuals' self-interest is pitted against other-regarding preferences. Contrary to the textbook assumptions of economic analysis, other-regarding preferences often prevail.[35] For example, in "public goods" games, each of several participants is given a sum of money; each is told that he or she may keep it or contribute any part of it to a common pool, and that whatever amount is contributed to the pool will be multiplied by some factor (less than the number of participants) and then distributed among all participants, however much each contributed. The game is structured so that the only rational individual strategy is to "defect," or contribute nothing; yet "cooperation rates," as captured by the average individual contribution, are typically between 40 and 60 percent.[36] So, too, with the "ultimatum game": An individual is given a sum of money and is told to offer some portion of it to another participant on the understanding that, if the offer is accepted, each gets to keep the designated share, but that, if the offer is rejected, neither gets anything. The "rational" offer is a trivial share, which the rational offeree should accept. Yet offers are typically closer to 50 percent, and offers that are significantly below 50 percent are often rejected.[37] Finally, in the "dictator game," the individual is given a sum of money that he or she may divide in any way with another person; the division is final. Here, too, even where there is no risk of rejection, offers are typically much closer to 50 percent than to the "rational" offer of zero.[38]

What these experiments suggest is, first, that most people exhibit a much greater propensity for other-regarding behavior—and especially for cooperation with and altruism toward others and for trust that others will reciprocate—than do the stylized rational, self-interested actors who populate much economic and legal analysis. But these experiments teach much more, for they have been run under a wide variety of conditions, yielding varying degrees of cooperation and defection. It turns out that social context exerts a strong and fairly consistent influence on the willingness to cooperate. In particular, the studies have shown that, even when the payoff for defection remains obvious and unchanged, levels of cooperative behavior rise dramatically simply in response to an authoritative instruction, or even a suggestion, that cooperation is appropriate or expected. Levels of cooperation also rise when the participants have the opportunity to communicate with each other, or even merely to see each other, before or during the game, and when the participants are somehow made to perceive a common identity with the others with whom they can choose to cooperate or not.

If we can extrapolate from these stylized experiments to the workplace—and that is a big "if"—the implications are encouraging. There are plenty of occasions in which an individual could act either selfishly or cooperatively toward his co-workers or toward the organization as a whole. But there is also, often, strong and authoritative encouragement of cooperation, at least insofar as it serves the organization; one's job, advancement on the job, or compensation may depend on taking the path of cooperation, and on trusting and being trustworthy. (Of course, "looking out for Number One" might also be rewarded and implicitly encouraged; that would often be contrary to the interests of a firm, but it does happen.) There is also lots of communication among co-workers as well as efforts by the organization to encourage its members to identify with their organization or work group. (Of course, we can also find backbiting, divisions, ostracism, and harassment among workers; that is unlikely to be a productive working environment, but that, too, happens.) To the extent we do find these pro-cooperative conditions, we would expect the workplace setting to bring out and build on the deeply rooted human propensity for cooperation and trust.

But let us return to the harder question of whether the experience of cooperation and reciprocated trust in one setting carries over into a greater propensity for trust and cooperation outside of that setting. There is evidence that it does. For example, many studies have shown that participating in a cooperative undertaking is associated with more cooperative behavior in a subsequent "public goods" game, while participating in a competitive undertaking is associated with less cooperation and more defection in the subsequent game. But these artificially induced conditions of "cooperation" or "competition" cannot be expected to leave as strong an imprint as do the conditions that prevail in one's daily economic life. In the words of Samuel Bowles, "preferences learned under one set of circumstances become generalized reasons for behavior. Thus economic institutions may induce specific behaviors—self-regarding, opportunistic, or cooperative, say—which then become part of the behavioral repertoire of the individual."[39]

Some intriguing evidence of this dynamic is found in the results of social dilemma experiments run in a wide variety of small-scale preindustrial societies throughout the world. The researchers found widely varying rates of cooperation among these societies—all higher than predicted by the assumption of rational self-interest, but most lower than those found in industrial societies such as the United States. They found that "behavior in the experiments [was] generally consistent with economic patterns of everyday life in these societies."[40] Specifically, cooperation levels were higher in societies in which the system of economic production required and rewarded cooperation and in which market exchange was a common part of daily life. The researchers surmise that daily life, and specifically economic life, forms a kind of "template"—a set of habits and emotional responses—that favor or disfavor cooperation, sharing, and trust, and that individuals resort to that template when faced with a new situation.[41]

The results pose an interesting contrast with another set of experiments that seek to replicate the *idealized* conditions of competitive markets, especially their impersonality and anonymity. In a variety of studies, "the more the experimental situation approximates a competitive . . . market with many anonymous buyers and sellers, the less other-regarding behavior will be observed."[42] But it is easier to create those conditions of anonymity and impersonality in the laboratory than it is to observe them in many actual market interactions. So while "*market-like situations* induce self-regarding behavior,"[43] daily participation in the institutions of *actual market societies*—such as the more market-oriented preindustrial societies and especially modern industrialized market societies—appears to be associated with rather high levels of cooperation.

This apparent paradox points to the fact that cooperation and trust—tacit and explicit—are endemic and necessary to the functioning of most actual market institutions. As compared to a life of subsistence farming, for example, economic life in modern society is vastly more social and more collaborative; it is comparatively rich with opportunities to show trust and trustworthiness. In particular, one of the most universal adult experiences in modern industrial society is a daily life of working with others. Where one's daily work life calls for a high degree of cooperation and mutual trust, this experience of working with others may be expected to produce at least a provisionally higher level of cooperation and trust outside of work life.

Of course, as the qualifier suggests, that is good news for modern industrial society only if the largely sanguine portrayal of workplace relations that I have sketched so far holds true for most real workplaces. For the corollary is also true: A daily work life that is pervaded by mistrust, competition among co-workers, and authoritarian and adversarial relations with supervisors may promote alienation, mistrust, and "defection" in the rest of one's social interactions. Further inquiry along these lines must await, first, a more varied and realistic portrait of the workplaces in which people work today, and, second, a closer examination of the significance of group differences in the workplace.

There is undoubtedly a disturbing underside to the growing centrality of work as compared to other forms of association and engagement in the lives of many citizens. But that is not because the workplace is a civic wasteland or a realm of strictly instrumental human relationships. Ties among co-workers provide social and emotional sustenance; they generate lasting friendships, even marriages, as well as a network of acquaintances; and they give many people "a real sense of belonging." The sheer amount of sociability and cooperation that takes place every day in workplaces should place them at the center of any account of what holds a complex, modern democratic society together.

The social significance of workplace ties is magnified by the comparatively diverse context within which they form. I will turn to that issue in chapter 4. But first it is necessary to fill in some of the broad strokes in the foregoing portrait of "the workplace," and to take note of some of the rich complexity of actual "workplaces," and of some of the changes that are affecting the organization of work.

FROM "THE WORKPLACE" TO WORKPLACES

Variety and Change in the Organization of Work

"The workplace," as described so far, is an intensely social environment. Co-workers routinely cooperate in doing the work itself—the most literal meaning of "working together." They socialize informally during the workday and sometimes afterward. They discuss shared terms and conditions of employment and are sometimes moved to make common cause and to seek a collective voice in these matters. Some modicum of cooperation, sociability, and communication about shared work conditions is virtually endemic to "the workplace" as we know it. But there are plainly many different kinds of workplaces and many different kinds of jobs, and they vary enormously in their hospitality to each of these forms of human interaction. So, too, workplaces are changing to meet the challenges of a dynamic and increasingly global market. Do the actual workplaces of the twenty-first century look anything like "the workplace" I have described? Do they foster the kinds of social ties on which I stake my claims here?

A convincing answer to those questions requires a closer look at the changing and varied nature of working environments.[1] The challenge is to do so without either lapsing into gross oversimplification or drowning in the complexity of the emerging picture. The difficulty of the enterprise is underscored by a preliminary look at two trends—toward "telecommuting" and toward team-based and collaborative work practices—that might be thought to have clear and simple implications—negative and positive, respectively—for the experience of "working together." On closer examination, these trends turn out to have surprisingly mixed implications for that experience. Moreover, they appear to be running up against features of human psychology that are likely to curb their transformative potential.

Much the same can be said of the broader trends that are said to be transforming the organization of work. The "bureaucratic" models that prevailed during much of the last century within the primary sector—the large private enterprises that dominate leading sectors of the economy—were relatively hospitable to the development of strong and stable workplace bonds. Those models are succumbing, under the pressure of economic competition and fast-changing product markets, to trends toward greater volatility and contingency, and toward greater sociability and collaboration. Yet the two trends are in tension with each other. And the disquieting trend toward volatility and contingency is in tension as well with some resilient features of human psychology that may be slowing their advancement. Employers still need to motivate workers, and workers still have deep-seated needs for security and sociability.

Unfortunately, this chapter will conclude on a discouraging note by looking at the low-wage model of workplace organization. The low-wage model is a relatively constant feature of the changing landscape and seems to have real staying power in some pockets of the American economy. A brief look at the conditions that prevail in those workplaces will serve as a useful corrective to what might otherwise seem a too-sanguine depiction of "the workplace." In particular, its characteristic form of governance by fear and threats stands as a harsh counterpoint to the picture of more or less cooperative and sociable relations among co-workers.

The following description of old patterns and new trends in workplace organization is highly abbreviated and is not intended to break new ground. Still, it is worth surveying this familiar landscape through a new lens, focusing on each model's capacity to foster cooperation, collective voice, and informal sociability. In that landscape there is cause for both optimism and caution. It is plain that workplaces vary widely in their tendency to foster cooperative human interaction. So, too, current trends vary in their implications for the "working together" thesis. But the basic human impulses behind cooperation, collective voice, and sociability are powerful and persistent enough to show themselves even in some highly inhospitable environments. The forces that tend to foster constructive and amicable bonds among co-workers are neither confined to the workplaces of the privileged few nor are they fading into history.

Telecommuting and Teamwork: A First Cut at the Complexity of Emerging Trends

One trend that seems unambiguously threatening to the role that I stake out for workplace relations is the growing phenomenon of "telecommuting" and the broader development of "virtual" communication among co-workers. I argue here that the unique integrative potential of workplace relations arises out of the regular, multidimensional, face-to-face communication and cooperation that is common among co-workers. Yet the specter of the "virtual workplace" threatens to transform co-worker relations into something far thinner, less personal, and more one-dimensional.[2] Indeed, it seems possible that, as technology proceeds at its breakneck pace and as the children of the Internet era begin to dominate the labor force, "the workplace" may become a mere metaphor for many workers. If the workplace and the ties that form there are as important to civic life as I argue here, this would ill-serve human needs and would fray the social fabric of a diverse society.

Of course, telecommuting has virtues as well, particularly in easing the conflict between work and family that burdens many parents, especially mothers, and impedes their career progress.[3] Moreover, some observers have pointed to the peculiarly egalitarian quality of electronic communication: Among the non-verbal cues that may be lost in cyberspace are the speaker's race, age, and sometimes gender.[4] Of course, this is less true among co-workers than in true cyberspace conversations. Even so, the etiquette of e-mail seems to be liberating for some: Subordinates seem to "talk back" more readily on their computer terminal than in person or by telephone. Moreover, these media and their uses are obviously still evolving. The quality of the relationships that are cultivated by e-mail and the like may eventually prove to be much like those that are cultivated over the water cooler. The addition of pictures and sound may even make the computer terminal of the future look and feel more like the water cooler.

More likely, however, the actual water cooler will be with us for some time. At least for the generation that came of age before the Internet, there persists a craving for interpersonal contact that has led firms and workers to create regular opportunities for face-to-face interchange among telecommuters and between telecommuters and others at the actual workplace.[5] One commentator says, "Forget what you've heard: the office isn't going anywhere. We like it. It's the place where we have friends and sandwiches. Where we feel important." According to Hani Rashid, a workplace architect, "[t]he promise of the virtual office was a grand mistake."[6]

It is not just that people like the office; they also work better when they work together, face-to-face. Most workplace learning occurs informally, in the unplanned and incidental interactions among co-workers during a shared work day. And regular face-to-face communication is equally essential to building the intangible qualities of trust and connectedness on which many organizations depend:

> Coworkers define and redefine who they are as a group in part by sharing and monitoring reactions to events at work, news of the outside world, weather, the behavior of bosses and subordinates and the thousands of other subjects that form the currency of daily communications. They solidify and redefine group membership, strengthening connections in hundreds of small ways and making new connections, often by chance. Telecommuters have fewer opportunities to tend and expand their personal networks. They are excluded from the accidental meetings that occur in the cafeteria or the unanticipated conversations with a new employee . . . that may uncover mutual interests.[7]

These accidental encounters do not take place in a virtual workplace environment. And the encounters that do take place among telecommuters—

the teleconferences, e-mails, and other purposeful exchanges of information and opinions—lack the rich visual and auditory cues that supplement the verbal content of communications and that are essential to building human relationships.

For now there seems to be an emerging consensus that telecommuting has its limited place, but that for most jobs and most people, face-to-face meetings and informal, unplanned interactions among co-workers are essential to building trust, cooperating effectively, and getting the job done. More essential than ever, it seems: "[H]otels report they are building more meeting space than ever, and corporate offices designed today include at least three times more conference rooms and collaborative space than 15 years ago."[8] To the extent that collaborative work processes are on the rise—and we will turn to that question below—face-to-face communication has become more, not less, important in many jobs.

All this suggests that electronic communications are more likely to supplement than to replace face-to-face communication among co-workers. In that more limited role, virtuality may have real virtues. The injection of electronic communications into workplace relationships that also have a significant face-to-face dimension may expand and equalize those relationships rather than eroding them. So the trend toward telecommuting, and toward virtuality in general, has troubling features. But it is apparently in tension with, and thus far limited by, basic features of human psychology and basic trends in the organization of the workplace: Face-to-face sociability and cooperation remain important for human happiness and for productivity and are unlikely to go away.

The trend toward more collaborative and team-based production methods, beyond putting the brakes on the movement toward virtuality, seems to hold great potential for enriching the workplace community and enlarging the scope of communication and cooperation. There would thus seem to be nothing but good news in the movement many observers report toward flatter and more fluid hierarchies, increased reliance on trust and on workers' own accumulation and sharing of knowledge through cooperative mechanisms, and emphasis on problem solving through group interaction rather than management fiat. In some of the most thoroughly innovative schemes, job classifications and hierarchy are largely erased; project-based teams of workers make their own decisions about hiring, scheduling, and production, and deal directly with customers. Other firms pick a few items from the menu of alternative practices and make more incremental changes in their traditional production methods and organizational structures.

The actual impact of various innovative work practices on both productivity and worker attitudes and welfare is much studied and hotly debated. Proponents of these practices claim that they enhance workers' well-being and commitment to the organization (as well as their productivity).[9] Critics argue that these practices—particularly those associated with "lean production"—amount to "management by stress" and undermine employee welfare.[10] Insofar as the expected productivity gains from these practices turn partly on their contribution to workers' feelings of well-being and commitment, questions about the latter are of intense interest to managers as well as to others interested in the impact of work life on the welfare of workers and of the society as a whole. Much of the empirical evidence so far has been mixed and offers some support to both proponents and skeptics. Some proponents have argued that these mixed results are a product of the very partial dissemination of the new practices and that a thorough reorganization of work that encompassed the full range of advanced workplace practices would show a clear positive impact on productivity.[11]

For our purposes, the crucial question is how these much-touted but varied practices affect workers' relationships with each other and their sense of community and connectedness. That question is much illuminated by one recent study that focused on the effects of various "alternative work practices" (AWPs) on workers' experiences of and attitudes toward their work and their organizations.[12] This study, by Canadian professor John Godard, sought to disaggregate both the varied AWPs—for example, "just-in-time" and "total quality management" programs, various team production methods, and information-sharing, quality circles, and other participatory structures   and the varied behavioral and psycho-social impacts on employees—for example, job satisfaction, motivation, commitment, and stress. Most importantly here, the study looked at the effect of various AWPs on employees' feelings of "belongingness" among co-workers and on their "citizenship behavior," that is, their willingness to volunteer help, to be considerate of others, and to participate in group activities beyond what is strictly required by the job.[13] Together, these two variables correspond quite closely to the qualities of sociability and connectedness with which we are concerned here.

The Godard study found that certain moderately innovative practices, such as traditional, supervised team- or group-based production and information sharing, were significantly correlated with workers' sense of belongingness and organizational citizenship behavior, as well as feelings of empowerment, task involvement, job satisfaction, self-esteem, motivation, and commitment. But many of these gains declined, and were seemingly canceled out by higher levels of employee stress, with the more advanced practices. One particularly unsettling finding was that "team autonomy" was significantly and *negatively* correlated with belongingness and citizenship behavior, as well as task involvement, job satisfaction, motivation, and commitment. Traditionally supervised teams did much better on these scales.[14] Godard concludes:

> Overall, . . . the results suggest that, when compared to "bad" practices associated with traditional individualized work, the so-called "best" practice associated with high levels of AWP involvement, with lean and autonomous team work organization, and with the provision of team autonomy and re-

sponsibility may have a number of positive (as well as some negative) implications for employees. But when compared to what might be referred to as "good" practice, or low to moderate levels of AWP adoption, and especially traditional group work organization and information sharing, their implications tend, if anything, to be negative.[15]

This study suggests that the much-touted movement toward more cooperative modes of work turns out to have surprisingly mixed implications for the formation of socially valuable workplace bonds. These practices do promise a more rewarding, sociable, and connected workplace; but they may work best, at least for workers and the workplace community, in moderation.

The ambiguity and limitations that emerge when we look more closely at the phenomena of telecommuting and of teamwork will be replicated many times over as we examine emerging trends and patterns of workplace organization. In particular, some trends that seem unambiguously hostile to workplace cooperation, solidarity, and sociability turn out to be coupled with more encouraging developments and to be limited by basic features of human psychology and productivity. On the whole, there may be somewhat less to the story of change and variation than meets the eye.

Bureaucratic Workplace Organizations in Twentieth-century America

To put the new practices and trends in perspective, it will help to look back briefly at the landscape out of which they arose. For much of the twentieth century, the dominant models of workplace organization among major American business enterprises were what we can call the "bureaucratic human relations model" and the "bureaucratic collective bargaining model." Both fit within predominantly hierarchical firms, with stable organizational pyramids and job descriptions. From the perspective of fostering socially valuable human relationships, these bureaucratic models had the virtue of promoting workforce stability and job security, and consequently long-lasting and multifaceted relations among co-workers. The union version had the added virtue of actively promoting solidarity among co-workers. It is perhaps too soon to declare the demise of these bureaucratic models; but I will use the past tense in describing them, for they are receding from the scene and are being supplanted by a different array of models of workplace organization.

The Bureaucratic Collective Bargaining Model

William Kornblum's powerful account of interracial ties in a Chicago steel mill came out of a blue-collar, unionized environment.[16] We will see other examples of this in chapter 4. Why might that be? Part of the answer may lie in the sheer physicality of the work—the dependence of each worker's health and safety on his co-workers and the mutual trust that this both required and fostered. But some features of the mass production model of workplace organization also contributed to the ability of the workplace to serve as an arena of social integration. In particular, the powerful presence and influence of unions in the core of the industrial economy—and the model of lifetime employment that unions championed—laid the groundwork for greater stability, solidarity, and egalitarianism in workplace relationships.

In the mass production economy, unions traditionally bargained for egalitarian and seniority-based compensation schemes, strict seniority in layoffs, a greater role for seniority (as opposed to discretionary judgments of merit and skill) in pay and promotions, clearly and narrowly defined job descriptions, and limits on disciplinary power.[17] All of these terms were backed by a system of "industrial due process" through grievance arbitration.[18] The standard "just cause" provision and the arbitral law surrounding it tended to push management toward more rule-based governance of the workforce. Disciplinary measures and especially discharge, to stand up to arbitral scrutiny, had to be based on reasonable, clearly announced work rules and had to follow principles of notice, progressive discipline, proportionality, and equal treatment of like cases.

These traditional union terms tended to produce a bureaucratic organization with inflexible, narrowly defined job descriptions, rules of behavior, and qualifications.[19] These terms supported a blue-collar version of the now-familiar "lifetime employment" model, which came to describe the career patterns of both unionized employees and many managerial employees. Workers during their most productive mid-career years accepted a wage that was less than their marginal product in exchange for an implicit promise of job security and a rising wage profile, even after productivity tailed off in later years, and of a decent retirement income.[20] The union version of "lifetime employment" was often punctuated by periodic seniority-based layoffs during slack periods. But job security rose with seniority; in the prosperous core industries, workers' careers within a firm typically lasted until retirement. This model appeared to work in the post–New Deal industrial economy for firms as well as workers. Firms gained labor peace, workforce stability and experience, and a willingness on the part of workers to invest in firm-specific skills and to train junior co-workers. The late-career wage premium was more than paid for by the surplus of marginal product over wages during workers' mid-career.

The traditional union terms also tended to align worker interests, to minimize interpersonal competition, and to limit managerial discretion that could be used to target union activists, favor compliant workers, and divide the workforce. The resulting co-worker relationships provided fertile ground for the cultivation of solidarity, which was crucial to the workers' ability to exert or threaten economic pressure on behalf of collective goals. Those periods of collective mobilization themselves created experiences and memories of shared sacrifice that further bonded workers to each other.[21] Unions' internal structures of self-governance brought about additional opportunities for cooperation and compromise among workers from different backgrounds and racial and ethnic identities.[22] All of these features of unionized industrial employment contributed to the bonds among Kornblum's steelworkers.

That is not to say that unions and their members were always champions of racial equality. They were not. Especially among craft unions, which sought to monopolize the relevant labor supply by controlling access to job skills, the economic impetus toward exclusion converged with racist and nativist impulses, and discrimination was endemic.[23] By contrast, the industrial unions of the Congress of Industrial Organizations (CIO), which sought to organize unskilled and semi-skilled workers who could be replaced off the street, pursued a consciously inclusive strategy. In the crucial years leading up to the New Deal, the CIO fostered a "culture of unity" across racial and ethnic lines in defiance of entrenched contemporary norms.[24] But the industrial unions did not control entry to the job and often did little to combat racial discrimination by employers in hiring and job placement.[25]

Absent racism in hiring and entry-level job assignments, the traditional union patterns of job security, rigid job descriptions and promotion ladders, and heavy use of seniority could have operated as built-in protections against discrimination and division among workers. The enactment of the Civil Rights Act of 1964, Title VII, which prohibited discrimination by both unions and employers, began to realize some of that potential. Litigation under the civil rights laws, together with federal government pressure for desegregation by its contractors, brought about real advances in the employment opportunities of black workers, especially in the heavily unionized manufacturing and transportation sectors.[26] As increasingly diverse workforces came under the traditional collective bargaining model, that model exerted a deliberate pressure toward solidarity, equality, and long-term bonds among co-workers.

The combination of the employment discrimination laws and the collective bargaining regime might have proven over time to be an ideal framework for the formation of interpersonal bonds across lines of social division. Unfortunately, that combined regime barely had time to take root before its foundations began to crumble, for desegregation got underway just as deindustrialization began to take its toll. As flexibility and agility became the keys to economic survival in a more competitive and fluid economy, the traditional union model, with its intentional rigidities and elaborate constraints on flexibility and discretion, became a liability in many industries.[27] I will return to these developments below. But let us turn to the nonunion component of the "primary sector," in which personnel management practices sought to provide some of what unions supplied in the collective bargaining model.

The Bureaucratic Human Relations Model

Among the nonunionized workforces of many major companies, including the white-collar workforces of companies with unionized components, what prevailed can be called a "bureaucratic human relations model." The model had disparate pre–New Deal origins, from the "scientific management" principles of Taylorism to Elton Mayo's famous Hawthorne experiments and his "human relations" school of management.[28] By the 1950s these strains had settled into an archetypical pattern that was memorably described in William H. Whyte, Jr.'s *The Organization Man.*[29]

Theory and philosophy aside, the human relations model reflected in part a strategy of union substitution and avoidance.[30] The model sought to reduce turnover, to displace or divert union sentiment, and to compete with union firms for the best employees by satisfying many of the employee desires that otherwise led employees to quit or to unionize. Even for segments of the workforce for which unionization was no threat, the union model helped to establish certain norms, such as the importance of seniority and principles of job security and due process, that could not feasibly be confined to the rank-and-file. The result was the creation of internal labor markets structured around the norm of "lifetime employment," or, more precisely, employment until a predictable mandatory retirement age. The model included a rising wage profile, job security that increased with seniority, progression along a well-established job ladder, and eventually retirement funded largely by deferred compensation plans. Outside hiring was largely confined to the entry level, and higher positions were filled from within. Unlike in the union version, periodic layoffs were rare.

The bureaucratic human relations model, like the collective bargaining model, fostered long-lasting and stable relationships, both among co-workers and between workers and the firm. Loyalty was actively cultivated and was rewarded with increasing job security and compensation and with deferred compensation plans. Loyalty was also compelled, however, by an implicit threat of banishment—for example, in the case of "whistleblowing"—that gave upper management a powerful upper hand even while it proclaimed values of fairness and security. Moreover, the norms of job security and the forms of due process were typically unenforceable, given the strong presumption of employment at will that prevailed through this period.[31] Employee expectations of job security were sometimes crushed without legal recourse.

This reminds us of the bleak underside of the much-touted "lifetime employment" model: It coexisted with a rather torpid external labor market, especially for the mid-career managers and professionals who were its chief beneficiaries.[32] The dearth of outside opportunities reinforced a strong internal pressure to conform to managerial demands and majoritarian mores. It helped produce "The

Organization Man," whose ingrained loyalty and conformity made him a standard target of postwar social criticism.

So, too, the bureaucratic human relations model initially flourished in an era of widespread and largely unchallenged discrimination against racial and ethnic minorities and women. Indeed, the esprit de corps that these organizations sought to inculcate was founded partly on the homogeneity of their white-collar workforces. The civil rights laws challenged those practices. As in union workplaces, some of what those laws did was to push organizations in the direction of procedural fairness and clear rules, job descriptions, and promotion ladders, and to diminish the role of supervisory discretion.[33] Change in the demographics of white-collar workplaces was much slower than in blue-collar workplaces. But the combined regime of antidiscrimination law and strong internal labor markets provided a potentially promising foundation for the development of long-term ties among increasingly diverse groups of co-workers.

The law was changing on other fronts as well. By the 1970s and 1980s, state courts began to come to the aid of employees—especially long-term employees—who were fired in the face of explicit or sometimes implicit assurances of job security. The courts eventually softened some of the sharp and cutting edges of the legal presumption of employment at will for these employees. So, too, the courts developed wrongful discharge doctrines based on "public policy" and occasionally rescued employees who were fired for noxious and socially irresponsible reasons. These legal reforms brought a small dose of "civil liberties" and an extra margin of security to the nonunion white-collar workplace.[34]

The combination of the bureaucratic human relations model with the reforms of antidiscrimination law and of tort and contract law might have strengthened the model's capacity to foster cooperative and egalitarian ties within an increasingly diverse workforce. But the opportunity to test that combined model was short-lived, as in the case of the traditional collective bargaining model. The rigidities of the bureaucratic human relations model, though less binding than those built into the traditional collective bargaining model, were similarly dependent on the comparatively stable and protected competitive environment that prevailed in the American economy for several decades after World War II. Both models began to give way in the face of increasing international competition. Waves of blue-collar and then white-collar layoffs in the 1970s and 1980s crushed the assumptions of lifetime employment and undermined the foundations of internal labor markets.

Contingency, Free Agency, and the Market-Infused Workplace: "*The* New Deal at Work"?

Increasingly unbounded competition and the growing need for flexibility in the production process has brought about an epochal shift away from mass production toward what Professors Piore and Sabel call "flexible specialization."[35] The new flexible forms of production are evidently incompatible with rigid bureaucratic models of workplace organization. But what is taking their place? Some observers see different models taking hold in different sectors.[36] Others see convergence toward a single model: the highly contingent, market-infused workplace. For Wharton School Professor Peter Cappelli, this is "*the* New Deal at Work."

The Rise of Contingent Employment

The market-infused model is partly captured in the rise of "contingent employment." Putting aside a vigorous dispute over the extent and the definition of "contingent employment," there is little doubt that the use of temporary employees, outside contractors, and independent contractors is on the rise.[37] There has long been a "secondary" or "peripheral" labor market alongside the core or "primary" labor market; and in the "secondary" labor market job security was weak and many jobs were explicitly temporary or otherwise tenuous. But what we now call "contingent" employment had generally been the province of unskilled and semi-skilled workers and existed only at the margins of the large bureaucratically organized firms in the primary sector. What is new is the increasing reach of contingent or nonstandard arrangements into the ranks of professionals, technical employees, and even managers, and into comparatively central aspects of a firm's operations.

Some of these workers happily embrace the label "free agents"; many haplessly lament the lack of benefits and of security. The economic marginality and insecurity of many contingent workers has gained the attention of policymakers. But there has been less attention to the implications for the workplace as a social institution.[38] The rising use of temporary and contract workers means that the workplace community is less stable and less cohesive. Its members lack a common identification with a particular firm or its objectives, and they lack common terms and conditions of employment. Their workplace connection is more tenuous and temporary, and their motivation to get along and overcome differences is bound to be less compelling.

The term "contingent employment" connotes a much more unitary phenomenon than in fact exists. Some "contingent employees"—especially those who work side-by-side with "core employees" of innovative firms—are sharing in the trends toward greater collaboration and autonomous decisionmaking that also characterize the new workplace practices; they may be integral members of a production "team." Contingent workers may serve in some firms as a buffer for the core workforce, securing the latter's continued employment by absorbing the ups and downs of the firm's labor needs. Or they may serve as a source of internal competition for a core that is driven by collective anxiety—as tangible daily reminders of the insecurity of the core employees' jobs and privileges. In short, the rise of contingent employment may be only the tip of a massive iceberg: the invasion of the external labor market into workplaces.

The Erosion of Internal Labor Markets

The bureaucratic models of workplace organization that dominated within the primary sector of the economy sought to promote longevity and stability by insulating participants from the pressures of the external labor market. In a world in which longevity and stability are less valued than up-to-the-minute skills and flexibility, these patterns are eroding. According to Cappelli:

> What ended the traditional employment relationship is a variety of new management practices . . . that essentially bring the market—both the market for a company's products and the labor market for its employees—directly inside the firm. And once inside, the market's logic quickly becomes dominant, pushing out of its way the behavioral principles of reciprocity and long-term commitment, the internal promotion and development practices, and the concerns about equity that underlie the more traditional employment contract. The policies and practices that buffered the relationship with employees from outside pressures are gone.[39]

Firms increasingly recruit from the outside rather than promote from within; they "outsource" work that is outside of their core expertise; they actively compete with other firms to retain key workers. Workers, for their part, compete with outsiders to keep their jobs and advance within the firm.

The more sanguine version of this "New Deal" entails a shift from the "lifetime employment model," with its implicit promise of security and longevity with the firm, to a new implicit promise of employability and career advancement through the acquisition of skills, knowledge, and connections.[40] The individual's attachment is less to the firm than to a team or a project, which is of finite duration and which may include participants from different firms. In a bleaker version of the "New Deal"—what one commentator has called the "disposable workplace"—firms set up explicit or implicit "tournaments" among several workplaces or work groups, in which only the highest performing groups will survive. Collective insecurity is used to spur performance, and contingent and contract workers are used not only to maintain flexibility and lower costs, but also to bring the competition for continued employment into the workplace itself.[41]

The implications of these developments for social relations within the workplace are mostly disheartening. On the bright side, they may increase the sheer number of co-workers with whom a given individual will interact; workers in these fast-moving short-term relationships may gain some facility in forming usable relationships with strangers from a variety of backgrounds. That is not a negligible skill. But those relationships are likely to be very thin and weak. Workers with no job security are bound to feel less free to discuss job-related issues and complaints with co-workers, to bring shared concerns to management, and to take any other kind of collective action in support of those concerns. The trade-off for workers is a more vibrant external labor market. That may give some workers a comparable or even greater share of the growing economic pie, at least in a seller's market. Alan Hyde's rich depiction of what he calls the "high-velocity labor market" of Silicon Valley leads him to conclude that the breakdown of internal labor markets in favor of highly fluid and competitive external labor markets has worked well for Silicon Valley's skilled workers, as well as for the growth and vitality of its information-based regional economy.[42]

For those with sought-after skills and real opportunities in the external labor market, those opportunities might counteract some of the insecurity of the new implicit contract and embolden workers to take risks. But for whom should they be expected to take those risks? In the Silicon Valley of the 1990s, workers with high mobility and no expectation of long-term employment took entrepreneurial risks; they left firms to work for or form high-risk start-ups. But without the expectation of long-term membership in a stable workplace community, workers can hardly be expected to risk their own prospects for the sake of their fellows within the workplace community. The prospects for solidarity in this kind of environment appear dim.

One way to think about these changes is in terms of the familiar trilogy of exit, voice, and loyalty.[43] In a firm with a strong internal labor market—both the union and the nonunion version—exit was discouraged and loyalty to the firm was rewarded; at least among union workers, voice was protected and institutionalized. What evolved among rank-and-file co-workers as a result could also be described in terms of loyalty and voice: mutual loyalty, or solidarity, and the cultivation of collective voice. A shift from strong internal labor markets to a more active external labor market entails a shift away from loyalty and voice and toward exit as a worker strategy for dealing with frustration and discontent, and toward "banishment" as an employer strategy for dealing with inadequate performance or economic downturns. Whatever its economic payoff, this shift seems clearly to undermine the capacity of the workplace to cultivate interpersonal bonds among diverse co-workers.

The sheer reduction in job tenure alone is bound to take a toll on workplace connectedness. Part of what makes workplace relationships distinctive is that they form under the imperative of getting along over the long haul. If there is no long haul, workplace relations may become more casual, low-stakes interactions with less transformative potential. The market-infused workplace described by Cappelli and others would rob the social experience of working together of much of what makes it most valuable for society.

Constraints on the Market-Infused Workplace

It is important not to overstate the case, however. First, the evidence does not indicate that internal labor markets have collapsed throughout the economy.[44] The high-velocity job market of Silicon Valley may be a harbinger of things to come, but they have not yet come. Average job tenure has declined only modestly in recent years, and the decline has been concentrated among men; women's job tenure has risen.[45] By some accounts, the downward trend may have already peaked. In the face of the labor shortages of the late 1990s, many companies that had sought to promote the "boundariless career," and to discourage expectations of long-term employment, found themselves trying to reestablish bonds of loyalty and to re-create rewarding career paths.[46] More recently, in the wake of evaporating "dot-coms" and other start-ups, many young job seekers are reportedly looking for more established organizations that offer less risk and greater security.[47]

Trends toward the supposed dissolution of the workplace community are thus subject to the ebb and flow of the labor market. But those trends also run up against some competing workplace imperatives and human propensities. For example, as firms move toward more cooperative and less hierarchical ways of working, they find that productivity depends increasingly on the quality of interpersonal relationships. Those relationships are a form of firm-specific "social capital" in which many firms find that they still need to invest. That takes time. People cannot be plugged into cooperative teams as easily as they could be plugged into a position on an assembly line. Professor Sanford Jacoby thus observes that, "to the extent these systems continue to proliferate, they create employer incentives to stabilize employment."[48] The evidence as to whether these systems do continue to proliferate is not uniformly affirmative, but there is no doubt that collaborative forms of production are much more widespread than they were a few decades ago.[49]

The move toward more cooperative and fluid ways of doing work highlights another side of recent trends in workplace organization: The erosion and fragmentation of long-lasting horizontal ties among workers has been accompanied by an expansion of vertical communication and collaboration between rank-and-file production and front-line service employees and the professionals, managers, and supervisors who formerly monopolized decisionmaking power and discretion over how the work was done.[50] The former have been compelled to develop new skills of communication and problem solving as they collaborate directly with management and professionals, and as they are given direct responsibility for dealing with customers to customize production and solve problems. This aspect of the new patterns of workplace organization puts a premium on social skills and employee commitment and morale, and builds both autonomy and the skills and relationships on which effective cooperation depends.

It brings a partial and paradoxical element of egalitarianism into the workplace in the form of amicable and reciprocal relations across class lines.

I do not mean to romanticize these emerging patterns. Friendly and egalitarian interactions often mask yawning gaps in privilege and power. Moreover, these new patterns are often essentially forced on employees. Some of these practices have been the vehicle for extracting greater effort and productivity without greater material rewards or a promise of job security and may make work itself more stressful and less rewarding. Even so, they may be embraced by many workers as the cost of survival in a more competitive economy and sometimes as real improvements in their working lives. Indeed, workers who are forced to hone skills of communication and collaboration both with higher-ups within their own organization and with customers report making use of these skills at home and in their religious and community organizations.[51]

But whatever the advantages and disadvantages of the cooperative work practices for workers, their proliferation seems to have put some brakes on the dissolution of internal labor markets. "Lifetime employment"—always qualified and limited to a privileged sector of the workforce—may be a thing of the past. But firms in the "primary sector" still generally adhere to many norms of the internal labor market: principles of pay equity and seniority within the firm, a rising wage profile rather than compensation based on marginal product, a preference for layoffs rather than pay cuts in slack times, and an unwillingness to selectively discharge employees without good reasons.[52] The reason managers give for their continuing adherence to these practices is simple: Employee morale, which is extremely important, would suffer if firms failed to abide by these widely shared norms of fair and equitable treatment. Or, as one manager put it, "At 6 P.M., 95 percent of our assets walk out the door. We have to have an environment that makes them want to walk back in the door the next morning."[53]

In short, managers' ability to indulge a preference for individualized, discretionary decisions, and to rely on the external labor market over the internal labor market to supply needed skills, is constrained by norms of fair play and patterns of human behavior that are still widely and deeply held. No group of employees can be perfectly monitored or motivated by carrots and sticks alone. In most workplaces, morale still matters. It may matter even more in the intensely cooperative, flexible, fast-moving, and hard-to-monitor work processes that are moving to the fore. Employee morale is deeply linked to perceptions of fair treatment, or so managers believe. And what counts as fair treatment corresponds to many of the key features of internal labor markets, such as internally equitable wages and benefits and a significant role for seniority. These propositions are least true in the lowest layers of the labor market, as well as in parts of the high-tech economy. In those sectors, attachments are weak, turnover is high, and investments in the job—economic and psychological—are minimal. But otherwise, some internal norms of fairness and equity and some modicum of security and stability appear to remain necessary to secure the employee goodwill that most employers need.

The Social-Capital-Intensive Workplace

In its extreme form, the new market-infused model fails to foster either the employee loyalty or the stable and productive relations among co-workers that are necessary for successful competition, at least in some sectors. The model also fails to induce adequate investments in training, either firm-specific or general. All of these—employee loyalty, cooperative relationships, and employer and employee investment in human capital—suffer in the absence of reasonable expectations of employee longevity.

For all these reasons, some firms take quite the opposite tack from the market-infused model: Rather than spurring performance through collective competition and insecurity, they seek to tap the productive potential that lies in cooperation, connectedness, loyalty, and experience. Some managers and consultants have discovered the value of "social capital" within the firm as a source of productivity. The point is made succinctly in the title of a recent Harvard Business School book by Don Cohen and Laurence Prusak, *In Good Company: How Social Capital Makes Organizations Work.*[54] Everything these writers advise and everything their favorite firms do is done in the economic interests of the firm. Most of what they do, however, builds interpersonal bonds and habits of cooperation that are bound to spill beyond the workplace.

Social Capitalism in the Nonunion Setting

Following scholarly uses of the term, Cohen and Prusak define "social capital" as "the stock of active connections among people: the trust, mutual understanding, and shared values and behaviors that bind the members of human networks and communities and make cooperative action possible."[55] The benefits to an organization are manifold:

> Social capital makes an organization, or any cooperative group, more than a collection of individuals intent on achieving their own private purposes. Social capital bridges the space between people. Its characteristic elements and indicators include high levels of trust, robust personal networks and vibrant communities, shared understandings, and a sense of equitable participation in a joint enterprise—all things that draw individuals together into a group. This kind of connection supports collaboration, commitment, ready access to knowledge and talent, and coherent organizational behavior.[56]

How does an organization go about building this invaluable resource? Cohen and Prusak stress the importance of "giving people space and time to connect, demonstrating trust, effectively communicating aims and beliefs, and offering the equitable opportunities and rewards that invite genuine participation, not mere presence."[57] Their favorite companies—we may call them the social capitalists—assiduously follow these strategies.[58]

Among the social capitalist tenets most relevant here is the importance of creating the space and the time for co-workers to meet and communicate, not at weekend retreats and company picnics but during the work day: "Social capital is mainly created and strengthened (and sometimes damaged) in the context of real work. The conditions and durable connections that we experience day after day have vastly more influence on it than special events and team-building exercises."[59] Good social capitalists thus create plenty of formal and especially informal meeting spaces. They recognize the importance of face-to-face interaction (and hence the challenge that "virtuality" poses to social capital development). And they know the value not only of work-related talk but of storytelling, discussion of current events, exchange of baby pictures, even gossip, in building the mutual trust and connectedness that is then available for productive use.

The social capitalists also value longevity, and thus resist the movement toward "free agency," volatility, and contingency. Relationships, experience, and especially the shared experience that is embedded in lasting relationships, have value for organizations, and they take time to develop. Here, for example, is Stanford Business Professor Jeffrey Pfeffer's description of SAS Institute, a large, privately held software company:

> It has a turnover rate of less than 4 percent. SAS does not contract out very much of anything, use many part-timers or tell people they need to think about their next job. . . . Nor does it offer stock options, dole out big bonuses or do any of the other things that companies with toxic workplaces have to do in order to bribe people into staying.
>
> What SAS does instead is provide generous benefits like on-site day care, a full-indemnity health insurance plan . . . , a 35-hour business week, recreational facilities—as well as something much more important. While lots of companies say that "people are our most important asset," SAS actually believes it. People are trusted rather than monitored and controlled, given great equipment to work with, permitted to try new things, allowed to have a life as well as a job and, in short, treated with a respect all too rare in today's high-stress workplaces.[60]

To the extent that experience, loyalty, and stable relationships are as important to productivity as these managers believe, then more companies can be expected to compete for designation as "people-friendly workplaces."[61]

Even Professor Cappelli, while proclaiming the ascendancy of the market-infused workplace, recognizes that some employees are not easily replaced and that firms should try to keep their most valued employees from succumbing to the temptations of "poachers" by cultivating their ties to each other:

> Loyalty to companies may be disappearing, but loyalty to colleagues is not. By encouraging the development of social ties among key employees, companies can often significantly reduce turnover among workers whose skills are in high demand. . . . [Companies can do this] by developing programs that create a social community in the workplace. Golf leagues, investment clubs, and softball squads create social ties and bind workers to their current jobs. Leaving the company means leaving your social network of company-sponsored activities.[62]

Cappelli seems to suggest that firms use these strategies selectively to retain "key employees"—those "whose skills are in high demand"—while treating other workers as contingent and disposable. But that may be harder to do than it sounds. In a world of flatter and more fluid hierarchies, individually valued employees need to interact and cooperate with individually replaceable employees. The need to foster that cooperation may lead employers to extend their social capital building beyond the few who are favored by the current skill demands of the external market.

So among the tenets of social capitalism of interest here are those that emphasize "equitable" and even egalitarian values. For example, ideas about space and equity converged in the design of Alcoa's headquarters, which was intended to

> narrow the gap between bosses and employees in the process of making it easier for people to meet and talk. Because everyone uses the kitchens, open spaces, and escalators for the same purposes of eating, meeting, or moving around the facility, those facilities tend to be socially leveling. Old-style executive dining rooms reinforced difference and distance. . . . [By contrast,] these public spaces contribute not only to accessibility but to a kind of equality.[63]

This "kind of equality" was carried through in the design of offices: open spaces and cubicles erased the hierarchy of the windowed and the windowless. Then-CEO Paul O'Neill occupied "the same nine-by-nine-foot cubicle that everyone else has. He explains: 'The size of my cubicle says to the rest of the organization that they are as important as I am as measured by the workspace. That's what it ought to be to get the organization to work together.'"[64]

Of course, the size of the CEO's salary says something else. One might question whether minimizing the visible signs of status and power, and emphasizing transparency and open communication, genuinely reduces or merely obscures inequality within firms. But either characterization is probably too simple. In any event, the more cooperative, communicative, and trusting relationships that these firms foster for their own economic ends are likely to teach more coopera-

tive, communicative, and trusting habits of thought and patterns of social interaction that people will carry into the world outside of work. That would appear
to be the lesson of the experimental and field research reviewed in chapter 2.

Among the constellation of practices that characterize the social-capital-
intensive workplaces are those that aim to accommodate workers' lives outside
the workplace. Some of those practices are explicitly "family-friendly," such as
the subsidy or provision of child care or the provision of paid leave time for childbirth, infant care, and care of sick children or other relatives. These practices
may be part of an economically motivated strategy for attracting and keeping
good and committed employees; they may stem partly from a sense of corporate responsibility. But these practices are often part of a larger set of workplace
policies that simply make it possible for people to live decent lives while suc-
ceeding at work. These "human-friendly" policies may contribute to civic life
not only by enhancing the civic potential of the workplace environment itself,
but also by allowing people to be involved in their communities outside of work.
That is a different kind of good thing than I mean to emphasize here, but there
is reason to believe that these good things—civic-ness at work and the capacity
to maintain a rich family and civic life outside of work—go together. Both may
be prongs of an organizational strategy that responds to workers as individuals
with a range of human needs and aspirations.

On one important subject, Cohen and Prusak's extended paean to social capital building in the workplace is curiously silent: the significance of workplace
demographics and diversity. One is left to wonder whether these organizations
succeeded in building connectedness while ignoring issues of racial and ethnic
identity, or whether they simply had relatively homogeneous workforces. We
will return in the next chapter to the question of how increased racial and ethnic diversity within workforces intersects with the increased emphasis on teamwork, cooperation, and connectedness. For the moment, we can simply observe
that, in the context of an increasingly diverse labor force, the increasing importance of effective collaboration is spurring organizations to find ways of getting
individuals to get along and work productively across group lines.

While the penetration of the extreme "free agency" model may be limited by
the continuing importance of stable, trusting, and cooperative human relationships in economic production, there is little doubt that "lifetime employment"
is fading into history. So in these high-cooperation, high-trust workplaces, employees' relations with their co-workers are not as long-lasting nor as firmly
founded on shared working conditions and physical interdependency; but they
are more numerous, more fluid, and less hierarchical. The team leader on one
project may answer to another team member on the next project. The newest
and youngest member of the team may make more money than more senior
members of the team because of his or her market power. Work is more intensely
social, and social skills—the ability to get along and work productively with a

diverse and shifting array of people without the reassuring constraints of rules or fixed roles—are increasingly important to success.

The current competitive environment will put the social capitalist model of workplace organization in head-to-head competition with the lean-and-mean market-infused model. From the vantage point proposed here, it is clear who the good guys are. A workplace that cultivates long-term relations of cooperation and mutual trust and respect will also foster human connections that enrich social life outside the workplace. To the extent that the law can play a role in nudging employers toward this model—a question to which I will return in chapter 9—the whole society would benefit. But there is an important variant of the high-cooperation model that incorporates a role for formal institutions of collective employee voice.

Cultivating Cooperation in the Union Sector:
Joint Team-based Production

One of the companies held up by Cohen and Prusak as a model of social capitalism—indeed, the one with which they open their book—is United Parcel Service:

> People inside UPS attribute its lasting success to elements of its persistent "character." A low turnover rate . . . makes long careers typical and helps preserve and transmit the firm's values and behaviors. . . . A tradition of promotion from within means that leaders have direct experience with the work of drivers and their supervisors. . . . That promotion policy, good salaries for drivers, and employee ownership . . . contribute to a sense of equity in opportunity and reward and joint membership in a common endeavor. . . . [T]rust, understanding, connection, and a sense of membership are widespread. They make the company work and give it a reputation as a good place *to* work.[65]

UPS exemplifies the social capitalist ethos: "Although large and dispersed and dedicated to efficiency, UPS remains largely a face-to-face, 'conversational' organization, held together by personal contact."[66]

Of course, as the public was reminded during a nationwide UPS drivers' strike in 1997, much of UPS's operations, including especially the drivers who form the core of the workforce, are unionized. Just as one learns nothing from Cohen and Prusak about the significance of workforce diversity for social capital building, one learns nothing about the union or the collective bargaining agreements on which the terms and conditions of most UPS employees—the good salaries, employee ownership, and "distributed decisionmaking"—are based. Those readers schooled in the American managerial tradition of union avoidance are left to puzzle out for themselves how to reconcile this depiction of shared commitment and thoroughgoing cooperation at UPS with the conventional view of unions as rigid, polarizing, and adversarial.

That conventional view is not wholly groundless. As the traditional bureaucratic collective bargaining model has come under economic pressure, it has devolved in some cases—often where management has sought deep concessions and the union has dug in its heels—into a highly unstable and conflict-ridden struggle between the union and a management seeking to destroy or declaw it. Long and bitter strikes, permanent replacements of strikers, and decertification battles often punctuate these struggles, as they did at Caterpillar Corporation, Eastern Airlines, and International Paper.[67]

But that is not the only path available. In other cases—where both management and union leadership have chosen cooperation over conflict—the traditional union model has evolved toward a more fluid model of joint decisionmaking such as that found at UPS. Other examples are found in steel, electrical products, and paper, as well as in auto and telecommunications.[68] The Saturn agreement between General Motors and the UAW is perhaps the best-known example. At Saturn, the "extensive decentralization of employment relations . . . has led to extensive involvement by workers and union representatives in business issues."[69] In place of rigid job descriptions, there is a single production worker classification:

> Work units participate as a problem-solving group and make decisions concerning job assignments, job rotation, overtime, and recruitment. Workers perform a variety of job tasks in their work area and also perform some of the planning and control tasks traditionally carried out by supervisors. . . . [T]here is no formal role for seniority in matters such as job assignments, job bidding, overtime, and shift assignments. Most of these decisions are made informally by the work units (i.e., by workers themselves).[70]

Saturn has been described as "an extreme example" of autonomous team-based organization; most unionized firms seeking to follow the cooperative path hew a bit more closely to the traditional model.[71] Indeed, the Godard study reviewed above suggests that those more moderate practices may be *more* conducive to worker well-being, commitment, and sense of belonging than is Saturn's more "extreme" pursuit of team autonomy. Saturn's own experience may provide some confirmation: In 1999, local union elections at Saturn resulted in a defeat of the incumbents and a vote for a somewhat "more traditional approach to labor relations."[72] We should not overlook the remarkable fact that the workers themselves, first by majority vote and then by collective negotiations with management, effected this change in organizational practices.

In some industries and workplaces, then, unions and managers are experimenting with new kinds of contracts and new kinds of relationships. In the union workplace, employee voice—both deliberation among co-workers about shared concerns and dialogue between workers and management—is institutionalized.

Where that institutional voice is sufficiently rooted and stable and unionization is an accepted fact of workplace life, the pressures of competition can lead far-sighted leaders on both sides toward a collaborative equilibrium. That equilibrium, characterized ideally by joint decisionmaking from the shop floor to the directors' boardroom, represents a partial realization of workplace democracy—one that fosters all kinds of productive human interaction—within the constraints of private ownership of productive capital.

The Low-Wage Workplace: The Suppression and the Tenacity of Solidarity and Sociability in the Worst of All Workplaces

Unfortunately, one of the most enduring features of the landscape we are surveying is the low-wage workplace. In some sectors of the economy, what works at work is still minimizing the cost of labor per unit of production through low wages and a relentless work pace.[73] Examples may be found in textile and clothing manufacturing, in meat and poultry processing, and in much of the food service industry; but the low-wage model has at least a foothold in many sectors, from telecommunications to computers to retail and finance. These workplaces exemplify the persistence of the "race to the bottom" in wages and working conditions that New Deal reformers sought to curb. Given the disappearingly low cost of labor in developing parts of the world with which some American employers now compete, it is hard to know where the bottom is in this race.

In the typical low-wage workplace, the worker's pace is closely monitored, turnover high, training minimal, and promotional ladders tenuous or nonexistent. There are few formal policies regarding leaves, discipline, and pay, and decisions on all these matters are made on a case-by-case, discretionary basis by supervisors and local managers. Employer authority is exercised through ready resort to the stick of discharge rather than the carrot of long-term rewards. These workplaces often operate at the margins of the law, and often in violation of minimum economic and health and safety standards. The low wages and oppressive working conditions may stimulate a desire for unionization, but any whisper of such a desire is met with reprisals or the threat of reprisals. These employers regard unions not as dying dinosaurs but as fire-breathing dragons that must be vigilantly fought off.[74]

The conditions in these workplaces are toxic for individual workers, for their families, and for their communities for a host of reasons. But I want to emphasize the less familiar threat posed by the low-wage sector to the civic health of the society. For in seeking to maximize the output of unskilled workers and to squelch any whisper of unionization or dissent, these employers suppress all kinds of productive human interaction. Employers aggressively suppress communication among workers about their oppressive working conditions and poor wages, and particularly about the possibility of organized opposition, by close oversight and the ever-present threat of discharge. Intense supervision and monitoring and the pervasive threat of discharge supplant and suppress the voluntary cooperation that is otherwise commonplace at work. Workers are also left little time and space for informal sociability. Sociability itself is not especially threatening, but it is an incidental casualty of both the intensely driven and intensely monitored pace of production and the aggressive suppression of dissident union talk.

So, for example, in a North Carolina slaughterhouse, workers on the "cut lines work with a mindless fury. There is tremendous pressure to keep the conveyor belts moving, to pack orders, to put bacon and ham and sausage on the public's breakfast table. There is no clock, no window, no fragment of the world outside. Everything is pork."[75] Injuries, both from the knives and from the repetitive motions, were a fact of daily life. Not surprisingly, some of these workers thought they needed a union; but "[e]veryone [was] convinced that talk of a union will get you fired."[76] Or worse. During a 1997 union drive, Mexican workers feared that unionization would get them deported, while many native-born workers, black and white, were unhappy with the union's liberal stance on immigration. Workforce divisions might have been enough to defeat the union drive, but the company didn't take chances; on the morning of the vote, employees were met by a phalanx of deputy sheriffs in riot gear.

Or consider an entirely different sort of low-wage workplace: the Wal-Mart store in which Barbara Ehrenreich worked "undercover." She found many ways "of keeping low-wage employees in their place."[77] For example:

> Rules against "gossip," or even "talking," make it hard to air your grievances to peers or—should you be so daring—to enlist other workers in a group effort to bring about change, through a union organizing drive, for example. Those who do step out of line often face little unexplained punishments, such as having their schedules or their work assignments unilaterally changed. Or you may be fired . . . Wal-Mart employees who have bucked the company—by getting involved in a unionization drive or by suing the company for failing to pay overtime—have been fired for breaking the company rule against using profanity.[78]

The fact remains that workers do occasionally "buck the company," consciously risking their jobs in pursuit of a better collective future for themselves and their co-workers. Wal-Mart's own concerted efforts to suppress this activity have produced a string of adverse labor law rulings, but little by way of remedies.[79]

Stories like these stand as a harsh rejoinder to the uplifting depiction of "working together" with which we began. The demographics of the low-wage workplace often bear little resemblance to the "comparatively integrated" workplaces of the portrait sketched above. Their workforces, especially those in the worst-paid, most dangerous, and dirtiest jobs, tend to be overwhelmingly non-white and heavily drawn from recent and often illegal immigrants. So in the North Carolina slaughterhouse:

> The first thing you learn in the hog plant is the value of a sharp knife. The second thing you learn is that you don't want to work with a knife. Whites, blacks, American Indians, and Mexicans, they all have their separate stations.
>
> The few whites on the payroll tend to be mechanics or supervisors. As for the Indians, a handful are supervisors; others tend to get clean, menial jobs like warehouse work. With few exceptions, that leaves the blacks and Mexicans with the dirty jobs at the factory.[80]

Even within this bottom category, status and pay differentials tracked lines of race and ethnicity: Native-born black workers got the better paid jobs on the "kill floor," while most Mexicans were relegated to the even more grueling "cut floor" where the animals were quartered.[81]

Within these segregated low-wage workforces, managers assiduously minimize the need for cooperation, the possibility of collective dissent, and the time and space for sociability. Still, they have not managed to eliminate those impulses. Sociability arises out of basic human needs; and where workers share low wages, long hours, and grueling and dangerous work, sociability may lead to solidarity and individual discontent may coalesce into collective discord. Sometimes management's divide-and-conquer strategies work, as they seemed to do in the North Carolina slaughterhouse; sometimes they do not. Evidence of the resilience of sociability and solidarity even in a harshly repressive environment can be found in the pre–New Deal history of labor militancy in a pervasively low-wage, Tayloristic economy. Contemporary evidence can be found in the fact that low-wage workers still whisper of unionization, and employers still fire them for it.[82]

The point of this is not to counsel complacency. On the contrary, it is clear that these low-wage workers are enjoying at best a very impoverished version of the workplace experience that I contend is central to the health of our society. The society thus has a powerful interest—one that goes beyond the need to improve wages and material conditions of work in these workplaces—in containing and combating the low-wage model. That effort confronts many hard questions to which I will return in chapter 9 below. But it is also important to recognize that there is something powerful in the process of working together that resists repression—something that should be recognized and put to work for the society as a whole.

While low-wage production engages a bigger share of the labor market in the United States than in most developed economies, it does not predominate. Most employers still cannot do without some kind of internal labor market, at least for the core of their workforce. Neither, however, can most employers do without the greater flexibility and fluidity that the free agency model epitomizes. Many firms mix their strategies, cultivating community and maintaining rather strong internal labor market norms for the core of their workforce while making significant use of contingent workers for more peripheral parts of the operations or for short-term needs.

The picture that emerges is full of experimentation, variation, and uncertainty. There are parts of the economy in which workplace relations are deformed and absurdly incongruent with the idealized portrait of "working together" with which I began. And throughout the economy, the civic potential of workplace relations is under strain and incompletely realized. But there is enough sociability, cooperation, and solidarity in the workplaces of today to demonstrate the civic and integrative potential of working together and the value of building on that potential. One need not overlook the deficiencies in the emerging picture to conclude that it is well worth devoting energy and resources to the project of building up and building on the civic potential of the workplace.

WORKING TOGETHER ACROSS RACIAL LINES

How Much Does It Happen and What Difference Does It Make?

Who are the co-workers with whom we cooperate, communicate, commiserate, and sometimes militate? As we have begun to see, they often come from different neighborhoods and from different cultural, racial, and ethnic backgrounds. In particular, the workplace is the single most frequent site of close and ongoing interaction between black and white adults. That is not to say that most workplaces are highly diverse. On the contrary, many workplaces are overwhelmingly white or thoroughly segmented along racial lines. Discriminatory hiring, firing, evaluations, and placement, as well as harassment and social isolation, persist and plague the work lives of the underrepresented and less powerful minority group members. But the claim advanced here is a relative one: Integration appears to have proceeded further and more smoothly in the workplace than, for example, in neighborhoods and schools. I suggest some possible explanations for that relative success before turning to the consequences of interracial interaction at the workplace for social attitudes and social relations outside the workplace.

The primary focus here is on black–white interactions. Once we look beyond the black–white divide to the increasingly varied mix of racial and ethnic groups in American society, the picture becomes much more complicated. The extraordinary and increasing heterogeneity within American society, and even within nominally unitary subgroups such as "Hispanics" or "Asian Americans," multiplies the number of different intergroup interactions and defies concise analysis. So at some risk of oversimplification, I will take interaction between black and white Americans as my paradigm case of intergroup relations. It is not the only important line of social division, but it has historically been the most troubled, as well as the most studied, line of division. If "working together" works for black–white relations, we can be reasonably optimistic that it can work across other lines of racial and ethnic identity as well.

Not all of the important questions here are empirical in any simple sense. Nor is the complexity of racial inequality wholly captured in individual attitudes and personal relationships. Indeed, focusing on those attitudes and relationships might seem to divert attention from deeper structural underpinnings of persistent racial inequality—to "depoliticize" the problem of racial inequality.[1] I do not mean to do so. The political significance of "working together" is a major topic of this book, and one that I will address at some length in later chapters. And the policy implications of "working together"—what the society might decide to do differently if we take seriously the importance of that experience—are explored briefly in the final chapters and more thoroughly elsewhere. But the political *valence* of "working together"— the meaning of the personal experience of working across racial lines for the future direction of political change—is highly indeterminate. It depends on what people learn through those experiences, and what they decide to do as a result.

The picture of workplace integration that emerges is one of a glass half-full or a journey half-finished. Both the extent and the experience of workplace integration can be seen in more optimistic terms (at least as compared to decades past and as compared to other social arenas) or in more pessimistic terms. It is fitting that much of the focus of advocacy, commentary, and scholarship is on the half (or more) of the glass that remains empty and on the work that remains to be done. And it is tempting to see in the more optimistic assessments of the state of race relations an apology for inaction. But I mean to do something very different here. In highlighting the progress that has been made in the integration of workplaces and the good that has come of it, I aim to deepen our understanding of what is at stake and to help rejuvenate the faltering commitment to further progress.

Comparatively Integrated Workplaces in a Still-Too-Segregated Society

There has been a good deal of progress toward the desegregation of "public spaces" of American society—places of public accommodation, recreation, and transportation, public services, and the retail sector. But the social interactions that take place there are mostly fleeting and superficial. When we look at the places where people interact regularly and repeatedly with each other, the picture is far less encouraging. As shown in chapter 1, black and white citizens in particular still spend much of their time in families, neighborhoods, schools, and other organizations that are made up predominantly of their own racial group. For most adult citizens the single most likely site of integration—of genuine social interaction across racial lines—is the workplace.

The Comparatively Integrated State of Workplaces

People from different racial and ethnic groups—while often continuing to live, go to school, and worship in separate social spaces—increasingly work together.

That is not to say that the typical workplace can be fairly described as "integrated." There are obviously many overwhelmingly white workplaces, and many more in which African Americans, in particular, have at most a token presence; that is especially true outside of major metropolitan areas and in small workplaces.[2] There are also many workplaces that are thoroughly segmented along racial lines, with all of the good and clean jobs virtually reserved for white Anglo workers and the worst and dirtiest jobs held by African Americans, or recent Latin American immigrants, or for some diverse but decidedly nonwhite or non-Anglo combination of those groups.

The still-considerable racial segmentation of the workforce reflects the continuing effects of past discrimination as well as ongoing discrimination against minorities in hiring and promotions—some of it unconscious—and racial harassment.[3] It is obviously hard to quantify the "actual" incidence of discrimination out there, independent of prevailing legal standards and their application in litigated cases. But a useful benchmark may be suggested by studies using "auditors," which come about as close as possible to bringing the laboratory conditions of "all else being equal" into the actual workplace. In one 1990 study, for example, pairs of "auditors," one black, one white, responded to "help wanted" advertisements in the Chicago and Washington, D.C. metropolitan areas. The auditors and their resumes were carefully matched in terms of experience, education, age, physical strength, and size; the auditors were trained to display similar demeanor, openness, articulateness, and energy level; and they presented identical objective job qualifications. So how did they fare in the job market? In more than two-thirds of the 576 hiring audits, black and white auditors were treated equally; that is, they advanced equally far in the hiring process. In 7 percent of the tests, the black auditor got farther in the process; and in 5 percent, only the black auditor received an offer. But in 20 percent of the cases, the white auditor advanced farther; and in 15 percent, only the white auditor was offered the job.[4]

Even more striking are the results of a 2002 study in which researchers responded to 1,300 help-wanted ads in Boston and Chicago by submitting résumés—typically four for each job—with equivalent education, skills, and experience but with different names.[5] The researchers assigned names that, according to birth certificates issued in the relevant birth years, were either common among blacks but not among whites (e.g., Tamika, Ebony, Aisha, Rasheed, Kareem, and Tyrone) or vice versa (e.g., Neil, Brett, Greg, Emily, Anne, and Jill). They found that applicants with white-sounding names were 50 percent more likely to be called for interviews than were applicants with black-sounding names. While about 3.8 percent of employers treated black-sounding applicants more favorably, nearly 9 percent favored white-sounding applicants. Overall, 10.1 percent of applicants with white-sounding names and 6.7 percent of those with black-sounding names were invited to interview. The significant advantage in call-back rates for white-sounding names held in both Boston and Chicago, for all sectors and all kinds of jobs, for large and small employers, for those who called themselves "equal opportunity employers" and those who did not, and for both men and women. Especially disturbing is the finding that call-back rates for black-sounding names did not improve significantly with improved credentials.

Together these studies provide a rough and ready gauge of the contemporary incidence of discrimination, at least hiring discrimination against black job applicants: While a few employers may favor black applicants, nearly three times as many appear to disfavor them even when they present identical qualifications.

I will have more to say below about the continuing existence of prejudice, discrimination, and what could be mildly termed the "asymmetry" of interracial relations at the workplace. Still, few would dispute the proposition that workplaces are more integrated than they were 30 years ago and more integrated than almost any other setting involving close personal interaction. Both the progress and its limits are shown in patterns of occupational segregation. Many professional and managerial occupations remain overwhelmingly white,[6] while African-American (and Latino) workers remain concentrated in low-wage, low-skill, and often highly insecure jobs.[7] But African Americans' employment in professional, white-collar, and skilled blue-collar occupations has risen significantly since World War II and since the enactment of Title VII. This is especially true in public employment and among large private sector employers that are most subject to governmental and judicial oversight in the form of federal contract requirements and large-scale litigation.[8]

Consider the changes in certain higher paid occupational categories from 1975 to 2001 among large private sector employers. During that period the percentage of "officials and managers" who were black rose from 3 percent to 6.5 percent; of professionals, from 3.2 percent to 6.9 percent; of "technicians," from 7.5 percent to 11.8 percent; and of craft workers, from 7 percent to 9.8 percent.[9] These numbers are all well under the percentage of black workers in the workforce as a whole, which rose during that same period from 10.7 percent to 14 percent; they reflect an overrepresentation of black workers, relative to their percentage in the workforce, among office and clerical workers (17.3 percent black in 2001), "operatives" (17.3 percent), laborers (18.9 percent), and especially service workers (24.2 percent). These figures suggest increasing though far from complete integration of occupations; they provide only a rough proxy for workplace integration. Together with the survey data reviewed in chapter 1, they confirm a decidedly mixed picture of both progress and disappointing distance from genuine equality and integration.

There are also some disturbing countertrends that threaten to widen the divide between black and white employment and economic success. As whites have left urban centers, and as inner-city workforces have changed complexion, employers sometimes follow white workers to the suburbs.[10] There they find a whiter but increasingly diverse workforce, as middle-class black workers as well as Latino and Asian-American workers also leave the cities for the suburbs in search of both jobs and more congenial environs. But those ex-urban employers leave behind an increasingly isolated and increasingly black urban population. The suburbanization of employment, together with the dramatic shrinking of the manufacturing sector and its reservoir of well-paid blue-collar jobs, pose serious questions about the extent to which African-American inner-city residents do or will in the future share in the experience of working in racially and ethnically mixed workplaces—or perhaps in any stable workplaces at all. Those concerns necessarily qualify claims about the *prevalence* of the experience of working together in contemporary America. But if my claims about the *significance* of that experience for the vitality of democratic life are persuasive, then they suggest added reason to decry the economic isolation of urban African Americans and to redirect public policy and public resources toward the reversal of these disturbing patterns.

All the qualifications and caveats, however, should not obscure the truth in the proposition that workplaces are comparatively integrated and becoming more so. In view of the sadly segregated state of much of American society, even this very partial degree of integration means that the workplace is where working adults are most likely to have genuine interaction across racial lines. The evidence reviewed in chapter 1 indicates that a large majority of black workers have white co-workers, and that most white workers—especially those who work for larger companies—have co-workers of another race, including one or more black co-workers. In particular, the workplace is the most frequent source of significant contact and especially friendships between black and white citizens.[11] This is precisely the pattern one might hopefully expect to follow from the existence of at least some racial integration among the co-workers from whom most working people, as we saw in chapter 2 above, draw many of their "close friends" and "discussion partners." Again, this book is not about friendship as such. But the development of friendships across racial lines attests to the more diffuse conditions of familiarity, sociability, communication, and cooperation that attain among co-workers in somewhat-integrated workplaces.

Why Are Workplaces More Integrated than Neighborhoods and Schools?

It is worth pausing to consider why there appears to be more racial integration in workplaces—more demographic integration and especially more actual social integration—than in many other arenas of social life. The law is clearly one factor. The enactment and enforcement of federal equal employment laws significantly advanced the employment status and economic conditions of black workers.[12] Those laws did much of their work in the first decade or so after their enactment, in dismantling policies of wholesale exclusion and segregation. African-American progress in the labor market has been comparatively slow in recent decades; "deindustrialization" has taken a particularly heavy toll on black employment, which was disproportionately concentrated in blue-collar and especially manufacturing jobs.[13] Still, antidiscrimination law has played a major role in bringing about more racially integrated workforces.

But that is only part of the answer, for the antidiscrimination mandate was extended into housing and schools (as well as public accommodations, which produce little close personal interaction) during the same period of civil rights activity. Residential segregation has persisted more stubbornly than segregation in employment, and moves toward housing integration have often been marred by outbreaks of violence. Professor John Calmore says flatly, "[a]mong the modern civil rights laws, fair housing law persists as the least effective."[14] Similarly, school desegregation became a major legal and political battleground, and in many areas simply failed.[15] By contrast, desegregation of workplaces, while slow and partial, has proceeded comparatively peacefully. So how is it that desegregation seems to have taken hold in the workplace more effectively and with less turmoil than in neighborhoods and schools?

The integration of schools has been frustrated precisely by its close dependence on residential integration, and thus by the same factors that have impeded the integration of neighborhoods. So a closer look at the comparison between housing desegregation and workplace desegregation will prove instructive as well on the question of school desegregation. One key to the greater success of employment discrimination laws may lie in the greater ability to police discrimination in the workplace than in housing. While the cause of persistent residential segregation is a complex matter, illegal discrimination by landlords, developers, real estate agents, and individual sellers surely contributes.[16] But the racial makeup of a neighborhood typically reflects the accretion of individual decisions over many years by buyers, sellers, real estate agents and developers, as well as government officials. Many of the race-conscious decisions that contribute to the continuing segregation of neighborhoods—for example, individual white homeowners' decisions to flee or avoid racially mixed neighborhoods and to pay a premium to live in an overwhelmingly white neighborhood—are not even open to legal challenge.[17] And discrimination in those decisions that are subject to the laws is often very difficult to detect. Whereas the racial composition of a particular workforce can be presumptively attributed to the decisions of a single employer and may be powerful evidence of discrimination, the homogeneous racial makeup of a neighborhood or community cannot be traced to any one actor.

Of course, just as housing discrimination law fails to reach an individual white homeowner's decision to leave a newly integrated neighborhood, employment discrimination law would fail to reach the decisions of white employees to flee a newly integrated workplace. But the latter doesn't seem to happen much. Therein lies another possible clue to the greater success of workplace integration. "White flight" has been a widely publicized impediment to integration of schools and neighborhoods; but it has not been much of a force, or else it has largely escaped notice, as a response to workplace integration. To be sure, what we might call "white flight" by employers does pose a serious potential threat to black–white integration. But white people appear less inclined to dislocate themselves in order to avoid working in the same workplaces with black people than they are to avoid living in the same neighborhoods or sending their children to the same schools with black people.

On the contrary, survey data reflect widespread support among white workers for racial and ethnic diversity—not just "equal opportunity" but demographic diversity—in the workplace. In one recent survey, 63 percent of all workers, and 60 percent of white workers, agreed or strongly agreed that "the diversity of a company's employees should reflect the diversity of the city in which it is located." Indeed, more than half of all workers (56 percent), and nearly half of white workers (49 percent) agreed that "employers should be *required by law* to maintain a certain level of diversity in the workplace."[18] On its face, that is a remarkably strong endorsement of demographic diversity at work; it goes far beyond voluntary affirmative action efforts, and verges on an acceptance of "quotas." These results should not be overinterpreted; survey data are notoriously superficial on such issues.[19] Moreover, support for workplace diversity does not translate into support for some obvious means of achieving diversity: In the same survey, only 15 percent of white respondents agreed that "because of past discrimination, qualified African Americans should receive preferences over equally qualified whites in such matters as getting jobs."[20] Finally, it must be noted that, for most of those white respondents, a workforce that reflects "the diversity of the city in which [they themselves] are located" may leave them comfortably in the majority. Still, white workers appear at least tolerant and often supportive of racial integration at their workplaces to a greater degree than in their neighborhoods or their children's schools.

We might speculate about why this is so. Part of the answer may lie in that which is absent from the workplace: White anxieties about children and schools and about declining property values, whatever their source, motivate some white flight from integrated neighborhoods; integrated workplaces trigger neither concern. But much of the answer may lie in that which is present in the workplace but not in neighborhoods: managerial authority. We have noted that the existence of a single gatekeeper who can be held legally accountable for the racial makeup of workplaces enhances the efficacy of employment discrimination law. That same fact may quell white fears that integration will go "too far." Maybe white workers trust overwhelmingly white managers to act as gatekeepers and to keep the workplace from becoming "too black." Maybe, too, the presence of rules, discipline, and (overwhelmingly white) authority structures in the workplace curbs fears that spur white flight from less regulated environments.

It is not only white attitudes and preferences, however, that affect the prevalence of integration. Another reason for the comparatively integrated state of the workplace may lie in the comparatively robust commitment to workplace integration among black Americans. There is more ambivalence about integration in other spheres of social life. Powerful voices in the black community have questioned the importance of integration in public schools and in neighborhoods, and the supposedly implicit presumption that contact with white people is necessary for black people's flourishing.[21] These commentators have celebrated the virtues of distinctively minority schools and neighborhoods, provided they have comparable services and resources.

The ambivalence about integration is perhaps most evident in connection with public education, the site of the first great desegregation battles. Over a quarter-century ago, Derrick Bell famously questioned the decisions of civil rights lawyers to press single-mindedly for school integration in the face of a strong current of support among their clients in the black community for more resources within racially identifiable schools.[22] Similarly, there is widespread support for the role of historically black colleges in fostering the aspirations of black students. Justice Clarence Thomas, joining in the decision to terminate a desegregation decree, questioned the priority of school integration over school quality and resources: "It never ceases to amaze me that the courts are so willing to assume that anything that is predominantly black must be inferior."[23]

A parallel view has emerged in housing. At least some part of the substantial residential segregation that exists can be traced to voluntary "self-segregation"— that is, to a preference among some black people for living in majority-black neighborhoods.[24] Of course that preference is often shaped by the "preference" that some white neighbors express—in the form of unfriendliness or hostility or worse—for living in overwhelmingly white neighborhoods. That preference is also shaped by the felt burdens and anxieties of integration in other spheres of life—what Professor Calmore has called "a profound integration fatigue."[25] But it also represents a genuine choice to live and to raise children in a sort of cultural comfort zone in which skin color and identity are a source of shared pride and not a daily source of tension.

This same preference is expressed in other arenas of civil society, such as religion and associational life, where it is backed by constitutional protections. In recreational life, too, the case has been made for accommodating racially identifiable leisure activities. In the words of Professor Regina Austin, "[t]here is safety in numbers; a bunch of black folks are more likely to get better treatment; and they can carry their sense of homeyness and intimacy with them."[26] Many black people may simply prefer to live and socialize with other black people.

The retreat from integrationist goals is hardly unanimous.[27] But claims for the value of integration are often met with arguments for the cultivation of distinct racial and cultural identity, or at least for the greater comfort, acceptance, and respect found within predominantly black social settings. There is simply no consensus that complete social integration is where we are or should be headed. But there is comparatively little ambivalence attending the struggle for integration of workplaces, and comparatively little talk of voluntary withdrawal into majority-black workplaces. True, there have been calls for greater economic self-reliance, black entrepreneurship, and the promotion of black-owned businesses.[28] But there has been no serious debate within the black community about the importance of integrating good jobs in good workplaces in both the private and public sectors of the economy. To a great extent, that is because too much, in terms of basic economic resources, is at stake in the labor market; too many of the good jobs are in institutions dominated by whites. There is simply no viable separatist option for most people.

A particularly sobering perspective on the contrasting "taste" or tolerance for integration in one's workplace and in one's neighborhood is offered by a black female accountant who lives in a black middle-class suburb of Atlanta:

> By living in an all-black middle-class community, it lets us know that we're good. There are not any white people around here staring us in the face and trying to prove we don't matter. So much goes on at the job that we have to endure, the slights and the negative comments and feelings that we're unwanted. When I have to work around them all day, by the time I come home I don't want to have to deal with white people anymore.[29]

Unfortunately this is not an unusual sentiment: Part of the reason some middle-class blacks seek out predominantly black suburbs lies in the tensions they confront in predominantly white workplaces, in "integration fatigue."[30]

Clearly the experience of workplace integration has been marked by pain and friction as well as friendship and cooperation. But people put up with more pain and friction in the workplace than in other spheres in which they might interact across race lines. They look for ways to work through or work around conflict rather than simply walking away, as they might do if some civic group or advocacy organization in which they participate, or even their neighborhood, becomes a site of conflict or tension, racial or otherwise. This may help to explain the degree of integration achieved thus far in workplaces. It may also encourage optimism that efforts to promote further workplace integration may take hold and accomplish their aims.

Whatever its explanation, the fact remains that integration of workplaces has proceeded further and with less overt controversy than integration of other social domains, both those that are and those that are not subject to antidiscrimination law. Given the amount of cooperation, sociability, and sharing of common concerns that occurs among co-workers, the presence of meaningful racial and ethnic diversity among those co-workers makes the workplace an exceptionally important location in the landscape of race relations in the society.

Some Consequences of Workplace Interaction across Racial Lines

At this point, fellow fans of the popular television drama *NYPD Blue* may find themselves thinking about New York detective Andy Sipowitz. One of the most compelling subplots in the series has been the transformation of Sipowitz's bred-in-the-bone racism as he struggles to assimilate his daily experience of comradery, cooperation, and life-and-death interdependence, as well as discord and conflict, with his African-American and Hispanic co-workers and superiors. *NYPD Blue* is only one of several popular television dramas, such as *ER*, *Law and Order*, and *The Practice*, that depict diverse groups of co-workers depending on each other, sharing jokes and celebrations, forming friendships and romantic ties, confronting ethnic and cultural differences and prejudices, and getting the job done. That is in striking contrast to the monochromatic hues of popular television series that revolve around groups of friends who are not co-workers, such as *Seinfeld* and *Friends*.

Television is hardly a reliable barometer of social reality. It may present a wishful illusion of liberal integrationism.[31] But to the extent that many people seem to find these fictions believable, it may be because they resonate to some degree with personal experiences. We have already seen evidence of the fruitfulness of workplace ties as a source of interracial interaction and friendships. Let us add some depth to this depiction of the consequences of "working together" by turning to the social science literature on intergroup relations. That literature ranges from ethnographic accounts of particular workplaces to field studies and laboratory experiments.

Real Stories of Integrated Workplaces

Let me begin with a story I myself heard from Marvlieu Hall, with whom this book began. About twenty years ago, Marvlieu's first job, with a Fortune 500 manufacturer of medical and personal care products, took her to a nearly all-white town outside of Dallas, Texas. She was put in charge of warehouse operations, with a workforce that was all-white, except for one African American, and all-male. "When the boss first introduced me as the new supervisor, I saw nothing but cold stares and jaws dropping in disbelief. I was twenty-two years old, black, and female, and that's all they knew about me." Not surprisingly, they did not immediately accept her. In her words, "they tried me." But she stood her ground, and management stood behind her. "They knew they were stuck with me." In rather short order, Marvlieu won them over by convincing key employees that she respected their skills and experience, but that she could help them do their jobs better. "They were pretty committed to their jobs. Besides, they were all on incentive pay, and knew they would make better money if we operated more efficiently. Pretty soon they could see that the changes I was pushing would show up in their paychecks." Respect and cooperation, and in a few cases something like friendship, followed.

Marvlieu Hall is an extraordinary person who has made extraordinary opportunities for herself. A story like hers could have, and probably usually would have, had a very different ending. But it is almost unimaginable that she could have formed these relationships, gained the respect of these individuals in this time and place, and overcome their stereotypes and biases, outside the workplace. She connected with them through a common interest in getting the job done, and she carried with her the authority of her workplace position and of the managers who stood behind her. Both the objectives she shared with the workers and the authority that she and higher-ups exercised over them were necessary conditions for her success.

Recall William Kornblum's account of South Chicago steelworkers in the early 1970s. At a time and place in which race relations were tense at best and neighborhoods were largely segregated, workers formed attachments "over a lifetime in the mills [that] often cut across the racial, ethnic, and territorial groupings which may divide men in the outside community."[32] Forced to depend on each other at work, they formed ties that were simply unimaginable outside the mill. And yet they sometimes carried those ties to the outside world: Black and white workers "routinely share[d] wakes, funerals, retirement parties, weddings, and a host of family activities over the course of their lives in the mill."[33] Racial hostility became at least leavened with feelings of solidarity, respect, friendship, and affinity.

Similar factors were at work in a New Jersey steel plant in the mid-1970s, when it became the site of several dramatic "wildcat" strikes. Rick Fantasia, a worker-turned-sociologist working in the plant at the time, found a remarkably diverse workforce, including roughly equal numbers of black, Hispanic, and non-Hispanic white workers, with each of those groups encompassing various ethnic subgroups.[34] Fantasia found, however, that "the actual activities and requirements of work, combined with certain patterns of social interaction, served to minimize . . . divisions" among these diverse workers.[35] Among the "patterns of social interaction," Fantasia found that "[k]idding and joking about racial, ethnic, and cultural matters provided a safe outlet for the expression of prejudices and differences," and often led to "a real sharing of culture."[36]

This is not to say there was no racial tension at the plant. Racial dynamics were complex, and individual attitudes contradictory.[37] But the divisions that remained did not prevent large and diverse groups of workers from joining in two spontaneous "wildcat" strikes—actions in which each participant could have lost his job—in support of fellow workers. Fantasia emphasizes that this soli-darity was as much a product of the collective action as it was a condition for it. Still, "the conditions of work and the day-to-day social interaction they shaped created at least a surface level of mutuality, a foundation of trust among the workers."[38] Working together created bonds of connectedness; acting together galvanized and strengthened those bonds.

Both of these last two workplaces were unionized industrial facilities. Aver-age job tenure was long and much of the work entailed an unusual degree of physical interdependency. Moreover, the presence of a union created additional ties among workers and promoted egalitarian practices and sentiments. To the extent that these features of a workplace tend to engender positive interracial interactions, it is especially troubling that unionized manufacturing jobs like this are disappearing. But these depictions of intergroup amity and respect in an era marked by interracial tension and conflict provide auspicious evidence of the possibilities that lie in working together.

Even more striking evidence of those possibilities may be found in the expe-rience of the workers who eventually made up the Congress of Industrial Orga-nizations (CIO) and helped to bring about the New Deal. The conditions seemed inhospitable: Ethnic loyalties were strong and reinforced by language differences; racial subordination was widely institutionalized; and employers often sought to exploit racial and ethnic divisions to thwart collective action. But employers also sought to break down ethnic loyalties and substitute loyalty to the firm. They did so partly by deliberately mixing ethnic groups both at the workplace and in ethnically mixed, company-based social programs—company-sponsored base-ball and bowling teams, social clubs, English classes, and other educational pro-grams. Employers' positive efforts to build loyalty to the firm in place of ethnic loyalties often backfired, however, when firms failed to deliver on paternalistic promises; for those very efforts had created common ground among the work-ers and multiplied their opportunities for interaction across ethnic divisions. The convergence of diversity within work groups, the increasingly centralized and integrated organization of work, and broader opportunities for sociability among co-workers encouraged closer cooperation across racial and ethnic lines and helped to bring about the explosive growth of the CIO and eventually the suc-cess of the New Deal.[39]

Indeed, recognizing the divisive potential of racial and ethnic divisions, the CIO deliberately fostered a "culture of unity" among diverse workers in the 1930s. Historian Lizabeth Cohen recounts this honorable chapter in organized labor's history:

> Racial unity became a watchword of the CIO's campaign in the 1930s, and to an astonishing degree in those early years . . . it became a reality in locals everywhere. A black butcher in Armour's sheep kill, filled with optimism,

boasted to a WPA interviewer in 1939 that whereas once "the white butchers hated the Negroes because they figured they would scab on them when trouble came, . . . with the CIO in, all that's like a bad dream gone. Oh, we still have a hard row, but this time the white men are with us and we're with them."[40]

The CIO unions organized their own racially and ethnically integrated recreational activities. Some even took it upon themselves to integrate the taverns and restaurants surrounding their factories—using the familiar tool of the boycott—so that they could be used as meeting places.[41] Cohen concludes: "The CIO hardly created a racially integrated society, but it went further in promoting racial harmony than any other institution in existence at the time."[42] It did so on the foundation of workplace integration, interdependence, and cooperation.

The transformative potential of workplace cooperation is perhaps most striking against the backdrop of the unreconstructed racial and ethnic divisions of the 1930s or of the fractured and volatile race relations of the 1970s. But that potential can be seen in more contemporary workplaces as well. Indeed, it can be seen in virtually any successful union organizing campaign in a racially mixed workforce, where management seeks to exploit racial divisions and the union must forge solidarity across those divisions. Race is not submerged in those campaigns; indeed, successful unions have learned to appeal to racial and ethnic loyalties and commitments in ways that do not divide workers from each other.[43] That story is well told by Professors Lani Guinier and Gerald Torres.[44]

Guinier and Torres recount, for example, the struggle to organize a union and secure a contract at a K-Mart distribution center in Greensboro, North Carolina, in the 1990s. The union organizers found that "the Greensboro plant—the only K-Mart distribution center with a majority nonwhite workforce—received the worst wages and benefits of any center in the country."[45] The challenge for organizers was to use the issue of racial injustice to unite rather than to divide workers and the community.

> Both labor and their allies in the Pulpit Forum [a group of black ministers that had been formed in the civil rights struggles of the 1960s] were convinced that K-Mart management believed it could get away with underpaying workers at the distribution center because the black workforce would passively accept this treatment. But they worried that . . . organizing the union effort solely around the issue of discrimination would alienate some whites and play into the divide-and-conquer strategy that opponents of the organizing effort were counting on.[46]

The black ministers' case to their parishioners was that "K-Mart's refusal to pay a living wage was a threat to all those in Greensboro who wanted to build a sustainable community."[47] The black ministers' framing of the issue opened the door for white workers and community members to join in the ministers' weekly protests on K-Mart's property and in the resulting arrests. A turning point came when K-Mart sued to enjoin the protests, but, in accordance with its "divide-and-conquer" strategy, named only black workers and black ministers. Rather than succumb to the company's bid to further racialize the dispute, the black community reached out to the white workers and their ministers, who promptly held a news conference asking why they were not sued for their participation in the shared struggle.

Much of the drama, as it is recounted by Guinier and Torres, takes place in the black churches and in the campaign of civil disobedience that they helped organize, and not within the workplace in which white and black workers worked together under the same wage structure day after day. Clearly this is not a simple story of common workplace bonds overcoming racial divisions. Guinier and Torres make a powerful case that racial solidarity and the black community's shared experience of racial injustice proved to be crucial resources in mobilizing the larger community against injustice and deprivation—that "racializing" this struggle in this way was an essential part of broadening and energizing it. Seen one way, the story they tell might be seen as more of a counterpoint to than an example of the unifying power of workplace bonds: common economic interests at the workplace had proved insufficient to unite the workers and to overcome employer resistance without the infusion of race consciousness—consciousness of racial injustice and how it harms the broader community.

At the same time, it is striking that many of the stories that Guinier and Torres use to develop their argument arise out of workplace struggles and organizing efforts. They describe, for example, another organizing drive at the largest textile plant in the United States that first failed when it sought to ignore racial issues, and then succeeded:

> It was only when union organizers found they could draw on the strengths of Chicano and black communities that the organizing effort made progress. By highlighting the willingness of blacks and Chicanos to work together and take a stand, the organizers helped white workers see that the racial pride of minority communities strengthened the coalition. . . . Racial pride became a vehicle for building worker, and ultimately community, solidarity.[48]

The power of shared workplace experiences and concerns often supplies the foundation for the challenging project that Guinier and Torres outline: that of building empathy and solidarity that both draws on and transcends racial identity.

It is not, however, only in blue-collar workplaces or only in union organizing drives or, for that matter, only in opposition to hierarchical authority, that the power of workplace connectedness can be seen. The experience of working together across racial lines operates more diffusely and less dramatically on the attitudes, beliefs, and preferences that people bring into the workplace and that they in turn carry out of the workplace into their personal, civic, and political lives. That is a claim I will develop theoretically in chapter 6.

The foregoing examples of workplace cooperation, communication, solidarity, and friendship across lines of social division may strike some readers as painting far too rosy a picture. It could certainly be countered with a far bleaker account—complete with its own litany of anecdotes—of hostility and harassment of racial minorities and of women, especially at predominantly white or male workplaces. So let us step beyond stories and surveys, and examine the social psychology of intergroup relations.

The Social Psychology of Intergroup Relations

A leading early theory of prejudice posited that negative stereotypes and hostility toward other racial groups flourished in ignorance and that close contact between members of different races improved racial understanding and racial attitudes.[49] Segregation was thus as much the cause as the result of racial tension and division. Integration and positive interracial contacts were the answer. Not all contact was expected to have salutary effects. According to Gordon Allport, a leading proponent of the contact hypothesis, "[o]nly the type of contact that leads people to *do* things together is likely to result in changed attitudes."[50] More specifically, Allport predicted that prejudice

> may be reduced by equal status contact between majority and minority groups in the pursuit of common goals. The effect is greatly enhanced if this contact is sanctioned by institutional supports . . . , and if it is of a sort that leads to the perception of common interests and common humanity between members of the two groups.[51]

The contact hypothesis provided one pillar of social scientific support, as did the more famous "doll studies" of the stigmatizing effects of segregation, for the legal assault on school desegregation in *Brown v. Board of Education*.[52]

The contact hypothesis has been much tested, criticized, and refined over the years. Early research in the school context, in which conditions were thought to be quite favorable for positive interracial contact, reached mixed results. Later generations of social scientists criticized the contact hypothesis for its individualistic focus, its seemingly naïve confidence in the value of experience and knowledge, and its neglect of issues of group power and status.[53] The notion that interracial contact and changes in individual attitudes could "solve" the problem of racial inequality in America is a lost illusion.

Still, it may be time, as Professor Calmore has urged, to "give the contact hypothesis another chance."[54] For as a simple empirical matter, the contact hypothesis has proven to be quite robust over the years. It has been tested, and usually confirmed, in a large number of empirical studies—field studies, survey research, and laboratory experiments—in a wide range of settings.[55] One recent survey of the research concludes that "there is undoubtedly a positive correlation, generally speaking, between reported interaction of members of an ethnic out-group and positive or friendly attitudes toward that group."[56] The research has yielded a consensus that intergroup contact tends to reduce prejudice when individuals interact in conditions of equal status and "cooperative interdependence" and when there is "normative support for friendly intergroup relations."[57] Another theorist has suggested that the single crucial condition for positive interracial contact is that it take place in a setting with "friendship potential."[58] Numerous controlled studies have shown a positive relationship between even short-term cooperative interaction with equal-status partners and feelings of respect and liking for the other-race individual.[59]

How does the workplace stack up as a site for constructive intergroup contact? The requirement of equal status is obviously problematic within any hierarchically organized institution. It is especially problematic where workplace status distinctions correspond to racial distinctions. Still, when there is diversity among peers, the workplace would seem to hold ample potential for positive interracial contact under this theory. We have already observed that there is more sustained interracial contact in the workplace than elsewhere and that interracial contacts on the job often lead to "social relationships and even enduring friendships."[60] A good deal of on-the-job contact meets the basic conditions for positive interracial contact: It is generally cooperative; it is sustained, personal, informal, and one-to-one; it is often in a context of equal status; and it has the approval of managers and the society as a whole. Indeed, in the world outside the laboratory, the workplace is virtually unique in its capacity to convene individuals who would not otherwise choose to interact and compel them to cooperate.

The idea of compelling people to get along may sound paradoxical and potentially counterproductive. But the success of integration in the armed forces—probably the most successful natural experiment in institutional integration that this country has seen—suggests that people can in fact be ordered to get along.[61] The military service is, to be sure, a very unusual kind of workplace. But the military's experience with integration suggests that, while "normative support" for interracial interaction is important, hierarchical command may sometimes be even better.

Relevant experimental research is harder to come by. Work relationships—which can develop over the course of many hours a day over weeks, months, or years—are particularly difficult to re-create in a controlled experimental setting. But one study sought to approach those workplace-like conditions in what a prominent scholar describes as "the most extensive laboratory test of the intergroup contact hypothesis."[62] Each subject—a white adult identified as "highly prejudiced" in initial tests—was "hired" for what was described as "part-time work" with two partners, one white and one black, both research confederates. The work took place over the course of 20 days and 40 sessions, each lasting 20 to 30 minutes, and consisted of operating an imaginary railroad system for which the "co-workers" planned routes and shipped merchandise. They received regular reports on their joint profits and losses and eventually received a bonus at the end. At several points, after the "co-workers" had developed a good rapport (which they typically did), the black confederate reported a personal experience with racial discrimination, and the white confederate expressed disapproval of such discrimination. At the end of the study, the subjects rated the black "co-worker" in highly favorable terms. More striking, these positive attitudes tended to generalize beyond the well-liked confederate. Several months later, in a context unrelated to the original experimental interaction, the subjects were tested on general attitudes toward black people, and, as compared to controls, expressed significantly more positive attitudes.[63]

One can certainly criticize this or any experiment for failing to capture the messy world of work. But some of the ways in which these experiments fail to replicate workplace realities—especially the limited amount and duration of contact and the lower stakes in getting along—seem likely to understate rather than overstate the potential value of workplace contact. Moreover, the experimental results point in the same direction as the anecdotal, ethnographic, and survey research cited above: Close, cooperative, and constructive interaction among individuals tends to reduce prejudice and hostility toward the groups those individuals represent.

Since the appearance of the contact hypothesis over 50 years ago, we have seen the desegregation of major social institutions. The types of interracial contact that were posited to reduce prejudice, once rare, are no longer so rare. In a broadly parallel development, expressions of overt racial prejudice have declined; white attitudes toward black people in particular, and attitudes toward racial integration and equality, have improved dramatically. The evidence cited above gives some reason for believing those two developments are causally connected.

The Persistence of Prejudice and the Asymmetry of Intergroup Relations

At the same time, all is evidently not rosy on the race relations front. The society remains stratified to a great extent by race and ethnicity. In part, that is the legacy of past segregation and discrimination. In part it reflects basic social and economic forces that tend to perpetuate the effects of past discrimination. In a market-based society, people with more money get more and better of everything—health care, education, housing, and more—for themselves and for their children. But at least part of the explanation lies in the persistence of prejudice and discrimination in the workplace and elsewhere in the society.

The Stubborn Persistence of Bias

Alongside the relatively sanguine "contact" studies are other studies showing the durability of prejudice and stereotypes, particularly by whites toward non-whites, even in the face of interracial contact.[64] These studies reveal the deep roots and the resilience of bias and have fundamentally changed the way many social scientists understand the nature of prejudice and discrimination.

Consider, for example, the unsettling disjuncture between increasingly tolerant explicit attitudes of whites toward blacks and toward integration and the persistence of "white flight" from integrated neighborhoods and other manifestations of white avoidance of and discomfort with black people. This disjuncture reflects what some social scientists call "aversive racism"—"the racism of people who would vote for a black president but might unconsciously steer away from sitting next to a black person on the Metro," or from living in racially mixed neighborhoods.[65] It is hard not to see "aversive racism," thus understood, as a big step forward from the overt and conscious racism that was widespread a few decades ago. But that is not the only way to see it. Says John Dovidio, one of the leading theorists in this area:

> You can see this as a new form of racism which is a necessary step toward its elimination—people who haven't yet been able to overcome their natural biases. . . . The other possibility is that this could be the mutant of the virus that is resistant to change. We used to [challenge] racism by saying it was bad, illegal or immoral. But with modern racism, that message doesn't produce any real change in behavior because people don't think it applies to them.[66]

This form of bias is not only more resistant to moral suasion; it is more resistant to legal challenge, for much of it is either beyond the reach of the law (as in the case of "white flight") or beyond the reach of ordinary means of proving discriminatory intent.[67]

Further insight into the origins of subconscious biases is found in research within the "social cognition" paradigm. According to this leading contemporary theory of intergroup relations, the human mind is essentially hard-wired to simplify and categorize events, things, and people, and to respond quickly based on these categorical judgments. In short, "human cognitive organization predisposes us to stereotyping."[68] Stereotypes "function as implicit theories, biasing in predictable ways the perception, interpretation, encoding, retention, and recall of information about other people."[69] Positive interracial contact thus does not eliminate prejudice because prejudice acts as a filter through which contact is experienced. These processes of bias in judgment and decisionmaking operate against "out-groups"—groups of which the subject is not a member—and in favor of the "in-group."[70] Similarly, research within the "similarity/attraction" paradigm finds that individuals tend to be more attracted to people whom they see as similar and to feel greater affinity and ease of communication within rather than across ethnic categories.[71]

These social psychological tendencies operate subconsciously among people who believe themselves to be unbiased. When those people are in charge of hiring, firing, promoting, and evaluating others in a workplace setting, these tendencies can infect the job prospects of "out-group" members without ever manifesting themselves in an overtly or even consciously discriminatory comment or act. A black employee may, for example, be denied a promotion based on mediocre evaluations by a supervisor who was unconsciously biased against him or her. If challenged, the employer would point to the inferior evaluations to show the legitimate and race-neutral basis for the decision, and there would be no smoking gun in sight to prove otherwise. A white team leader who feels greater affinity and ease of communication with white members of the team may believe that those members contribute more to the team's success, and might recommend them for the next big project on that basis, without attributing those feelings to race.[72]

Even assuming that these unconsciously biased decisions violate the antidiscrimination laws in principle—and there is some controversy over that question[73]—they can rarely be proven discriminatory.[74] The net effect of these stubborn cognitive and affective tendencies is to perpetuate the disadvantages of racial outgroups that are not well represented among workplace decisionmakers and to do so in ways that lie beyond the reach of conventional antidiscrimination law.[75] The social science of intergroup relations thus underscores the need for the law to reckon with the persistence of bias, especially unconscious bias, even as conscious attitudes have become much more tolerant and egalitarian.

These same cognitive and affective dynamics take a toll on the experience of workplace cooperation across group lines. This is documented in the burgeoning empirical literature on organizational diversity and its effects on group performance. There is evidence that group diversity—including racial diversity—improves some aspects of decisionmaking by expanding the range of ideas considered and of alternatives generated. But demographic diversity has also been associated with "lower levels of satisfaction and commitment, lower performance evaluations for those who are different, and higher levels of absenteeism and turnover."[76] As one comprehensive review of the literature concluded, "the preponderance of empirical evidence suggests that diversity is most likely to impede group functioning," particularly in the implementation as opposed to the decisionmaking phase of group performance.[77]

These studies are chastening. But the lesson we learn from them depends on the question we ask. If the question is whether diverse groups are likely to perform and get along better or worse than more homogeneous groups, the answer is dispiriting: "Unless steps are taken to actively counteract [the negative] effects, . . . by itself, diversity is more likely to have negative than positive effects on group performance."[78] But if diversity is a given—as it is in the society as a whole—then the more important question is whether intergroup relations will be better with more rather than less interpersonal interaction and cooperation across group lines. The answer to that question is quite clear: Constructive, cooperative contact tends to improve intergroup attitudes and relations and to reduce (though probably not eliminate) prejudice.

But what does all of this mean for organizations that are becoming increasingly reliant on the quality of interpersonal relations at the same time as their workforces are becoming increasingly diverse? My main concern here is not with the productivity of diverse work groups. But that is a major concern of managers, and that makes it a concern here. For the decisions managers make about how to organize work and foster intergroup cooperation and efficiency have ripple effects throughout the society. The literature on organizational diversity is vast, and I make no effort to synthesize it here. But I do want to draw out a few crucial implications from the intergroup relations literature for the organization of workplace relations.

Reckoning with Intergroup Bias and Friction within Organizations

The psychology of group identity and bias is obviously very complex. The experience of positive interracial contact does not magically dispel long-held beliefs and unconscious categorical distinctions. Experience and perceptions are filtered through the lens of preexisting expectations, and uncertainty and ambiguity tend to be resolved consistent with those expectations. Intergroup contact can lead not only to improved interpersonal relations and attitudes but also to conflict and antagonism. In the workplace all of these complexities can translate into lower performance and productivity "[u]nless steps are taken to actively counteract [the negative] effects." As organizations have increasingly accepted diversity—whether they accept it as a fact of life, as a feature of good corporate citizenship, as a shield against discrimination liability, or as a tool for reaching an increasingly diverse customer base—they have turned their attention to how to make diversity work for their bottom line, or at least not against it. They have turned to research showing that biases, while "hard-wired," are also malleable.[79]

The intergroup relations literature thus suggests that unconscious stereotypes loom larger in some contexts than in others, and that organizations can take steps to reduce their impact on group processes. For example, while competition between groups exacerbates biases, cooperation can reduce them. Also productive, according to this literature, are "attempts . . . to deliberately promote identification with the larger group and minimize subgroup identification."[80] So, for example, promoting identification of diverse workers with their team, department, or company, or with their union, can help combat biases and tensions.

The cognitive research also highlights the role of a trait's "salience" in intergroup interaction.[81] The more salient the group trait, the more these cognitive processes affect perception, memory, and judgment about individuals. Moreover, the group trait is more salient, for example, when the evaluator has little individuating information about the other-race individual being evaluated; the more particularized and personal information the evaluator has about the individual—the sort of information gained through sustained, personal, cooperative interaction— the less the role of racial bias. The group trait is also more salient, and stereotypes are particularly likely to operate, in the case of a "token" minority than in more integrated settings. The group trait is also more salient when it "converges" with other significant distinctions, such as job category or socioeconomic status; contact is more productive and less distorted by bias where categories are "crosscutting"—where race (or sex) does not typically correspond with job function or with lower status.[82] Similarly, researchers have found that intergroup relations are shaped by the distribution of power among identity groups.[83] All of these results suggest that more thoroughly integrated organizations will be less plagued by unconscious cognitive and affective biases.

The results might also suggest that the less said in the workplace about racial identity, the better. To complicate the picture further, however, other research suggests that confronting issues of identity, intergroup tensions, and racial attitudes among cooperative work groups can sometimes do more to combat subconscious biases and tensions than can simple cooperation in shared tasks and emphasis on shared interests and goals. Field studies of workplaces have found that some organizations are able to use demographic diversity as a kind of diagnostic tool—as a way to identify organizational frictions and pathologies and to learn better ways of functioning.[84] Recall the thesis of Guinier and Torres that racial disadvantage serves as a "miner's canary"—a warning of broader forms of disadvantage and a potential resource in mobilizing mixed-race groups to achieve social change. So, too, some managers find that racial diversity and even intergroup friction can be a resource in identifying and revamping unsound organizational practices and in improving the capacity of organizations to deal better with the conflicts that are endemic to group decision making.[85]

These findings may point the way for organizations seeking to overcome the friction and distance that, notwithstanding the generally positive role of cooperative interaction on intergroup relations, still plague diverse work groups. These lessons are particularly relevant for organizations that rely on highly collaborative, team-based ways of working. Recall that "the preponderance of empirical evidence suggests that diversity is most likely to impede group functioning," unless steps are taken to address these problems. That is an unsettling proposition for firms that have placed "group functioning" at the heart of their operations.

Once again, the lesson they take from this depends again on whether demographic diversity is perceived as a choice or as a fact of organizational life. For firms that perceive diversity as a choice, it may not be the obviously profit-maximizing choice. But for firms that see demographic diversity as a positive virtue or as a fact of organizational life, the increasing importance of effective collaboration will spur them to find ways to improve intergroup relations.

For present purposes, it is less important to understand what works best to promote cooperation and productivity within diverse work groups than it is to appreciate the significance of firms' devoting resources to finding out what works best. Fortunately, the increasingly diverse labor force from which firms draw, along with some pressure from the law of employment discrimination, are helping to make diversity inescapable. Given growing workforce diversity and growing reliance on interpersonal cooperation, more and more firms are impelled to find ways of overcoming some of the friction that comes with heterogeneity. In doing so, they are also doing good work for the society as a whole.

Firms are also impelled—and the law needs to impel them—to seek new ways of insuring equal employment opportunity in the absence of the fixed job categories and promotion ladders around which employment discrimination law developed. For it is not only true that diversity can pose a potential threat to team-building and teamwork; team-based decisionmaking can also pose a threat to intergroup equality and to the ability to detect and police discrimination. Particularly given what we know about the continuing power of subconscious bias, the diffusion of decisionmaking power—the power to hire workers and to assign them to or freeze them out of important projects—among fluid groups of workers threatens to entrench bias in its most subtle form. Antidiscrimination law has yet to catch up with these changes in organizational practice.[86] This is a complicated topic that will bear closer scrutiny in the programmatic part of this project.

The Asymmetrical Experience of Intergroup Relations

This also brings us to an obvious but important observation. On the one hand, stereotyping and bias can be found both among insider groups—groups that dominate an organization (and the society) by their numbers, their power and status, or both—and among outsider groups. White workers may hold stereotypes about black workers, and vice versa. But the *vice* is not the same as the *versa*. In workplaces in which most managers and supervisors, and even most co-workers, are white, the burden of stereotypes, and the perceived need to defy them, falls disproportionately on the outsiders, whose economic fortunes are dependent on the approbation and comfort of the more powerful insiders.

The burden of hidden and unconscious bias falls most heavily on those minority workers who are excluded from desirable jobs and workplaces altogether by decisionmakers who may not be aware of their biases. But the burden also falls on those who cross that hurdle. For the experience of interracial interaction—even of positive and friendly interaction—is not symmetrical. The appearance of cooperation and amity may mask the persistence of racial prejudice among insider employees. And it may mask feelings of alienation, anxiety, and a sense of artificiality on the part of outsider employees.

So, for example, the white steelworkers of South Chicago observed by Kornblum cooperated with and depended upon and supported black co-workers at work; but they went home to segregated neighborhoods in which racial epithets were ubiquitous and resistance to the entry of black homebuyers was an article of faith. And their black co-workers knew this. Fantasia observed white factory workers engaged in day-to-day cooperation, good-natured joking, and spontaneous solidarity with their African-American and Latino co-workers. But among themselves, they sometimes reverted to overtly racist talk. Interracial cooperation, trust, and friendliness coexisted in these '70s-era workplaces with the racism and segregation that pervaded the society outside the workplace. We might hopefully speculate—and the experimental evidence suggests it is plausible—that positive workplace interactions contributed over the longer run, and continue to contribute, to the erosion of overt racial hostility in the decades since. But the picture is only partly sunny and clouded with ambiguity.

The burden of working under the weight of prejudice and stereotypes is greatest in workplaces that are overwhelmingly white, in which African-American or Latino or Asian workers, or even all of these groups together, make up a relatively small minority of the workforce. Black professional and managerial employees in particular—a comparatively privileged minority within a minority—have recounted experiences of hostility, denigration, and paternalism on the part of white co-workers who assume them to be less able.[87] These "integration warriors,"[88] to use John Calmore's term, report feelings of anger, resentment, suspicion, and anxiety in response to conflicting pressures to represent or to submerge their racial and cultural identity.[89] Social scientific studies and the firsthand accounts of outsiders confirm that it is token or near-token outsiders who suffer the most from stereotyping, and from the felt need to "act white," as well as from hostility and harassment. More thoroughly integrated workplaces can foster more symmetrical and more genuine cooperative relations. And of course the law can play a role in bringing about a more thorough degree of integration; that is a topic to which we will return in chapter 8.

As we have noted, the wearing and sometimes blood-boiling work of integrating workplaces has led some among the black middle class to retreat from integrationism and to move with their families to predominantly black communities. But it has not, nor is it likely, to lead to a widespread retreat from integrated workplaces. Most of the black middle class has little choice but to find ways of making integration work in the workplace. The law must do its part to insure that (predominantly white) managers have little choice as well.

So it is crucial to acknowledge that prejudice persists and that it continues to burden racial minorities and to taint their experience of interpersonal relations, within the slightly and moderately integrated workplaces that predominate. But that does not mean that the appearance of interracial cooperation in those workplaces is a mere illusion. The experience of working together, even in the far-from-ideal workplaces of today, does give rise, for example, to what both black and white workers describe as "friendship," and it does so far more often than any other social setting. Even where cooperation remains at the instrumental or superficial level, it has the proven potential to reduce stereotyping and bias, and to foster greater familiarity, greater empathy, and fairer judgments. The law has a limited capacity to prohibit, punish, or even detect the unconscious or well-hidden biases and stereotypes that often infect judgments about and relations among individuals and groups. But the law can help—and has helped—to create social environments in which these destructive attitudes gradually wane.[90]

Taken together, the evidence offers solid support for the integrative capacity of workplace relations in a diverse society. That is not to say that interracial bonds of trust, solidarity, and friendship are ubiquitous in the workplace. For it cannot be said either that workplaces are typically diverse and integrated or that positive social ties inevitably grow out of workplace diversity when it does exist. The evidence confirms a more modest proposition about the development of intergroup connectedness at work: It can happen, it does happen, and, because of the nature of work and the comparative diversity of workplaces, it happens more in the workplace than anywhere else.

The cultivation of interpersonal ties across racial lines is a "public good," one that enriches in diffuse ways the quality of civic and social life. It is not the solution to the enduring problem of group inequality, for the problem is not just one of wrongheaded or uncaring attitudes. In particular, the cultivation of those interpersonal ties will do little to disrupt the intergenerational transmission of advantage and disadvantage in a society in which even such fundamental goods as health care, housing, and education are allocated largely through markets. But the proliferation of warm and constructive interpersonal ties across racial lines helps cultivate a feeling of "being in this together." For reasons that I will develop further in chapter 6, that is an invaluable resource in any effort to redress some of the most insuperable obstacles to equality, and it is an indispensable feature of social relations in a diverse democratic society.

MEN AND WOMEN WORKING TOGETHER

Workplace Interaction across Gender Lines

(and Some Other Lines of Social Division)

There is ample evidence that the experience of working together across lines of social division such as race, though not untroubled by prejudice and hostility, tends to reduce prejudice and hostility. This experience fosters cooperative social ties and skills, conversations about a wide range of work-related, personal, and political matters, and bonds of empathy and affinity across salient lines of social division. Can anything like this claim be made in the case of gender?

Part of the powerful significance of interracial contact on the job stems from the relative paucity of close and cooperative interracial contact outside of the workplace. That is manifestly not the case as between men and women. Most importantly, men and women usually live together for much of their lives as spouses, brothers and sisters, and parents and children, not to mention as neighbors. There is not a general pattern of "gender segregation" in neighborhoods, most schools, and many other spheres of society from which workplace integration is an important departure. On the contrary, notwithstanding women's recent progress in the labor market, there is still more gender segregation in the workplace than in most of the rest of the society. Given the much more frequent and intimate connections between men and women within families and neighborhoods, what difference does it make that men and women increasingly work together in the same jobs and workplaces?

The key to this question may be found in the phenomenon of "role segregation." There is not much spatial segregation on the basis of gender outside the workplace. But role segregation—the assignment of positions and tasks on the basis of gender—remains prevalent, and largely unassailable through law, in many of the spheres outside of the workplace within which men and women interact closely. The workplace is different. Antidiscrimination law prohibits explicit role segregation; and although there is still a lot of de facto role segregation in the workplace, the law affords some leverage against it. The law's condemnation and partial breakdown of role segregation at work has helped to bring about women's advancement into previously male occupations and into relations of parity with or authority over male co-workers. That development has in turn challenged and tended to erode traditional gender roles, attitudes, stereotypes, and hierarchies outside the workplace, including those within the family.[1] To the extent that the equal employment laws are partly responsible for women's advancement within the world of work, the law thus has a powerful indirect influence on gender roles and relations outside of work, and even in the realm of intrafamilial relations, in which direct intervention is sharply limited.

There is one more striking difference between the experience of interracial interaction at work and the experience of interaction between men and women at work: The latter multiplies the manifestations of sexuality in the workplace— sexual attraction, sexual innuendo, sexual jokes, sexual assault, consensual sexual relationships, and sexual harassment. Of course all these things can happen in single-sex environments as well. But in a predominantly heterosexual world, the introduction of women into a predominantly male workplace (or, less often, vice versa) multiplies the possibilities for sexual attraction, tension, and conflict. I will return to this theme briefly below and in chapter 8.

I begin with some data about the extent of gender segregation and integration in the workplace, followed by a brief discussion of the role of antidiscrimination law in promoting the latter. I then turn to a discussion of the consequences of men and women working together outside of traditional gender roles—as peers or with women supervising men. I conclude with some very brief observations about the significance of workplace interaction across lines of social identity other than race and gender: ethnicity, language, religion, and sexual orientation.

Women's Progress at Work: A Glass Half Full

Whether women's progress in the labor force has been surprisingly fast or surprisingly slow is certainly debatable; but it has been substantial. In the past few decades, American women's workforce participation rates and incomes are up, and their occupational choices have expanded, especially in professional, managerial, and supervisory jobs. In those traditionally male jobs in particular, they more frequently work alongside or supervise men. They also make more money, work longer hours, stay in the workforce longer, undertake more responsibility, and exercise more authority at higher levels of the workplace hierarchy.

Women's participation in the paid workforce has of course risen steeply.[2] As of 2001, over 76 percent of women between the ages of 25 and 54, and 64 percent of women with children under the age of 6, were in the labor force.[3] There remains a significant wage gap between men and women, though it is declining; women who work full-time now earn an average of about 77.5 percent of what men earn.[4] The gap shrinks dramatically when the data are adjusted to account for the greater total seniority and continuity of workforce participation of male workers.[5] Most of the gap that remains is related to field of employment: Men are still more heavily represented in more highly compensated business and engineering occupations and in more heavily unionized skilled manual trades, while women remain disproportionately concentrated in education, social services, clerical work, and nursing.[6] So while the goal of "equal pay for equal work" is within reach, occupational segregation remains a significant obstacle to women's economic equality.

Neither the walls nor the glass ceilings that limit women's opportunities have come crashing down.[7] Female pioneers in previously—and still nearly—exclusively male work sites and jobs are especially likely to experience serious sexual harassment.[8] Harassment in these cases—which may take the form of overt hostility to women, pornographic displays, destruction of tools, or refusal to train—serves to mark the workplace as a male domain, to eject female interlopers, and to reinforce occupational segregation.[9]

The causes of occupational segregation are many and controversial; this is not the place to attempt to sort out the entangled roles of divergent occupational preferences, gender-related socialization, employer discrimination, and harassment. The continuing existence of harassment and other forms of discrimination—the targets of Title VII law—obscure any effort to discern the more benign role of choice. And the very meaning of choice is confounded by the persistence of gendered stereotypes and expectations that shape women's own choices throughout their childhoods, schooling, and careers. So we find that, according to one recent survey of teenagers, "73 percent of girls said the desire to help others would guide their career choices, while 70 percent of boys cited making money as the most important factor."[10] Girls may be making socially valuable and altruistic career choices, based on gendered socialization patterns, that yield lower future incomes. It is not easy to pinpoint the problem in that pattern, much less the solution. The fact remains that men and women often still occupy different fields of work, different jobs, and different work sites, and that men supervise women far more often than the reverse.

Still, these patterns are changing; and they began to change more dramatically in the 1970s after Title VII was enacted. Women have entered some of the most closely guarded male bastions, from the construction trades to the highest echelons of corporate management, albeit still in small numbers. One comprehensive recent study shows a gradual decline in the "segregation index"—the percentage of women or men who would have to change jobs to achieve an equal occupational distribution—from 68 percent in 1970 to 59 percent in 1980 to 52 percent in 1990.[11] The change in some occupations has been quite dramatic. Between 1970 and 1990, the proportion of financial managers who are women has gone from 19 percent to 46 percent; of public administrators, from 22 percent to 46 percent; of unspecified "managers and administrators," from 15 percent to 35 percent. Among professions, the proportion of architects who are women has gone from 4 percent to 15 percent; of physicians, from 10 percent to 21 percent; of dentists, from 5 percent to 27 percent; and of lawyers, from 5 percent to 25 percent. Nor are these isolated examples: In 1970, 55 percent of women and 71 percent of men worked in occupations in which the overwhelming majority (at least 80 percent) was of their own sex; by 1990 this was true for only about one-third of women and two-fifths of men.[12] Of course current figures include workers whose work lives began decades ago, when the paths of men and women diverged far more than they do now; even with no further convergence between the paths of men and women at the entry stage, levels of segregation are bound to fall further as the oldest cohorts in the workforce move into retirement.

Of course, important segments of the economy, especially upper management and skilled manual trades, remain overwhelmingly male while other sectors, especially clerical and lower-level health and child care occupations, remain overwhelmingly female. That pattern is self-reinforcing and hard to break, for when women are a small minority within a workplace or job category, they are much more susceptible to stereotyping, bias, and discrimination.[13] It is also a matter of some concern that the great bulk of the decline in gender segregation has occurred through the entry of women into traditionally male job categories; there has been comparatively little movement of men into traditionally female job categories.[14] To the extent that this pattern holds in the future, it will limit further progress toward gender desegregation.

All that being said, however, it is clear that women have advanced both higher and across a broader range of occupations in the last several decades. Of course gender integration of job categories is not the same as gender integration of workplaces; statistics on the latter are harder to come by. But common sense and experience suggests that the former tends to bring with it the latter. Not only are women working more, working in a wider range of occupations, and making more money; with increasing frequency they are working side-by-side with men and supervising men. It is also noteworthy that married women are increasingly likely to make as much as or more than their spouses: As of 1996, nearly one-fourth of wives earned more than their husbands, and another one-third of younger women (ages 25 to 34) earned roughly the same.[15]

This is a glass that is half-full and half-empty; there has been progress toward gender equality, yet full equality is still not in sight. Scholarly attention, at least among legal scholars, has tended to focus on the empty half of the glass, and on how to reduce the remaining gap between men and women's employment status and wages. But I want to focus for now on the half of the glass that is full: Given the significant progress that women have made in the labor market, what have been the effects of that progress outside the workplace? First, however, let us briefly consider a different question: What role has employment discrimination law played in bringing about women's progress?

The Role of Law in Women's Workplace Advancement

The employment discrimination laws were intended in part to secure better jobs for women by removing discriminatory barriers to their hiring and advancement. Title VII brought about in short order the demise of separate male and female columns in the want ads and of the categorical exclusions they signified. The government's related adoption of "goals and timetables" for the employment of minorities and women by government contractors clearly helped expand opportunities in the larger firms that were directly affected. The combined impact of remedial orders, consent decrees, out-of-court settlements, and employer efforts to avoid litigation and liability is surely appreciable but not easy to quantify. Attempts to measure the precise impact of antidiscrimination law on women's employment have been limited and have yielded indeterminate results.[16] Part of the difficulty in tracing the law's effect lies in the fact that the law has worked in tandem with other social, economic, and technological forces that have opened doors for women at work in recent decades. Two such developments come immediately to mind: improved techniques of birth control and the declining importance of physical strength in the labor market.

However hard it is to separate out the contributions of these economic and technological developments from that of the law, it is even harder to separate out the contribution of changing attitudes and social norms about "women's work" and gender roles, and changing educational and occupational aspirations of girls and women; for these changes are not independent of the law. For example, economists would predict that, as the prospect of discrimination in more lucrative and traditionally male fields declined (partly because of its illegality), young women should invest more in becoming qualified for such work.[17] Even changing attitudes toward women and gender roles are likely to be intertwined with legal developments. As a historical matter, the enactment of Title VII took place very early in the rise of modern feminism; the enactment of a national mandate of equal employment opportunity for men and women in 1964 may have "caused" as much as it was "caused by" changing attitudes toward traditional gender roles in employment. Then again, the causal links between the law and these ideas may be quite weak in either direction.

All in all, it seems fruitless to try to pull apart the converging social, economic, ideological, technological, and legal developments that have contributed to women's advancement in the labor market. The law may in fact be a relatively minor factor in the dramatic increase in women's workforce participation and continuity of workplace participation.[18] It seems likely, however, that the law has played a bigger role in opening opportunities for women in traditionally male jobs and in higher levels of the workforce hierarchy. It is simply hard to believe that the enactment of a law barring sex discrimination, together with public and private enforcement efforts that were intended to afford women access to better and more varied jobs, that were often successful, and that were costly for employer defendants, made no significant contribution to the dramatic advancement of women into better and more varied jobs in the years following the law's enactment.

The higher level and nontraditional jobs in which women have made significant advances are the jobs in which women are most likely to end up supervising men or working side-by-side with them. Those are also the jobs in which women are more likely to achieve something like parity of earning power with their spouses. To the extent that those changes in women's circumstances produce changes outside the workplace—a proposition to which I will now turn— it is likely that those changes can be traced indirectly and partially to the law of employment discrimination.

What Happens When Men and Women Work Together?

So what happens when women spend more time, make more money, exercise more authority, and work side-by-side with men at work? Of course, when women first entered all-male blue-collar workplaces, they often encountered overt hostility and vicious harassment. One of the fields in which men have most strongly and successfully resisted the incursion of women is in construction.[19] The experiences of women who, with the encouragement of governmental agencies and the assistance of special apprentice programs, sought to enter the construction trades encourage little optimism about the prospects for gender integration. At the same time, there were some hard-won gains, as suggested by this hair-raising experience by an experienced female welder, the only woman at a new job site:

> For three weeks no one except the general foreman spoke to me. If I sat down, everybody would move to another area. If I went up to work, they would actually try and move their work. . . . At the end of three weeks, we had this one particular job where you had to go between the thirteenth floor and the twelfth floor and weld what they call a "buck stay" to the boiler. . . . The man who was supposed to be my partner couldn't get his arm in there between the floors. So I told him, "I'm going to put the safety line on and you're going to have to hold it."
>
> He looked at me very strangely and he said, "You're going to let me lower you between the floors?" I said, "Whether or not I live or die is going to be totally up to you. You are my partner, this work is our responsibility, and I'm the one that can fit in there. So I'm going to hand you this end of the rope," I said, "and I am going to more or less take on faith the fact that you will not let me go."
>
> Between the grating and the boiler, it is just open all the way down to the bottom. Thirteen floors. Straight down. I took my shield in one hand,

I put my glove on, I got the welding rod ready to go, and I said to him, "Lower me down." And it was like this very pregnant pause. I went down. And I'm here. So we know he held onto that rope.

When I came up and undid the harness, he asked me if I would like to go for coffee. It was the first human contact with any kind of civility to it at all. I acted like the three weeks just hadn't existed, went for coffee. He sat there, asked me why the hell I would ever consider doing anything like this. I told him I had children, my husband hadn't been able to get a job, I had the expertise and I felt this was the way to use it. Then he talked to other people, and what evolved was a very good relationship with most of the men.[20]

Such an intense experience of "cooperative interdependence" is surely rare and is hardly a reasonable prerequisite for women's acceptance. But the story may tell us something about the potential power of working together, even in these worst of circumstances, to break through prejudice and exclusion.

Professor Julius Getman describes a more gradual but more thorough transformation of gender relations at a paper mill in Northern Maine, from "sexual teasing, innuendo, and hostility" when women first became a presence to acceptance and camaraderie:

Sharon Jacques recalls, "I was the first woman to go in the pulp mill—try that one! It was horrible. They didn't want any women, they were going to do everything to get rid of me. They used to urinate in the drains and they refused to quit doing that. But after about six months, we became a family, and I don't even know when it happened."[21]

Similarly, a field study of gender relations in underground mining found that, alongside persistent sexualization and stereotyping of work roles, there was "strong evidence that nonsexual, egalitarian relationships have developed between at least some of the men miners and their women co-workers."[22]

Of course, one can find countless tales of merciless harassment to temper any undue optimism.[23] The harassment that often meets women who enter male domains of work typically aims to preserve privileged male access to certain kinds of work and to resist female intrusions into masculine domains.[24] Some combination of harassment, discrimination, a limited pool of qualified female applicants, and declining levels of employment has operated to maintain a virtual male stranglehold on many occupational categories in construction, transportation, and manufacturing.

Still, it is encouraging to note that sexual harassment appears to be less common and less severe in genuinely integrated workplaces; as overwhelmingly male occupations and workplaces become less so, this form of backlash should subside.[25] Indeed, in integrated workplaces in which women enjoy status and authority, they often engage in and enjoy sexual banter, flirtation, teasing, and joking. This conduct comes within some broad definitions of harassment, but does not generally create a "hostile environment" where it is not part of a pattern of gender inequality.[26] The point is not to soft-pedal the frequency and virulence of harassment of women, especially pioneers in overwhelmingly male workplaces. The point is that the experience of working side-by-side in positions of approximate equality can sometimes bridge even deeply entrenched gender divisions in the workplace. Both men and women are likely to carry this experience with them outside the workplace.

One can envision several ways in which women's greater workplace authority, earnings, and presence in nontraditional occupations could tend to produce greater equality between men and women, even within the family. The sheer logistical pressures of women's work schedules, and the economic incentives that follow from their increased contribution to family income, might be expected to alter the traditional gender-based allocation of domestic responsibilities (and there is evidence that it has done so).[27] Moreover, women who achieve greater economic independence should be in a better position to avoid, change, or leave unsatisfactory relationships. We might also expect consequences for gender relations in the next generation. As compared to the children of the 1950s, children whose parents have relatively comparable commitments to and rewards from work, and more similar responsibilities at home, may expect and aspire to greater equality for themselves and may develop more egalitarian conceptions of gender roles and relationships.

I want to focus, however, on how women's expanded role in the paid labor market, and particularly the experience of men and women working together as peers, affects the broader civic sphere. Does gender integration at work promote cooperative social ties, civic skills, deliberation over political and other matters, and greater empathy *between men and women*? Does it foster more egalitarian and less gender-biased attitudes?

Women's greater and broader responsibility at work is linked to women's increasing involvement in civic and political life. Longer tenure, greater responsibility, and more cooperative interaction between men and women at work tends to widen women's social circles, bringing them into contact with other women and men outside the circle of family, neighbors, and mutual friends that they share with their spouses. This wider network, as well as the skills and sense of competence gained at work, is associated with greater involvement in some kinds of civic, political, and professional associations (though less involvement in associations, such as parent–teacher organizations, traditionally dominated by at-home mothers).[28]

The intergroup relations research on the effects of cooperative interaction gives further reason to believe that men's experience of working with women as peers in the workplace should make them more receptive to women's participation and leadership in civic and political life. Women are subject to discrimination and disadvantages that stem in part from prejudice and stereotypes about the proper role and the abilities of women.[29] To some extent the biases that women face reflect dynamics similar to those that plague interracial and other intergroup relations. Those workplaces that have been most transformed by the advancement of women would seem to offer relatively favorable conditions for positive intergroup contact between men and women: There is often intense and ongoing cooperative interdependence and the development of trust, empathy, affection, and friendship among co-workers. That interaction takes place under the aegis of a legal norm of equal opportunity without regard to sex: work roles are to be assigned on the basis of qualifications and interest, not sex. And indeed, there is evidence from field studies that men's experience of interaction—at least positive interaction—with women at work tends to yield more favorable attitudes toward women as workers.[30] Other field studies of gender bias in the attribution and assessment of female performance find unexpectedly low levels of bias in actual work settings.[31]

Interestingly, there appears to be a dichotomy between laboratory studies and field studies of gender bias: "The literature on women in employment is replete with instances in which gender effects found in the laboratory fail to be replicated in field settings."[32] Researchers suggest that this is based on the effect of long-term experience and face-to-face interaction at the workplace, as well as institutional support for women's authority. The lab studies may tend to overstate the influence of stereotypes: "Artificial, short-term laboratory situations tend to elicit subject responses based on readily available stereotypes, while long-term, real-life, field settings include extensive interpersonal contact that provides subjects with a more realistic basis for their behavior."[33] These observations offer some support in the context of gender for the contact hypothesis and the positive effects of intergroup interaction and cooperation on intergroup attitudes, at least within the work situation. They also suggest that stereotyping is a greater influence on hiring decisions, which come rather close to the laboratory setting, than in decisions about current employees. We will return to the significance of this surmise in chapter 8 in connection with the workings of antidiscrimination law.

But applying the research on intergroup relations and attitudes to men and women requires us to confront a fundamental difference between interracial interaction and interaction between men and women: In a society that is still rather segregated by race, many adults experience very little close, cooperative interracial contact. By contrast, there is a great deal of close, even intimate, contact between men and women within the family and elsewhere; yet prejudices and stereotypes demonstrably persist. So how can additional contact between men and women at work affect attitudes within the family and in other social contexts in which contact is already common?

Clearly, contact between men and women is structured differently than is interracial contact. Race relations—especially relations between black and white Americans—is characterized by "spatial segregation" between the groups, while gender relations are generally marked by a high (though declining) degree of "role segregation."[34] In the workplace, role segregation takes the form of occupational segregation and may be accompanied by a rather high degree of spatial segregation as well: The overwhelmingly female clerical pool has little informal contact with overwhelmingly male upper management. But especially within the family, there is often a high degree of role segregation coupled with what we can call "spatial integration."

It is also striking to note that women—at least adult married women—may have relatively little close and cooperative interaction *with each other* outside the workplace.[35] Women who are not in the paid labor force, in particular, may experience quite a lot of cooperative (though not necessarily egalitarian) interaction with their male partners, but rather little independent contact with other women. That is in sharp contrast to the structure of *intragroup* relations within racial and ethnic groups: High levels of spatial segregation produce little *intergroup* contact, but a great deal of *intragroup* contact both inside and outside the family. Intragroup contact helps enable the formation of a group identity, the perception and articulation of shared grievances, and the mobilization of collective demands. So women's entry into the workplace—even into overwhelmingly female occupations—may have provided a crucial catalyst for the growth of the modern women's movement and of feminist sensibilities, broadly understood. Women's experiences of working together with each other may have been at least as important as their experiences of working with men in bringing about such progress as there has been toward sex equality in the workplace and outside of it. My focus here, however, is on the significance of the experience of working together *across* group lines.

The problem of role segregation suggests a way to think about the relevance of the contact hypothesis to workplace contact between men and women. One of the crucial conditions that the contact hypothesis prescribes for improving intergroup attitudes and relations is that the contact take place under conditions of equality—that is, under conditions that do not replicate the status differential between the groups. Similarly, research has suggested the importance of "cross-cutting categories"—for example, role assignments that cut across rather than correspond with group membership—in reducing the salience of group membership and the influence of stereotypes. So, for example, the earliest proponents of the contact hypothesis cautioned that the intimate, sustained, and often cooperative contact between a white woman and her black housekeeper in the Jim Crow South held little potential for transforming racial attitudes.[36] Both the equality condition and the value of cross-cutting categories point to the same proposition: In order to promote more egalitarian and positive attitudes, con-

tact must take place in a context that has the potential to defy traditional stereotypes and status hierarchies.

Much of the extensive contact between men and women obviously fails to
meet these conditions. Much of it takes place in the context of family and sexual
relations, in which biological differences and sexuality are often salient, and in
which functional roles are very often assigned on the basis of sex. Even though
the typical division of domestic labor within the family is moving in an egalitarian direction, it has far to go before reaching parity. To the extent that is the case,
the family, for all its intimacy, may hold limited potential for undermining traditional stereotypes and hierarchies. Moreover, intimate family relationships lie
largely beyond the constitutional or practical scope of much legal reform. It is
thus hard even to imagine a law prohibiting the assignment of domestic tasks
on the basis of sex, or the imposition of unwelcome sexual propositions, within
a marital relationship.

The law has a former hold on the workplace. Title VII's prohibition of employment discrimination on the basis of sex aspires to make the workplace an
arena of equality, in which roles are assigned not on the basis of sex roles and
stereotypes but on the basis of skills, qualifications, and interests. Title VII seeks
to prohibit intentional "role segregation," thus reducing both occupational segregation and spatial segregation, in the workplace. The law has had only partial
success thus far in breaking down occupational segregation between men and
women. When formerly segregated workplaces and occupations are opened up,
however, the intergroup relations literature suggests that harassment and hostility sometimes gives way to, and sometimes exists alongside, the development
of mutually respectful and egalitarian peer relations.

Policing Relationships and Sexuality at Work

Title VII seeks to reform not just the process of filling and assigning jobs, but
also, through the doctrine of discriminatory harassment, patterns of interaction
among co-workers. While it is hard to imagine a law prohibiting "unwelcome
requests for sexual favors" between spouses, such conduct between co-workers
may create a hostile work environment and a form of discrimination in conditions of employment for which employers may be liable under Title VII. Title
VII's prohibition on sex discrimination and sexual harassment offers legal support for the development of peer relations—relations that are not imprinted with
the traditional dominance of men over women, in which gender is only an incidental factor.

More often than not, men still exercise authority over women in the workplace.
But sexual harassment law seeks in part to prevent men's exercise of workplace
authority over women as subordinates from being leveraged into an assertion of
male power and prerogatives over women as women. And as women increasingly

find themselves in positions of equality with or authority over men on the job, sexual harassment law stands guard (with only partial success, of course) against male employees' efforts to subvert these equal or reverse-hierarchical relations by the reassertion of male dominance. The law gives employers a powerful incentive to police against sexist conduct (and speech, on which more later), and the employer's disciplinary authority gives employees a powerful incentive to conform to employer demands. Once again, we find that both legal compulsion and internal economic compulsion play a potentially productive role in helping to make the workplace an important laboratory of more egalitarian relations between men and women.

On the other hand, the legal compulsion of harassment law has combined with internal economic compulsion to produce some counterproductive trends as well. The ambiguity in the term "sexual harassment" fosters a troubling confusion that Professor Vicki Schultz has explored in depth.[37] As the Supreme Court has recently made clear, what the law prohibits is the imposition of hostile working conditions "because of sex," meaning gender. Harassment that is "sexual" is not necessarily "sexual harassment."[38] But courts, lawyers, and commentators continue to urge employers to banish sexuality and all forms of sexual expression from the workplace (while sometimes overlooking gender-based harassment that is not sexual in nature). And employers, fearful of liability and suspicious of passions and preoccupations that might distract from production, are following their advice.

Many employers, driven in large part by a fear of harassment charges and litigation, have promulgated highly censorious antiharassment policies that threaten to purge the workplace of much of its prodigious potential for friendly and even intimate relations.[39] Professor Schultz has recently documented the pervasive movement to "sanitize the workplace"—to banish all mention or manifestation of sexuality, however friendly, egalitarian, or even welcome. Harassment law played a major part in setting these forces in motion, but they have acquired a momentum of their own and have become detached from and even hostile to the goal of gender equality.[40] This movement threatens to make real the seemingly innocuous but ominous motto that "the workplace is for work." We will return to these concerns below in chapter 8.

In spite of significant progress toward gender integration and equality in the workplace, the glass is still half-empty. Yet the overall picture gives reason for optimism. Women continue to make progress in the workplace. Given the amount of time that most adults spend in the workplace, and the economic incentive to accommodate themselves to the demands made upon them at work, their experience of relatively, and increasingly, equal relations at work may spill over into more egalitarian attitudes and relations outside the workplace and even in the home.

In the case of sex discrimination, more than with any other antidiscrimination doctrine, Congress led the way. It was at least partly a tactical miscalculation on the part of southern opponents of racial equality that produced the Civil Rights Act's sweeping condemnation of sex discrimination in employment in 1964.[41] That was well before the modern women's movement had the political wherewithal to secure such legislation—state or federal—on its own, before the development of any constitutional antecedents disapproving sex discrimination under the equal protection clause, and at a time when overt sex discrimination in hiring was utterly ubiquitous, not only in a single region but throughout the country. Many readers will recall, as I do, reading the unapologetically sex-segregated classified ads by which employers announced their discriminatory hiring policies well into the 1960s. Nonetheless, the law took hold, growing deep roots and strong branches that reach into virtually every sizable workplace in the country.

Equality between men and women at work is still far off in many sectors and many workplaces. Even so, the professed commitment to equal opportunity for women in employment, together with the striking progress that has been made in recent decades, suggests that the workplace presents a unique point of leverage in the broader struggle for equal power and opportunity in the rest of the society, including within the family. It is a place where the law can make a difference, and the difference that the law makes there can help reshape women's lives and their role in society well beyond the workplace.

A Brief Note on Workplace Relations across Other Lines of Identity: Ethnicity, Language, Religion, and Sexual Orientation

The experience of working together across group lines, and the consequences of that experience, is obviously not the same across all lines of division. Having examined two very different cases of race and gender, and found both common and distinctive features across the two cases, we may be in a position to reflect briefly upon the significance of workplace relations across some other significant lines of group identity.

Ethnicity and Language

Title VII bans discrimination on the basis of national origin (or ethnicity) and religion as well as race and sex. It is a short stretch from "race" to ethnicity, and thus from the significance of workplace relations across race lines to that of relations across other lines of ethnicity. Indeed, one might object to denominating even black–white relations as "interracial," and assimilate these into a larger category of more-or-less observable ethnic distinctions.[42] But however we denominate the move from black–white relations to relations across other lines of ethnic and geographic origin, it seems to take us in the same direction: The more those other lines are marked by visible (or audible) difference, the more they are troubled by prejudice, and the more they are associated with spatial separation in other spheres of social life, the more we would expect workplace relations across these lines to function like black–white relations, and to have similar potential for building bonds and improving relations in the society at large.

So how much spatial separation is there with respect to groups other than African Americans? No other large ethnic group shows signs of fully replicating the discouraging pattern of black segregation; with the exception of Mexican Americans in some border regions, by and large one sees more integration of neighborhoods and therefore of schools.[43] On the other hand, as I will discuss briefly below, among some recent immigrant groups one sees rather high levels of segregation within urban "ethnic enclaves."[44] In other words, at least as to some groups, spatial segregation outside of the workplace limits opportunities for cooperative intergroup contact. The research on intergroup relations reviewed in chapter 4 encompasses a wide range of ethnic differences and comes to the same conclusions about the value of intergroup contact and cooperation. A case for the value of workplace ties between Latino and non-Latino workers, or between those of Asian and non-Asian origin, for example, would closely track the case made here for black–white ties in the workplace.

The issues become more complex where ethnic differences correspond to language differences, which complicate the prospects for integration inside and outside the workplace. Much has been made here of the value of communication across lines of social identity. Not all communication is verbal, of course. But a common language would seem to be more than helpful, if not necessary, for the cooperation, sociability, and sharing of work-related concerns on which the "working together" thesis depends. Where language differences make conversation difficult or impossible, one of the main engines of social connectedness is stalled. And where language differences dictate social interactions—for example, if Spanish-speaking workers socialize only with each other—those differences may re-create ethnic "segregation" within an integrated workforce. Indeed, there is evidence that some employers with mostly immigrant workforces seek language uniformity within work shifts to facilitate communication among workers.[45]

One response to these concerns might be to support calls for "English-only" rules in the workplace. However, such rules burden already disadvantaged language minorities in the labor market, and they restrict the freedom of workers to communicate with each other within language groups. Because language is closely linked to ethnicity and national origin, such rules are justifiably suspect under Title VII.[46] On the other hand, the problem that language differences pose for workplace integration highlights the importance of fostering literacy in a common language, however that is best achieved.[47] Without entering into the controversy over the efficacy of bilingual education, I would suggest that the importance of intergroup ties in the workplace raises the stakes in that debate. One of the things schools should be doing is building the language skills that students will need to communicate with their eventual co-workers in diverse workplaces.

All of this sidesteps the crucial empirical question of how much interaction there is within the workplace between ethnic groups—and especially new immigrant groups—and native-born citizens from outside those groups. We have already noted the heavy concentration of new immigrants from some groups—especially poor, unskilled, and undocumented workers from Latin American and East Asian regions—in the low-wage sector. We have also noted the related phenomenon of "ethnic enclaves" in which some immigrant groups are concentrated, both living and working primarily with others of the same ethnicity and language.[48] To some extent these enclaves are a product of an inhospitable society—of discrimination and hostility, against which the law may be a more or less effective tool—and of inadequate educational and training opportunities, as to which public policy has an important role to play. To some extent these enclaves recapitulate patterns that proved functional for earlier waves of immigrants, who created ladders of progress within and eventually out of the ghettoes to which they were initially channeled.

The phenomenon of ethnic enclaves, which may envelope their residents for generations, obviously limits the extent of workplace integration and, to that extent, the potential good that can come out of workplace interactions across racial and ethnic lines. For purposes of my argument, the issue of ethnic enclaves largely recapitulates the more familiar phenomenon of inner-city concentrations of poor African Americans. In both cases, whatever cultural, economic, and psychic support is to be found within these relatively homogeneous communities, it is hard to believe that their residents would not welcome and pursue greater job opportunities outside their boundaries. In both cases, much good—including the particular good that is elaborated here—would come from drawing individuals from these communities into decent jobs in mainstream, integrated workplaces. Much good would also come from improving the conditions for collective self-help among workers in the low-wage sector in which these individuals are concentrated. Some aspects of labor and employment law that I will discuss in chapters 8 and 9 are relevant here. Otherwise, I will not have more to say about the complex questions posed by the existence and persistence of ethnic enclaves.

Religion

Religious differences present another variation on the pattern of intergroup relations. In the United States, religion has generally been less divisive, and a less persistent basis for discrimination, than race. But in most respects, the significance of religion seems analogous to the significance of ethnicity in this context. Indeed, it may be when religion overlaps with ethnicity, as it often does in the case of Jewish and Muslim workers, that it is most likely to be the basis for discrimination and stereotyping. We would expect the law's banning of religious as well as ethnic discrimination to bring about greater religious diversity in the workplace, and thus to make it more likely that people of different religious identities and beliefs will work as co-workers. We would similarly expect this to produce more cooperative and friendly relations, and reduced prejudice, across religious lines in much the same way as interracial relations at work lead to improved racial attitudes and relations beyond the workplace.

But the case of religion is more complicated. On the one hand, religious identity is often invisible to observers, including co-workers; intergroup contact across invisible lines of identity is not likely to have much effect. On the other hand, religious identity is sometimes expressed in distinctive religious practices or expression that may heighten the experience of group difference. Title VII not only prohibits employer discrimination on the basis of religious identity; it also requires some degree of employer accommodation of religion and religious expression and practices.[49] They may be forced to tolerate some religious expression, and may have to walk a fine line between the claims of overtly religious workers to freely exercise their religion and the claims of co-workers to be free from religious harassment.[50] Both sets of claims originate in Title VII's ban on discrimination on the basis of religion.

The law's limited accommodation of religious practices means that religious diversity may be more visible than it would otherwise be. Workers may be more aware of their Muslim or Sikh or Jewish co-workers' religious identity to the extent that the latter wear (and employers are required to permit) distinctive religious headwear. That may make religious differences more salient, and potentially more divisive, than they would otherwise be. But that potential is held in check in the employment context by the imperatives of production and efficiency, which the law also accommodates. From the perspective of distinct religious minorities, the balance struck by the law, and by employers acting within the law, may demand too much conformity with majority norms.[51] Limited as it is, the mandate to accommodate religious practices probably makes the experience of religious diversity at work more like the experience of racial or ethnic diversity, in that it may make the majority aware of group differences that would otherwise be invisible. If that is so, then religious diversity in the workplace may have much the same positive consequences as racial and ethnic diversity.

Sexual Orientation

A distinctive feature of homosexual identity is that it can be invisible to others—even family members.[52] To the extent that homosexuality triggers stereotypes, hostility, ridicule, and discrimination, many gay men and lesbians endeavor to keep their sexual orientation secret and invisible to co-workers, even to invent heterosexual relationships and other badges of sexual conventionality.[53] The possibility of concealment has meant that there has long been much more workplace interaction between heterosexual and homosexual workers than the former have been aware of. At the same time, the widespread invisibility of homosexuality has allowed heterosexuals to maintain misconceptions, stereotypes, and hostility that would be sorely challenged by daily cooperative contact with openly gay and lesbian co-workers.

Another distinctive feature of homosexual identity, as compared to the other lines of social difference examined here, is that no federal law yet prohibits discrimination on the basis of sexual orientation. But a growing number of state and municipal laws do so, and federal legislation may be on the horizon.[54] That trend, and especially the more tolerant attitudes that underlie that trend, have opened up employment opportunities and have made it increasingly possible for gay men and lesbians to live openly as such.[55] As changing laws and attitudes permit gay and lesbian workers to be more open about their sexual orientation, the experience of working together is changing and becoming a potentially transformative experience for straight employees. For it appears that the social psychology of intergroup relations works for gay-straight relations—that "cooperative interdependence" among gay and straight co-workers tends to reduce prejudice, defy stereotypes, and cultivate affinity and acceptance.[56] Indeed, workplace interaction across increasingly visible lines of sexual orientation may be making some contribution to the increased tolerance and support for civil rights for gay men and lesbians that are expressed in opinion polls and apparent all around us.[57]

A more powerful force in the erosion of anti-homosexual sentiment, however, lies within families and, again, in the distinctive nature of sexual orientation. Gay individuals grow up within biologically-related (and predominantly heterosexual) families; that makes sexual orientation like sex (and unlike race) in the degree of intimate "spatial integration." But sexual orientation is also, as noted above, unknown, invisible, or concealed for much of an individual's life, which makes it unlike both race and sex. That means that family members only learn that a loved one is gay after years, even decades, of intimate co-existence. This element of surprise or discovery within families with respect to a fundamental aspect of identity is almost unique to sexual orientation. Sometimes homophobia is strong enough to survive alongside, or even to destroy, intimate familial bonds. But those familial bonds put enormous pressure on prejudicial attitudes formed in ignorance. Where family love prevails, the parents and siblings of gay people not only may develop more liberal and accepting attitudes but may promote those attitudes within their own social circles.

So what happens outside the workplace and especially within the families of gay men and lesbians is probably the main engine of increased tolerance and acceptance of homosexuality. But what happens within the workplace between gay and straight co-workers, at least with the extension of workplace equality norms to sexual orientation, is roughly analogous, and is likely to have analogous consequences, to what happens between black and white co-workers. The workplace can be an important, albeit secondary, incubator of more tolerant social attitudes.

The difference that the law makes in promoting workplace interaction between men and women and between gay and straight employees, and the societal consequences of workplace interaction between men and women and between gays and straights, is not the same as in the case of race and ethnicity. As I turn to the more theoretical dimensions of my argument in the next part, the focus returns to the paradigm case of race and ethnicity, with its defining features of spatial segregation and limited interaction outside the workplace. I leave it to the reader to recognize that the argument translates only imperfectly to the case of other intergroup relations. With that caveat, let us proceed.

Part Two

HOW WORKPLACE BONDS ENRICH DEMOCRATIC LIFE

Thus far we have seen that workplace associations can and often do foster cooperation, sociability, and connectedness across boundaries of family and neighborhood and, critically, across cleavages of race, ethnicity, and other lines of social division. Yet the argument so far has only hinted at the relationship between the interpersonal ties that form at the workplace and the healthy functioning of a democratic society. Before launching that more theoretical inquiry, let me restate in general terms my claim about the relationship between workplace ties and democratic life.

The success and vitality of the democratic project depends on some sense of interdependence and common fate and some ability to empathize, cooperate, and communicate among citizens from different families, neighborhoods, and communities. These interpersonal ties are especially important, yet less common, across lines of social division such as race that have been the basis for discrimination and segregation. A liberal democratic society that is devoted to freedom as well as to equality necessarily tolerates discrimination and self-segregation in many spheres of private life—in individual decisions about where and with whom to live and form families, friendships, and other private associations. That freedom has contributed to a continuing legacy of racial separation in families, neighborhoods, and many voluntary associations. Segregation, in turn, limits the society's store of shared knowledge and empathy regarding the conditions of life across group lines.

Personal ties across those lines of division are essential to building the citizens' will and ability to overcome divisions, to craft compromise and consensus in the face of conflict, and to combat the subtle and intransigent sources of inequality that remain in American society. The proliferation of those ties depends upon the existence of a domain in which people find it necessary to get along and get things done with others with whom they would not otherwise choose to associate, or with whom they would not choose to associate on terms of equality. The workplace stands virtually alone in its capacity to foster those ties. The process of working together leads to sharing of experiences and beliefs, and it does so in the context of ongoing cooperative and constructive, even friendly, relations among citizens whose daily lives may not otherwise intersect. The workplace thus performs a distinctive kind of mediating function—an *integrative* function both in the older sociological sense of connecting individuals with the larger society and in the newer sense of connecting individuals from different racial and ethnic groups.

To be sure, the capacity of the workplace to perform this function is not fully realized. Some workplaces are structured to minimize the freedom of interaction among co-workers and to minimize the importance of cooperation in production. Moreover, workplace harassment, discrimination, and occupational segregation on the basis of race and gender still exist. But while the success of the antidiscrimination laws is hardly complete, there is little question that those laws have traction in the workplace. Without overstating its success, Title VII has put forward an ideal vision of the workplace, and some tools for its reconstruction, as a realm of comparative equality and comparative integration across lines of race, sex, and other traits that have traditionally been the basis for subordination and widespread inequality.

SITUATING THE WORKPLACE IN CIVIL SOCIETY

Social Integration, Social Capital, and Deliberation at Work

Having articulated in general terms what workplace connectedness does for a diverse democratic society, I want to sort out some discrete but related threads of the argument and link them to some old and new lines of thought about the role of associational life in a democracy. It will be useful, albeit conventional, to begin with Alexis de Tocqueville's elucidation of the role of associations in the early American republic. For Tocqueville's account contains the seeds of several modern strands of thought about the functions of associational life in a democratic society: democratic deliberation, social capital formation, civic skills, and social integration.

In his justly celebrated study of democracy in America, Tocqueville marveled at the rich collective life among the avowedly individualistic Americans. He was struck by the proliferation of voluntary political, social, and economic associations through which they engaged in a constant quest for collective self-improvement and prosperity:

> Americans of all ages, all stations in life, and all types of disposition are forever forming associations. There are not only commercial and industrial associations in which all take part, but others of a thousand different types—religious, moral, serious, futile, very general and very limited, immensely large and very minute.[1]

In Tocqueville's view, much of the success of the American experiment in democracy, as well as much of its prosperity, could be traced to the vitality of associational life.

Tocqueville's recognition of the instrumental utility of associations anticipated the modern concept of "social capital." In a relatively egalitarian democratic society, he observed, there were no wealthy aristocrats to carry out the building of infrastructure, commerce and industry, and other large undertakings. Associations grew in America to fill the role that concentrated wealth and power played in

Europe; they allowed citizens of modest means to pool their wealth, energies, and ingenuity to get things done, both through and outside of the institutions of government. Tocqueville also recognized that it was through associations that citizens exchanged ideas about common goals and undertakings and learned the skills and habits of cooperation. Finally, Tocqueville saw in voluntary associations the social glue that held together this avowedly individualistic society: "Feelings and ideas are renewed, the heart enlarged, and the understanding developed only by the reciprocal action of men one upon another."[2]

There is no doubt that economic and commercial associations were among the voluntary groups that Tocqueville celebrated.[3] When we turn, however, to contemporary accounts of the role of associations in democratic life, we find that the workplace is largely ignored or excluded from many of these accounts. That is traceable in part to the emphasis of many contemporary accounts—especially those accounts that hearken to a legal or constitutional perspective—on the separateness and the independence of associations from the state. Associations are said to provide a buffer between individuals and the state—a free space for the development of individual personality, distinct group identity, and dissident ideas—and a potential source of opposition to the state. I have called these the "sword and shield" functions of associational life, and I will return to them below in chapter 7.

But associations are also said to play a critical role in *linking* individuals to the rest of the society and to its governing institutions. The contemporary literature, echoing Tocqueville, identifies several related "linking" functions of associational life:

- Associations operate as sites of public discourse and of the deliberations that are essential to democratic governance in a complex society. Associations serve as a primary locus for the formation, exchange, aggregation, and amplification of opinions about society and its governance.
- Participation in associations builds interpersonal connections and norms of reciprocity and cooperation that allow people to overcome collective action problems, thus contributing to the success of collective undertakings, including political undertakings.
- Participation in associations cultivates civic skills and a sense of political efficacy, assets that can then be deployed in the political sphere. Civic skills—vested in individuals and unequally distributed throughout the society—amplify groups' and individuals' ability to get what they want from the political sphere. But the wide dissemination of civic skills among the citizenry can also enhance the overall effectiveness and responsiveness of government.
- Associational life cultivates diffuse but essential feelings of connectedness, empathy, and common fate that induce individuals to forego immediate self-interest for long-term collective well-being.

These claims about the virtues of associations are obviously interrelated; indeed, they are all intertwined in Professor Robert Putnam's influential articulation of the concept of "social capital" and the social and political benefits of a multiplicity of formal and informal associations. Within a very capacious understanding of "social capital" that combines many different functions of associational life, Professor Putnam highlights a crucial distinction between "bonding" ties and "bridging" ties. This distinction partly tracks and partly cuts across the distinction I draw here between the "sword and shield" functions and the "linking" functions of associational life.

"Bonding" associations are "inward looking and tend to reinforce exclusive identities and homogeneous groups," while "bridging" associations are "outward looking and encompass people across diverse social cleavages."[4] In Putnam's evocative formulation, "[b]onding social capital constitutes a kind of sociological superglue, whereas bridging social capital provides a sociological WD-40."[5] Some associations both bridge, in the sense that they bring people together from different social groups, and bond, in the sense that individuals join them on the basis of what they already share with the group. A religious congregation, for example, may be founded on the common bond of religious affiliation, but may bring together individuals of different racial groups who share that affiliation.

Both bonding ties and bridging ties are essential in a healthy democratic society. Bonding associations are crucial in the formation of individual identity, the aggregation and articulation of separate or dissenting group interests, and the protection of minorities against a potentially overreaching and homogenizing state. They perform many of the essential "shield" functions of associational life. But bridging ties—the ties that arise out of demographically diverse associations—are equally essential in a complex and heterogeneous modern society. Returning to the several ways in which associational life links individuals to democratic society (as opposed to shielding them from it), it is evident that "bridging associations" make a distinct contribution along each of those dimensions:

- Bridging associations operate as sites of public discourse and deliberation across lines of social difference; they permit the exchange of diverse experiences and opinions and the formation of political preferences that take better account of a broad range of interests.
- Bridging associations build connections, trust, and norms of reciprocity and cooperation across lines of social division and enable people to cooperate for the good of diverse collectives, including the society and the community at large.
- Bridging associations build civic skills of cooperation, negotiation, persuasion, and organization within diverse groups; these civic skills may

differ from the skills required for operating effectively within homoge-neous groups and are especially useful in the political life of a diverse society.

- Bridging associations cultivate feelings of connectedness and empathy across rather than simply within lines of social division; they cultivate a willingness to compromise and to sacrifice in the interest of broader and more inclusive collectivities.

Because they engage diverse individuals in regular, ongoing, cooperative activity and enable individuals to get to know each other and to care about each other, workplaces are particularly well-situated to foster deliberation, social capital, civic skills, and simple empathy across lines of social division. Let us take up these "linking" functions of associational life.

Social Integration and "The Ties Formed by Sharing in Common Work": An Old Idea Renewed

Tocqueville's most profound observation about the virtues of association was also the most ephemeral: "Feelings and ideas are renewed, the heart enlarged, and the understanding developed only by the reciprocal action of men one upon another."[6] What is often overlooked is the fact that, for Tocqueville, productive and commercial associations were clearly among the forms of "reciprocal action" through which "[f]eelings and ideas are renewed, the heart enlarged, and the understanding developed." In his view, association and interdependence in the economic realm helped to foster the remarkable capacity for self-governance that he observed within the young American republic.

So, too, for the founders whose achievements Tocqueville was assessing, the capacity for self-governance was firmly rooted in the productive sphere. Their emphasis, however, was less on *interdependence* than on *independence*—the independence of the yeoman farmers and the free artisans who owned the property on which their livelihood was based. For the republican founders, citizens' political independence and civic virtue rested squarely on the solitary forms of production that were soon to be overtaken by the emerging factory system and increasingly social forms of production.[7] For the modern reader seeking democratic resources within the domain of production, there lies greater promise in Tocqueville's contrasting appreciation for the virtues of interdependence within the economic sphere.

Tocqueville's insights in this regard echoed in some measure the optimism of the "*doux commerce*" thesis, prevalent in eighteenth-century Europe and influential among some American founders.[8] According to that thesis, commerce and exchange in free markets worked to "soften" and civilize men and manners by bringing individuals from disparate origins into close and repeated contact with one another, engaging them in a web of mutually beneficial transactions and relationships, and weaving individuals, communities, and even nations together through ties of economic interdependence. In the words of Montesquieu, "Commerce . . . polishes and softens barbaric ways as we can see every day."[9] Thomas Paine echoed his words across the Atlantic: "[Commerce] is a pacific system, operating to cordialise mankind, by rendering Nations, as well as individuals, useful to each other."[10]

This sanguine thesis prefigured Tocqueville's celebration of "reciprocal action" and cooperative activity, as well as the powerful idea of the "invisible hand": Even as each participant in this network of commerce pursued his own interests, the common interest was served, not only by greater prosperity but by the civilization of manners, the growth of mutual understanding, and the shared commitment to peace and stability. The *doux commerce* idea thus contained threads of what was to become, in the hands of Adam Smith and his modern descendants, the triumphant economic justification for capitalism and free markets. But the human relationships and their "civilizing" potential of markets were eventually swept away, like useless cobwebs, leaving behind a cleaner and colder world in which rational, self-interested individuals, by the operation of "the invisible hand," produced greater prosperity for all.

The liberal economists' spare vision of frictionless, arm's length exchanges among atomistic individuals offered no comfort to those who worried about the demise of community and social solidarity in modern capitalist society. By the time Tocqueville wrote in the 1830s, the notion that the individual pursuit of economic gain was innocuous, even salutary, for society appeared increasingly naïve as that pursuit seemed to overtake all others and to corrode the civic spirit. Tocqueville himself dissented sharply from the enthusiasm for the pursuit of material self-interest that underlay both the *doux commerce* thesis and its leaner and meaner Smithian successor.[11]

Among the greatest indictments of the individual pursuit of wealth was its evident tendency to degrade and impoverish those employed in the pursuit. Both Tocqueville and the early American republicans were thus alarmed—alarmed for the sake of democracy—by the growth of the factory system.[12] This new form of economic organization was creating a growing class of wage laborers—and, since the abolition of property qualifications for the franchise, a growing segment of the electorate—whose mindless, repetitive, and grueling work under conditions of subsistence seemed to render them unfit for citizenship. They manifestly lacked the economic independence that underlay the founders' vision of citizenship, for they did not own the material basis for their own livelihoods. But neither did they partake of the kind of economic interdependence that was extolled by the *doux commerce* thesis and by Tocqueville.

Their subservient role in industry rendered them dependent, exploited, and alienated and cast a shadow over the idea that democracy was served by relations within the productive sphere.

The relentlessly increasing division of labor was typically blamed on both sides of the Atlantic, most famously by Karl Marx, for the social evils of industrial production.[13] In the view of one acute observer, however, the division of labor was, over the long haul, the basis not only for greater prosperity but also for increasing social solidarity. In his first major work, *The Division of Labor in Society*,[14] first published in 1893, Émile Durkheim observed that modernization and the increasing division of labor had made each person "more of an individual" by loosening "the bonds that attach the individual to his family, to his native heath, to the traditions that the past has bequeathed him, to the collective practices of the group."[15] But this increasing differentiation had also undermined the traditional basis for morality and social cohesion, which lay in the homogeneity of persons and beliefs within small communities. For Durkheim, however, the cause of the crisis carried the seeds of its own solution: The increasing division of labor brought with it a new basis for social cohesion and morality. As individuals assumed different functions within the division of labor, they became at the same time increasingly interdependent and cooperative beings. Through the division of labor, "the individual is once more made aware of his dependent state vis-à-vis society."[16]

Durkheim's analysis of the division of labor set him apart from his contemporaries in several camps—from those who longed for the "mechanical solidarity" of the village community, as well as from those who would rely solely on the "contractual solidarity" of free exchange. Durkheim thus proclaimed the vision of the liberal economists to be impoverished in its neglect of social cooperation and solidarity within the economic sphere. He observed that "exchange . . . is not the whole of contract; there is also the harmonious working of the functions that are co-operating. These are not only in contact in the brief time when things pass from one person to another. More extensive relationships necessarily result from them . . ."[17] These relationships engendered feelings of solidarity and of altruism upon on which social life depended:

> Thus, altruism is not destined to become . . . a kind of pleasant ornament of our social life, but one that will always be its fundamental basis. How indeed could we ever do without it? Men cannot live together without agreeing, and consequently without making mutual sacrifices, joining themselves to one another in a strong and enduring fashion.[18]

Durkheim thus placed cooperation within the economic sphere at the center of the process of social integration and empathy-building.

In so doing, he set himself apart as well from the anticapitalist critics of the division of labor. Durkheim conceded that the realities of industrial life at the turn of the century fell far short of the promise of social solidarity that he saw in the division of labor. In particular he acknowledged the tendency of capitalist production to "diminish the individual by reducing him to the role of a machine."[19] But he insisted that "the division of labor does not produce these consequences through some imperative of its own nature, but only in exceptional and abnormal circumstances."[20] On the contrary,

> normally the operation of each special function demands that the individual should not be too closely shut up in it, but should keep in constant contact with neighbouring functions, becoming aware of their needs and the changes that take place in them, etc. The division of labour supposes that the worker, far from remaining bent over his task, does not lose sight of those co-operating with him, but acts upon them and is acted upon by them.[21]

For Durkheim, the "normal" division of labor promised to extend to ordinary workers the virtues of interdependency and cooperation that had been traced to associational life by Tocqueville.[22]

What was it that prevented the "normal" division of labor and the active and conscious cooperation it was supposed to engender? Durkheim concluded that the organization of society had not caught up with that of the economy. Echoing Tocqueville, Durkheim asserted the importance of associations: "A nation cannot be maintained unless, between the state and individuals, a whole range of secondary groups are interposed. These must be close enough to the individual to attract him strongly to their activities and, in so doing, to absorb him into the mainstream of social life."[23] But the same pressures that had destroyed village society tended toward the fragmentation of many such secondary groups: extended families, religious and educational institutions, and voluntary associations. Durkheim concluded that the foundation for social solidarity among autonomous individuals had to be located in the actual processes of work and in associations of those who perform similar functions within the division of labor. There was simply no other place in the society, outside the embattled family, in which the ties of interdependency were sufficiently durable to lay the foundation for social integration.[24]

Durkheim's analysis would seem to resonate with then-emerging patterns of industrial and professional self-organization.[25] But he had in mind a more ambitious reorganization of society along corporatist lines, with "occupational groups"—groups "constituted by all those working in the same industry, assembled together and organised in a single body"—serving as the basic institutions of governance.[26] This prescription may have doomed the prospects of his more subtle diagnosis taking hold on this side of the Atlantic. Moreover, the prescription was in tension with the diagnosis itself, for industry-wide occupational groups posed much the same problem of remoteness between the individual and the larger society that these "secondary groups" were designed to cure.

This feature of the corporatist vision later prompted a pivotal American observer, John Dewey, to dissent:

> There is at present, at least in theory, a movement away from the principle of territorial organization to that of "functional," that is to say, occupational, organization.... *It is true that ties formed by sharing in common work, whether in what is called industry or what are called professions, have now a force which formerly they did not possess.* But these ties can be counted upon for an enduring and stable organization, which at the same time is flexible and moving, only as they grow out of immediate intercourse and attachment. The theory, as far as it relies upon associations which are remote and indirect, would if carried into effect soon be confronted by all the troubles and evils of the present situation in a transposed form. There is no substitute for the vitality and depth of close and direct intercourse and attachment.[27]

In recognizing the power of the "ties formed by sharing in common work," Dewey might have rescued and revived Durkheim's early insights into the integrative possibilities of working together, face-to-face and side-by-side, from Durkheim's own turn to corporatism. But that was not to be. For it seems that, in rejecting the turn to corporatism, Dewey turned away as well from the "ties formed by sharing in common work" as an important medium of social integration. Still, his views on this matter warrant a closer look.[28]

Dewey was seeking to locate "the public" in an increasingly complex and heterogeneous democratic society. Like his modern descendants, Dewey placed great importance on the cultivation of a vibrant sphere of public discourse, not only to fuel and legitimize democratic political processes but also to link together the members of a diverse and pluralistic society. But he recognized that, if public discourse was to help cultivate communal bonds among individuals with no familial or ethnic or religious ties, the concept of public discourse needed to be brought down to earth. For the foundation for social cohesion lay inescapably in "the vitality and depth of close and direct intercourse and attachment," of "face-to-face intercourse."[29] These personal relationships formed a sort of template for the more abstract relations between citizens and more remote others with whom they were engaged in common political endeavors: "Democracy must begin at home, and its home is the neighborly community."[30]

Dewey's focus on "the neighborly community" both echoes Tocqueville's praise for local government and anticipates a lively contemporary discussion of the prospects and realities of participation, deliberation, and solidarity among diverse citizens through local governments.[31] But in hindsight, if the aim was to cultivate social connectedness, Dewey may have hitched his hopes to the wrong vehicle, much as the American framers may have done in yoking their conception of republican citizenship to a political economy of farmers and artisans. For today's sidewalkless neighborhoods and bedroom communities foster less "face-to-face intercourse" than the "neighborly community" that Dewey idealized, and certainly less than "the ties formed by sharing in common work."

Dewey's recognition of those workplace ties and of the importance of face-to-face relations might well have led him to the workplace, for he was a strong proponent of industrial democracy both as a "school for democracy" and as a vehicle for realizing human potential. Yet Dewey did not in his writings link the problem of "the public" with the potentialities of a reconstructed workplace.[32] To be sure, the integrative possibilities of working together were much obscured by the grim state of the American workplace in the early twentieth century. The workplace of "laissez-faire" America, with its prevailing Taylorist principles of organization, may not have appeared to be a promising medium for building social solidarity and transcending social divisions.

Change was in the air, however. By the 1930s, the "human relations" school of industrial management had rediscovered "group dynamics" and the importance of employee morale and motivation to productivity. Its adherents set about better satisfying workers' basic social and economic needs in order to reduce turnover, to increase productivity, and to quell interest in unions. Some employers also sought to break down ethnic loyalties that competed with the desired identification with the employer; but their efforts tended to produce stronger bonds among diverse workers. These developments helped secure for workers some of the common ground they needed to mobilize their collective power and form effective unions in critical industrial sectors. Once financial collapse and economic depression unsettled confidence in the "free market" and emboldened the proponents of government intervention, the stage was set for the New Deal.[33]

At least through the New Deal era, the link between one's role in the productive sphere and one's capacity for self-governance was a recurring theme in American political discourse.[34] The nature of that link was necessarily transformed as the founders' commitment to economic independence collided with economic developments that corralled citizens into a system of production that fostered abject dependence at worst and interdependence at best. The increasingly complex and collective nature of production brought forth an increasingly social, cooperative, and participatory conception of industrial life in a democracy. It brought forth, in particular, calls for "industrial democracy" as an indispensable complement to political democracy.

The shape that "industrial democracy" took was largely the handiwork of Senator Robert Wagner, the intellectual architect and driving force behind New Deal labor policy. Senator Wagner's own distinctive vision of industrial democracy—and particularly his conception of collective bargaining as an essentially cooperative enterprise—reflected in part the influence of his contemporary and fellow democrat, John Dewey.[35] The version of "industrial democracy" within capitalism that Senator Wagner brought into being was in many ways remote from the "genuinely cooperative" alternative to capitalism to which Dewey himself aspired.[36] Still, having left unexplored in his writings the capacity of work-place ties to foster connectedness in modern society, Dewey nonetheless provided some of the intellectual impetus for the framing of a new legal constitution for the workplace that might better realize that potential.

As explored further in chapter 9, the New Deal "constitution" of the workplace has not worked as its framers imagined. The optional form of democracy that it instituted has proven to be either unattainable or undesirable for most workers, and the freedoms of speech and association that it extended to the union and non-union workplace alike have been chronically underenforced. But the legislation did bring about a dramatic and lasting change in the organization and conditions of major industrial establishments and put upward pressure on the labor relations policies and conditions even within many nonunion workplaces. Moreover, the New Deal labor legislation firmly established the regulability of the workplace— the power of the government to intervene in private employers' decisions about whom to hire and fire and to regulate the allocation of rights and power within the workplace. It laid the groundwork for crucial amendments to the constitution of the workplace with the Civil Rights Act of 1964 and its progeny, and for the rash of regulatory statutes and individual rights that followed.

Even as it turned away from the more ambitious quest for a thoroughly co-operative and democratic social order, the New Deal's reconstitution of the workplace, together with the crucial Civil Rights Era amendments, effectively recast the role of workplace relations within American society. Those laws helped to make the workplaces of today comparatively promising venues for the face-to-face connections that Tocqueville, Durkheim, and Dewey, each in their own day and their own way, deemed necessary for the vitality of democratic society.

Social Capital and Civic Skills in the Workplace

The concerns of Tocqueville have gained renewed attention under the recently popularized rubric of "social capital." Social capital refers to "connections among individuals—social networks and the norms of reciprocity and trustworthiness that arise from them" and that help people to accomplish things together.[37] Some dimensions of social capital consist of highly diffuse feelings of empathy and "being in this together."[38] Some dimensions correspond to the processes of po-litical deliberation that I will discuss below. Yet the very term "social capital" suggests an aspiration to greater rigor and precision; it seeks to place social capi-tal on a par with human and physical capital in our assessment of the resources of a society, a community, a group, or an individual. The concept of social capi-tal echoes the instrumental theme in Tocqueville's celebration of associational life in American society.

Just as with economic forms of capital, social capital is unequally distributed among groups and among individuals. And as with economic capital, social capital—in the form of "connections"—helps individuals and groups compete with each other for valuable goods, including good jobs. The more one has, the more one gets. But Putnam has focused attention, and adduced a great deal of data, on the benefits of social capital to communities and to society as a whole—on social capital as a public good rather than simply a private good. Even acknowledging the unequal distribution of social capital, a society that has more of it is better off in many respects. My claims here hearken mainly to the latter dimension of social capital—to the value of workplace connectedness to the society or the community as a whole, not the private value of "connections" to individuals and discrete groups within the society. But there is no getting away from the problem of inequality, and we will return to it.

Social capital is valuable primarily because it allows people to accomplish things together. It helps to overcome problems of collective action: the tragedy of the commons, underinvestment in public goods, and prisoners' dilemmas. The problems are familiar: All would benefit from cooperation, but cooperation will not be forthcoming unless people can trust others to cooperate rather than to "defect." In Putnam's words, "[t]he greater the level of trust within a community, the greater the likelihood of cooperation. And cooperation itself breeds trust."[39] The question is how trust is developed and maintained in a complex modern society. According to Putnam, the answer lies in "norms of reciprocity and networks of civic engagement." Norms of generalized reciprocity—"I'll do this for you now, knowing that somewhere down the line you'll do something for me"—serve to build trust and to enable cooperation. Dense networks of civic engagement provide fertile ground for the evolution and enforcement of norms of reciprocity. These networks punish defection and reward cooperation by multiplying opportunities for repeat transactions among individuals who are loosely related through the network of associations and by translating acts of cooperation (or of defection) into a reputation for trustworthiness (or untrustworthiness). These associations operate in more diffuse ways as well. They shape the culture; they educate and socialize individuals in the norms of reciprocity and cooperation; and they demonstrate by their success the benefits of cooperation.[40]

Putnam marshals a formidable body of statistical evidence to show that a rich endowment of social capital—dense civic networks and a high level of generalized social trust—is linked to an array of social goods, including greater prosperity, health and well-being, safe neighborhoods, and better government.[41] Unfortunately, he also makes a powerful case that the conventional Tocquevillean portrait of America as a land of "joiners," of volunteers, of a robust civil society, is fading. Americans are devoting less time to informal socializing, joining fewer clubs and organizations, engaging in less political activity, and expressing less trust in their fellow citizens in recent decades.[42]

But connectedness in the workplace stands as an important exception to the pattern of decline. As we have observed, it is holding steady as a place where people "get a real sense of belonging," while feelings of connectedness in other social settings, such as neighborhoods, clubs, and religious congregations, are declining. As Putnam recognizes, "[t]he workplace is a natural site for connecting with others."[43] It exposes people to a wider social network and brings them into contact with opportunities for other kinds of civic engagement. The significance of workplace ties is magnified by the fact that, as elaborated at length here, "the workplace is much more diverse, racially and even politically, than most other social settings."[44] As a consequence, "[w]orkplace integration, for all its difficulties, has been by far the greatest success" in creating bridging social capital.[45]

The workplace is also a well-documented source of "civic skills"—skills of communication, compromise, and collective decisionmaking, and a sense of political efficacy. The introduction of "civic skills" as part of the content of social capital helps to elucidate the link between civic engagement and democracy. The civic skills story often emphasizes the individual resources rather than the social ties that arise out of social interactions within civic groups. It leads back to questions about the unequal distribution of these assets within a society. But civic skills are overwhelmingly relational in nature; their development both depends on and promotes the development of cooperative social ties. And a society or a community that is richly endowed with civic skills will benefit from more effective and articulate communication of collective needs, grievances, interests, and opinions between the governed and the government and more effective resolution and implementation of public policies. Whether it is social ties or civic skills we are looking for, they are likely to be found in the same places. And it is clear that both are found in the workplace. That is especially true for higher level workers with greater involvement in decisionmaking; but it is also true for many production-level workers, who increasingly participate in collaborative workplace processes.[46]

All this would seem to make the workplace a central site of social capital building in contemporary society.[47] Indeed, recognizing the workplace as an important source of social capital helps to address some criticisms of the social capital story. The claim that societal well-being and governmental efficacy depend upon the vitality of informal voliability and autonomous voluntary associations may tend to foster political complacency and skepticism toward the use of government power and public policy as instruments of social reform. But if the workplace is a major source of social capital, the law may play a significant role in rebuilding it. For the workplace is clearly amenable to regulation and has gone through significant transformations in the last century, often by the purposeful operation of law. Consider the contribution of the Civil Rights Act of 1964 to the desegregation of workplaces. The comparative diversity of workplaces is no accident; it is the deliberate product of public policy. Consider, too, the initial contribution of the National Labor Relations Act to the unionization, and in that sense democratization, of major industrial firms. This history suggests that the workplace is one locus of associational life where public policy can have a significant impact on the process of social capital formation.[48]

The idea of work-based social capital avoids another major criticism of the social capital story: its neglect of the economic foundations of social well-being. For some commentators, "the call for higher social capital as a solution to the problems of the inner city misdiagnoses the problem. . . . It is not the lack of social capital, but the lack of objective economic resources—beginning with decent jobs—that underlies the plight of impoverished urban groups."[49] The recognition that work, as well as civic voluntarism, helps build social capital avoids this dichotomy. Jobs are important not only for the "objective economic resources" they bring, but also for the positive social ties, norms of reciprocity, and feelings of trust, mutual responsibility, and solidarity that they engender.

Yet there is ambivalence toward workplace ties in many modern accounts of civic life.[50] That ambivalence stems in part from serious concerns about the nature of those ties. To begin with, relations among co-workers are mostly what sociologists call "weak ties."[51] Weak ties are good for helping people find jobs, but they may be thought too weak to do the yeoman's work assigned to social capital. On the other hand, if it is important to cultivate ties that cross lines of social division—to build "bridging" social capital—we have no choice but to start with weak ties. The evidence reviewed in Part I shows that weak ties have a power of their own in bridging social divisions. Moreover, weak ties that begin at work often grow into stronger ties—including cross-racial ties—of friendship and intimacy.

A more serious concern with the quality of workplace ties lies in the instrumental and the hierarchical context in which they form, and in the broad power of employers to monitor, censor, and punish communication and association among co-workers.[52] The hierarchical dimension of workplace relations may train people to get things done by giving or taking orders. It also creates huge disparities in the amount of trust and discretion people enjoy and widely disparate opportunities to form meaningful social ties with resourceful individuals and to participate in well-endowed interpersonal networks. To the extent that the workplace is a major site for the formation of social capital, it contributes very unequal portions of those assets to individuals and groups at different rungs of the socioeconomic ladder. These concerns are mitigated but not dissolved by trends toward greater collaboration and less rigid hierarchies in the workplace. On the other hand, we have begun to see that hierarchy and power in the workplace do not cut in only one direction, for compulsion and authority and the sheer need to get a job done can and often do help to forge ties and enable cooperation that takes place nowhere else in the society.

On the whole, we may agree with Putnam in rejecting "the hopeful hypothesis that American social capital has not disappeared but simply moved into the workplace."[53] That would indeed be too hopeful and too simple. Workplace ties are not interchangeable with the ties that arise out of religious associations, community groups, voluntary membership organizations, or the like. On the other hand, the workplace is a large and crucial pocket of resilient social ties that should be closely examined and cultivated. It fosters an enormous amount of sociability, cooperation, and solidarity among working adults. The sheer amount of time spent there, the economic motivation that sustains one's commitment to a job, the psychic meaning of work to individuals' identity, and the comparative diversity of workplaces all magnify the value of any improvements in the civic potential of the workplace.

Public Discourse in Work Clothes

One of the things that is supposed to take place in civil society, and largely through associations, is political deliberation and public discourse. Public discourse has come to occupy an increasingly central place in democratic theory.[54] It offers a way to engage citizens in the political process, to improve the quality of political decisions, and to elevate the nature of political decisionmaking above the sheerly opportunistic contest among self-interested political actors that is envisioned by public choice theorists. For some leading political theorists, the legitimacy of democratic decisionmaking, and the moral obligation of the losers to abide by majority decisions they oppose, depends on the existence and vitality of a realm of public discourse in which all citizens can participate as political equals. Moreover, the norms and practices of communication that prevail in public discourse serve to link together the citizens of a complex and heterogeneous modern society.

Much of the discourse about discourse delves into two related questions, to which I will return: First, what is the value of deliberation in a democratic polity?[55] Second, what are the necessary conditions for a functioning deliberative domain?[56] But I want to begin with a different question that receives comparatively little attention in the deliberation literature: Where, if at all, do ordinary citizens participate in public discourse? In particular, do the millions of conversations that take place every day among co-workers count as a form of public discourse or deliberation?

If the question were simply where citizens converse with each other about shared concerns, social issues, and public affairs, one would have to conclude that the workplace is a leading site of public discourse.[57] People practice skills of deliberation at work—they communicate their views, listen to others, compromise, and often participate in making decisions. They learn and do those things, in part, through the communication that is part of performing the job. They also communicate about other workplace issues—matters of shared concern among workers who share terms and conditions of employment. Some of those workplace concerns have grown into major national policy issues in recent years. Consider health care, affirmative action, the minimum wage, family and medical leave, and workplace harassment. But citizens also discuss public issues that have nothing to do with the workplace. Studies show that, when people are asked with whom they discuss matters of importance, including politics, co-workers figure as frequently as spouses, and more often than any other category of nonrelatives.[58] At least if we are concerned about the participation of ordinary citizens, and certainly if we give any importance to face-to-face discussion, and particularly if we are concerned with conversations that reach across boundaries of family and neighborhood, workplace conversations are of great importance. For it is clear that citizens deliberate with each other at work far more than in the fabled public square and far more than through voluntary civic organizations.

Does any of this put workplace conversations on the map of public discourse? The deliberation literature suggests two ways of approaching this question. One is to ask what deliberation is supposed to do in a democratic polity, and whether workplace discourse does it. The second is to ask what are the necessary conditions for democratic deliberation, and whether workplace discourse does or can meet those conditions. The answers to those two sets of questions are complex and linked.

What deliberation is supposed to do, in part, is to engage the citizens in the processes of political decisionmaking.[59] The deliberativists reject the elitist vision that dominated democratic theory in the postwar period, in which citizens' passivity is assumed and even applauded as a source of political stability. Public discourse is a medium through which citizens can participate in the political process and influence political decisions. If that is what democratic deliberation is for, then it cannot normally be found in the workplace. Indeed, it cannot normally be found anywhere in the daily lives of most ordinary citizens. Other than by voting, the ordinary citizen rarely attempts to influence the formal outputs of the political process.[60] He or she may write an occasional letter to the editor or participate in a political demonstration or may join—that is, in most cases, write a check to—an advocacy organization. But if the only deliberation that counts is that which is directly aimed at influencing political decisions, then, as a descriptive matter, ordinary citizens are largely left out of the picture; as a prescriptive matter, the deliberative democrats will have to start from scratch in constructing a role for those citizens.

But deliberation is extolled not only as a direct form of political participation but also as a more indirect way to improve the outputs of the political process. Deliberation is said to lead to better decisions, decisions that better approximate "the public good," or that at least better accommodate the varying interests and values of a diverse public.[61] Deliberation improves the outputs of the political process largely by improving what goes in. Deliberation and open channels of public communication bring more information about, and a greater understanding of, the varying experiences, grievances, values, and preferences of the diverse citizenry into the decisionmaking process.

Iris Marion Young is particularly illuminating in her discussion of intragroup difference "as a necessary resource for a discussion-based politics in which participants aim to cooperate, reach understanding, and do justice."[62] Through the process of deliberation, citizens discover shared concerns and conflicts and may come to understand and empathize with others who have different interests, experiences, and beliefs. As a result, they form political opinions and preferences that are more informed by and take greater account of the interests and experiences of others. The sharing and interaction of these individual opinions and preferences creates a public opinion that, while not unitary, is more truly public than a simple aggregation of private, self-regarding preferences.

The preference-shaping, opinion-forming function of deliberation suggests a broader conception of public discourse than does the participatory function. Clearly conversations that shape and challenge and modify political preferences take place in the workplace. Indeed, such conversations take place in the home, among close friends, and anywhere else that people experience the world and share their experiences. But certain features of workplace discourse give it a particularly valuable role in the process of preference- and opinion-formation in a diverse democratic society.

First, conversations among co-workers are less private, less particularistic, and in that sense more public than conversations among family members and close friends. Because people neither choose nor grow up among their co-workers, the norms of workplace discourse may be closer to the norms of public discourse than are the norms of discourse among family and close friends. Most workplace discourse occupies an important intermediate point on the spectrum from the most particularistic to the most public. It is more public than conversations within families, yet less public than self-conscious interventions in political decisionmaking. Perhaps in part for this reason, communication across these "weak ties" helps to weave private views and experiences into something more like "public opinion."[63]

Second, and relatedly, conversations among co-workers are more likely to cross lines of social division, such as racial, ethnic, or cultural identity, than are conversations with family and nonwork friends. The importance of dialogue across group lines has gained some attention from the deliberative democrats. But the workplace adds a crucial element: It fosters face-to-face conversation among people who have *both* different experiences, perspectives, and opinions *and* a reason to care about and get along with one another. The social science research reviewed above offers some empirical basis for the notion that the convergence of diversity and common ground that is found in the workplace (and almost only there) is particularly likely to challenge individual preconceptions, biases, and ignorance about others.

That brings us to the second set of questions that the deliberation theorists would pose in determining whether workplace conversations count as part of public discourse: What are the necessary conditions for democratic deliberation, and are they, or could they be, met in the workplace? The apparently clear answer to that last question would seem to doom any effort to bring the workplace inside the domain of public discourse. Professor Post, for example, is quite emphatic that the workplace lies outside of the domain of public discourse because of the conditions of inequality and unfreedom that prevail there. In the workplace, "an image of dialogue among autonomous self-governing citizens would be patently out of place."[64]

Professor Post's location of the workplace on (or, rather, off) the map of public discourse reflects a sharp dichotomy within modern social theory—and particularly in the influential work of Jürgen Habermas—between the domain of the market and the domain of public discourse and civil society. On this view, participants in the realm of public discourse must relate to each other as political equals and must appeal to mutually comprehensible reasons, shared values and interests, a common good.[65] By contrast, market institutions are internally organized to pursue the objectives of those with authority over and within these organizations. Inequality is endemic, and self-interest, guided by instrumental rationality, drives behavior. For public discourse to play its crucial energizing and legitimizing role in a democratic society, it must be shielded from the inequalities, power relations, and self-interested motives that necessarily prevail in the market. The location of the workplace in this scheme may seem to follow straightforwardly from this analysis: The pervasiveness of power, hierarchy, and inequality in work relations necessarily excludes the workplace from the domain of public discourse.[66] The problem of hierarchy and inequality in the workplace is a complex and recurring one to which chapter 7 is devoted. But some of what needs to be said on that problem bears quite specifically on the role of workplace conversations in public discourse and needs to be said here.

Clearly workplace relations are not a model of democratic engagement. Co-workers do not meet as free and equal citizens. But if concerns about inequality and hierarchy could somehow be allayed, there would be much to be gained by bringing workplace conversations into our conception of public discourse. There is certainly lots of talk among co-workers. The fact that this talk goes on in the context of working relationships—relationships that must remain at least constructive, cooperative, and civil if not friendly—imports a kind of discipline and constraint that does not exist in the core of public discourse. The fact that this talk goes on among comparatively diverse groups of co-workers is of momentous significance to the quality of public discourse.

Consider by contrast the voluntary civic, religious, political, and recreational associations that serve in most accounts as the primary arena for deliberation among ordinary citizens. Citizens join freely and, by and large, convene as equals. But those associations claim little of the citizens' time. Moreover, they are often rather homogeneous in terms of race and ethnicity. By definition, these voluntary associations draw individuals together on the basis of what they already share. Voluntary associations may meet the conditions of freedom and equality, but they may not supply the crucial element of diversity. That is not to denigrate their importance, but it does limit the kind of role they can play in public discourse.

Consider, too, the core of public discourse: the mass media and the storied "public forum"—the streets, parks, and sidewalks where citizens mount protests, distribute leaflets, or make speeches. There, the reigning mode of discourse is what Professor Post calls "critical interaction," or what the Supreme Court calls "uninhibited, robust, and wide open" debate.[67] In the "public square," nothing is sacrosanct and everything is open to question, unconstrained by existing community norms, including the very norms of civility and tolerance that make rational deliberation in a diverse society possible.[68]

The picture of public discourse that emerges from these accounts is highly fragmented. Civil, face-to-face exchange of ideas and experiences seems to take place within autonomous voluntary groups formed on the basis of shared identity or ideas. These groups then contend, and exchange ideas, in the unruly, unregulated, and rather impersonal "public forum"—the media of mass communication and the public square. One finds no place in the picture for civil, face-to-face conversations among individuals—acquaintances—of different identities, backgrounds, ideas and opinions.

The central role of the public forum within public discourse—its standing as the sole location for pluralistic exchange across group boundaries—gives rise to what Professor Post calls "the paradox of public discourse": "To the extent that a constitutional commitment to critical interaction prevents the law from articulating and sustaining a common respect for the civility rules that make possible the ideal of rational deliberation, public discourse corrodes the basis of its own existence."[69] The paradox arises largely from idea that the entire domain of public discourse must be one of "critical interaction," or no-holds-barred debate. If that is so, then workplace discourse is obviously outside of that domain. It would be silly to claim that the workplace is, or could be, or should be a domain of open and unconstrained debate. But it is not clear that freedom from constraint—either private constraint or public regulation—is a necessary condition for *all* forms of public discourse.

We can identify several ideal conditions for democratic deliberation. Among them are freedom—freedom from coercion by others and from state-imposed constraints—and equality, in terms of class as well as other group identities. I would emphasize, too, the importance of both diversity and connectedness among the participants. All of these conditions help to make it possible for people to learn from each other, to take each other's interests into account, to form political preferences and opinions that reflect a broader and better informed view of the world. The problem is that no social space that actually exists—not the core of public discourse, not the realm of voluntary associations, certainly not the workplace—can meet all of these conditions. Indeed, if there were many social spaces in our society that met all of these conditions—or even the single condition of, for example, equality—we would have less to deliberate about and more to celebrate. In the words of Professor Schauer, "[i]n an ideal world"—one in which views were "untainted by prejudice, selfishness, and related pathologies"— "people would not have the kinds of beliefs that deliberation would talk them out of."[70] But if an important subject of deliberation is the problem of inequality and how to address it, we have to be able to deliberate in a society in which inequalities of race, class, and sex impinge broadly and deeply on people's lives.

Moreover, while the workplace fails to meet some crucial conditions for democratic deliberation, it supplies a dimension that is missing from other sites of democratic deliberation and public discourse: a place for the informal exchange of experiences and opinions and knowledge among people who are both *connected* with each other, so that they are inclined to listen, and *different* from each other, so that they are exposed to diverse ideas and experiences. The convergence of diversity and connectedness, together with the legal mandate of equality, allows workplace conversations to make a particularly valuable contribution to democratic deliberation.

We can thus bring into the domain of public discourse the millions of conversations that take place in the workplace every day if we can reimagine that domain as a house of many rooms—different social spaces that meet different sets of deliberation-enhancing conditions. This more differentiated system of public discourse would still have a core in which freedom of expression is most unconstrained. But it might also have one or more rooms in which freedom of expression is subject to constraints—even government-imposed constraints— that are inadmissible in the core. Expanding our conception of public discourse, and of the speech that is relevant to self-governance, beyond the realm of unbridled "critical interaction" may allow us to expand the freedom of speech within institutions like the workplace without necessarily sacrificing competing virtues of restraint, civility, and connectedness.

For now, the essential point is that the conversations that take place within the workplace are important not just within the organization, and not just within the private lives of the people engaged in those conversations. Those conversations constitute a layer of public discourse—part of its deepest root system—in which ordinary citizens themselves participate in a regular and vital way. This way of thinking about public discourse should cause us to rethink how the law regulates or enables workplace speech, and how it shapes the workplace community, its demographics, and its forms of interaction. That is a project that I will sketch below in Part III.

In sum, the workplace must be considered, along with voluntary civic networks, among the chief incubators of social capital and vehicles of deliberation. The role it plays is distinctive. It cannot be relied upon to replace voluntary associations. But neither can voluntary associations do what workplaces do in building connections among people who may not otherwise choose to connect. That brings us to the heart of the matter: What does compulsion—the compelled association that follows from the employment discrimination laws and the compelled cooperation that is enforced by managers in pursuit of productivity—have to do with the building of these connections?

COMPULSION, CONNECTEDNESS, AND

THE CONSTITUTION OF THE WORKPLACE

To claim for workplace associations a more central role in democratic society, one must confront two distinguishing features of the workplace, both traceable to its firm footing in the market: First, workplaces are subject to pervasive regulation; they lack the autonomy from the state that civil society institutions need, on some accounts, to perform their crucial functions. Second, workplace relations are often undemocratic, unfree, and permeated by elements of economic coercion and power that are radically at odds with the egalitarian principles that must prevail—again, on some accounts—in the institutions of civil society.

These objections, and my response to them, go to the heart of the unique role of workplace relations in civil society. For it has become apparent that both the regulability of the workplace and the presence of economic pressure and authority play an ambiguous but largely constructive role in the cultivation of socially valuable workplace associations. These features of contemporary work life disable the workplace from doing some of what voluntary associations do in civil society; yet they enable the workplace to play a role that voluntary associations cannot play. In particular, the law's capacity to compel racial integration, together with the capacity of authorities within the workplace to compel people to get along with each other, help to make workplace associations distinctively important in a diverse democratic society.

The point is not, however, that authoritarian and hierarchical governance structures are necessary to produce these most valuable workplace bonds. Workplaces that are less hierarchical and more committed to building productivity through cooperation, commitment, and trust appear to produce more of the connectedness on which society thrives as well. So the role of workplace authority poses a puzzle, not necessarily a problem, for the "working together" thesis. The solution to that puzzle lies in the law's broad and legitimate role in governing the workplace, which opens up rich opportunities for building upon the partially realized potential of workplace relations to enrich social and political life.

The Regulability of the Workplace and the Value
of Compelled Association

Nearly any association of individuals can be said to "mediate" between individuals and the state or the larger society. But different kinds of associations play different mediating roles. Some accounts of civil society focus on the negative or oppositional functions of associations—what I have called the "sword and shield" functions. In these accounts, the chief function of associations, and of civil society itself, is to serve as a buffer between the individual and the state and as a potential source of resistance to the state. The leading role in these accounts is assigned to voluntary associations that bring together individuals who share ideas or interests or important aspects of their social identity into a common space. Such associations foster the formation of dissident opinion and distinct identity and form an essential bulwark against totalitarianism.[1] In order for these associations to provide a shield, and a potential sword, against the otherwise overweening power of the state, they must themselves be largely autonomous and shielded from state control.

The literature on civil society and associational life is positively bristling with tensions and paradoxes, many of which stem from the notion that autonomy from the state is a prerequisite to the ability of associations to play their part— their "sword and shield" functions—in democratic society. Stated most simply, it is impossible to insure that associations are *both* autonomous from the state *and* themselves respectful of democratic ideals of freedom and equality. Indeed, it may be impossible to secure associational autonomy anyway, given the role that law plays—necessarily or at least pervasively—in defining the boundaries and activities of many of the voluntary associations that make up civil society.[2]

It is surely true that, whatever degree of autonomy from the state is thought to be necessary for associations to play their oppositional functions, and whatever degree of autonomy voluntary associations are thought to have, the workplace has much less of it. Workplaces are subject to a plethora of regulations, including many that govern the composition and internal governance of the workplace, such as Title VII and the National Labor Relations Act. But the very feature of the workplace that impinges on its ability to serve the "sword and shield" functions—its susceptibility to extensive state regulation—turns out to support the ability of the workplace to play a different sort of mediating function by building connections between the individual citizen and the diverse body of fellow citizens.

Let us begin with the crucial fact that the workplace, unlike many voluntary associations, is subject to antidiscrimination law. One of the epic legal developments of the twentieth century has been the emergence of the principle of equal protection and its extension into a growing circle of public and private institutions. The Constitution demands nondiscriminatory access to public schools, employment, housing, and public services. Equal protection has been extended in the form of antidiscrimination statutes into other educational institutions, places of public accommodation such as hotels and restaurants, and the housing market, as well as into all but the smallest private sector workplaces.[3] Countervailing claims of private property, freedom of association, and privacy were long ago swept aside and are rarely echoed today.[4] The principle of equal opportunity in employment, in particular, enjoys nearly universal public support.[5]

Other associations—the family, religious institutions, political associations, and some private clubs and fraternal organizations—have fared differently. To a great extent, they remain free to discriminate, either because they lie beyond the scope of antidiscrimination legislation or because they enjoy a supervening constitutional right of freedom of association or both. The constitutional limits that freedom of association places on the equality principle, articulated most clearly in *Roberts v. United States Jaycees*[6] and elaborated recently in *Boy Scouts of America v. Dale*,[7] are based on an explicit judgment about the role of freedom of association, and of certain private associations, in our democratic society. But that explicit judgment has two indirect consequences that are important here: It limits the extent to which many voluntary associations can be counted on to foster connections across racial and ethnic lines, and it effectively shifts that crucial function onto those institutions such as the workplace that *are* subject to laws mandating equality and inclusion.

In *Roberts*, the Supreme Court identified two kinds of associational freedom protected by the Constitution. First, the freedom of intimate association is protected for its intrinsic value "as a fundamental element of personal liberty."[8] The majority explained that "certain kinds of personal bonds have played a critical role in the culture and traditions of the Nation by cultivating and transmitting shared ideals and beliefs; they thereby foster diversity and act as critical buffers between the individual and the power of the State."[9] The quintessential intimate association is the family; but some small and selective associations may come within the freedom of intimate association as well. The workplace, by contrast, anchors the other end of the "spectrum from the most intimate to the most attenuated of personal attachments."[10] Thus, "the Constitution undoubtedly imposes constraints on the State's power to control the selection of one's spouse that would not apply to regulations affecting the choice of one's fellow employees."[11]

The Constitution also protects the freedom of expressive association, which is recognized "as an indispensable means of preserving other individual liberties." In particular, "[a]ccording protection to collective effort on behalf of shared goals is especially important in preserving political and cultural diversity and in shielding dissident expression from suppression by the majority."[12] Expressive association affords a more limited shield against regulation, and its scope depends on the association's expressive mission. In *Roberts*, for example, the Jaycees' self-proclaimed expressive mission was not antithetical to the admission of women, so their right of expressive association was outweighed by the state's compelling state interest in promoting equality and "social and political integration" of women in public and economic life.[13] By contrast, in *Dale*, a majority of the Court found that the Boy Scouts' expressive mission *was* antithetical to the admission of avowed homosexuals and barred the application of New Jersey's broad public accommodation law banning discrimination on the basis of sexual orientation. However puzzling and problematic may be the line between the Jaycees and the Boy Scouts, there is little doubt about the location of the workplace on this axis. The ordinary workplace, organized around economic rather than political, social, cultural, or spiritual objectives, cannot claim the freedom of expressive association as a shield against antidiscrimination law.

It is hard to say how many associations lie within the zone of constitutional protection that *Roberts* delineated and *Dale* fortified. But the effective exemption of most private voluntary associations from antidiscrimination law is much broader. No federal law prohibits discrimination by such associations, and few states or municipalities have public accommodations laws as broad as the law at issue in *Dale*.[14] With or without a constitutional freedom of association, most of the associations that are celebrated by Tocqueville's modern descendants are legally free to discriminate.

Of course not all voluntary associations that are permitted to discriminate choose to do so. But nor do nondiscriminatory associations necessarily attract a heterogeneous membership. For it is in the nature of voluntary associations that they bring people together on the basis of views, interests, community ties, and aspects of identity that they already share. So while many voluntary associations are racially mixed, many are not, and there is usually nothing the law can do about it. Individuals can choose to join exclusionary groups, homogeneous groups, or even no groups. We have already noted evidence that individuals in more heterogeneous communities participate less in civic associations than do citizens in more homogeneous communities, perhaps because they wish to avoid the attendant diversity. Indeed, one criticism that is levied against the relatively narrow freedom of association recognized in *Roberts*, and the compelled association that follows from application of antidiscrimination laws to private associations, is that it may drive individuals who would prefer homogeneous associations to ever more marginal and alienated associations or even out of associations altogether.[15]

The liberty to join together based on common culture, identity, ideas, or objectives is an indispensable feature of a free society. Yet crucial as such voluntary associations are for securing a domain of liberty and independence of thought and expression, and for cultivating distinct identity and culture, they cannot be counted on to play the very different but critical function of bridging social divisions. The very voluntariness of these groups limits their ability to draw together individuals across lines of social division that they prefer not to cross.

The limits that freedom of association places on the antidiscrimination principle represent an explicit judgment about the function of intimate and expressive associations in a diverse and democratic society. But the denial of associational freedom and the validation of the antidiscrimination principle in other institutions, particularly the workplace, implicitly assigns to those institutions another function that is equally important. The workplace does not serve as a buffer between the individual and the state; it does not perform its mediating function by "cultivating and transmitting shared ideals and beliefs" among intimate associates, free from the intrusion of the state and societal norms. It functions rather as a link between individuals and the broader society by convening strangers from diverse backgrounds and inducing them to work together toward shared objectives under the aegis of the societally imposed equality principle. Its function is *integrative*, in the rich dual sense of drawing individuals into the broader society as a whole and drawing them into interpersonal relations across group, and especially racial, lines.

The workplace performs this integrative function in part because it cultivates relationships that are both more intimate and more communicative than those that arise within the other societal institutions that are subject to antidiscrimination law (except, perhaps, for schools). For while the instrumental nature of workplace relationships properly removes them from the reach of freedom of association, it is a mistake to see in the workplace *only* instrumental, market-driven behavior and relationships. Workplace relationships may begin as "the most attenuated of personal attachments," but they often yield bonds of empathy and affection that transcend family, neighborhood, racial, and ethnic identities.

The claim here is not that the Constitution, or the Supreme Court in *Roberts*, deliberately conferred on the workplace this role. *Roberts* suggests that it is by constitutional default that the workplace is subject to antidiscrimination legislation: workplace relationships are thought to lack the qualities of intimacy, expressiveness, or identity-formation that give other voluntary associations their distinct and protected constitutional functions. Nor is it my claim that Congress's *purpose* in enacting Title VII was to draw diverse citizens into cooperative endeavors. The proponents of Title VII pressed basic demands of justice and fairness and sought in particular to improve the economic status of black Americans.[16] They did not proclaim the value of social integration, which in 1964 would more likely have been seen as a threat to workplace discipline and productivity, or perhaps as a tolerable consequence of the law, than as a positive virtue. Yet the enactment of Title VII, and its constitutional blessing in the face of freedom of association claims, has effectively assigned to the workplace an important integrative function that no other major societal institution can perform as well.

The Ambiguous Role of Compulsion and Hierarchy in Workplace Interaction

The role of the workplace in a diverse democratic society thus rests in part on the norms of equality that govern the workplace by virtue of Title VII. But Title VII has nothing to say about the essential inequality at the heart of most workplace organizations: the inequality that stems from one's place in the workplace hierarchy. The hierarchical structure of many organizations limits employee freedom of action and interaction and inhibits the development of trust among managerial, professional, skilled, and unskilled segments of the workforce. More to the point, some employees are required to listen and submit to others who hire them and could fire them, and who control their advancement and conditions of employment. That is most brutally salient in the low-wage workplace; but elements of hierarchy and economic inequality are endemic to the workplaces we know. So we may aspire to make the workplace a realm of equality on the basis of race, sex, and ethnicity; but the workplace remains a bastion—indeed, a leading source—of class inequality.

The problem might be reframed in terms of intergroup relations. Segregation and inequality on the basis of wealth, or "socioeconomic status," are rampant in our society. In some ways, the story parallels that of race. As in the case of racial divisions, class divisions often correspond to spatial separation. That is true, and increasingly so, in residential patterns. The growing phenomenon of "gated communities," with their own private security forces and other private "governmental" services, is only the most pronounced form of residential separation based on wealth.[17] Elementary and secondary education is also becomingly increasingly segregated on the basis of socioeconomic status, as richer parents gravitate to more expensive suburban neighborhoods with better funded public schools, or simply withdraw from the public school system in favor of expensive private education. It is unclear how much class-mixing there is within private associational life; those groups that bring individuals together on the basis of common background and interests are likely to mirror the rather bleak state of class separation and inequality in the rest of the society. So far, the story of class separation runs roughly parallel to the story of racial segregation.

The parallel continues one step further into the workplace: For many working people, there may be more "interclass contact" inside the workplace than elsewhere in their lives. Managers and professionals may have more contact, more cooperation, and more amicable interaction with low-level clerical workers, for example, within the workplace than they have any place else. Of course, cooperation and amity exist, if at all, alongside organizational hierarchies in which class-like occupational distinctions determine one's rewards and authority. That is where the story of class in the workplace diverges sharply from the story of race. For class inequality not only continues inside the workplace; it is cultivated there and it flourishes free from any legal constraints.

The workplace, far from being a domain of relative egalitarianism and integration with respect to class, is typically the single most important *source* of an adult's wealth, class identity, and class status. One's place in the workplace hierarchy brings with it vast differences in income, status, and authority in the outside world; inside the workplace, it determines not only one's comforts, compensation, and privileges, but also who gives orders to whom, and who is empowered to hire or fire whom. In modern American society, at least, class is not primarily something that we bring into the workplace and hope can be set aside there (as in the case of race or sex); it is what we acquire, or at least reinforce, inside the workplace and take back to the outside world.

That points to another major difference between inequality and privilege based on class and that based on race: The law has little to say against the former, in the workplace or elsewhere. With a few exceptions, the Constitution—at least the Supreme Court's Constitution—casts no cloud of illegitimacy over the innumerable privileges of wealth in our society.[18] Nor does the law ban discrimination on basis of wealth in the workplace or elsewhere. On the contrary, the whole society rests on a foundation of private property and market exchange that is constructed by law and that assumes and insures the existence of wide disparities in wealth and all that it can buy for oneself and one's children.

It might be tempting simply to sweep aside concerns of class in the present context. The "working together" thesis builds largely on preexisting normative commitments to equality and integration along certain lines of social identity. Insofar as class and wealth distinctions are largely beyond the reach of those normative commitments, perhaps we need not worry too much about the workplace not serving the same integrative role with respect to class. But a number of uncomfortable questions stand in the way of that complacent response: What if interactions within workplace—the kinds of interactions I celebrate for their ability to transcend certain social divisions—actually exacerbate class divisions, class inequality, and class segregation outside the workplace? What if the increasing centrality of work in our lives, and of the workplace in our collective civic life, is bound to harden and widen class disparities? And what if the class structure of workplace interactions fatally distorts those interactions?

The problems of hierarchy and class inequality would seem to stand as major hurdles to the admission of the workplace into the realm of civil society and the overlapping realm of public discourse. Professor Putnam points to hierarchy and power as a major impediment to effective social capital formation in the workplace.[19] Professor Robert Post excludes the workplace from the domain of public discourse because "an image of dialogue among autonomous self-governing citizens would be patently out of place" there.[20] For Jürgen Habermas, the inequality and economic power that pervades workplace organizations violate the "conditions of communication" that define public discourse.[21] At every turn in this argument, it has been necessary to confront the problem that, at work, some people give orders and some follow them. How can these forms of interaction contribute to democratic self-governance in a society committed to liberty and equality?

Three possible but ultimately very partial answers initially suggest themselves. One optimistic answer might seem to lie in the trends discussed in chapter 3 toward more cooperative modes of organization, more diffuse authority relations, and flatter and more fluid organizational pyramids. But those trends themselves are only partial in their reach. Moreover, even the most cooperative and egalitarian of modern workplace organizations depend on a level of restraint and discipline in human relationships that seems at odds with the democratic paradigm of political freedom and equality.

Another more utopian response might be grounded in the ideal of workplace democracy: If hierarchy and lack of democracy impair the mediating role of workplace relations, then we should make workplaces democratic. But if the role of the workplace in a democracy depends on the institution of democracy in workplaces, the thesis speaks only to an imagined and elusive future. I mean to say something about the mostly undemocratic workplaces of the present and the role they play in democratic society. Workplace democracy is a worthy aspiration, and the attenuated legacy of democracy left by the New Deal "constitution"—the framework it supplies for unionization and collective bargaining—does provide some support for productive workplace ties. But that model is so beleaguered that it, too, can supply only a very small part of the answer to the problems of hierarchy and power that seem to plague my thesis.

By contrast, one might offer a realist response based on the lack of good alternatives: Where else do we see as much potential for constructive interaction among citizens across racial and ethnic lines? If that is an important dimension of social life in a diverse democratic society, as I have argued it is, then the best we can do—interaction under conditions of hierarchy—is good enough to warrant recognition and cultivation. But the response of realism and resignation is too simple, too. The problem of hierarchy in the workplace calls for a more subtle response.

The workplace is not a model of democratic engagement. Its organizing principles are not "congruent" with the organizing principles of democratic society. But workplace relationships can contribute to the vitality of a self-governing society in some ways that private, voluntary organizations cannot, and they can do so in part *because of* the presence of authority and economic constraint. So, for example, the fact that people "choose" their place of work and "choose" to stay there under the economic imperative of making a living and often supporting dependents precludes workplace relations from serving some of the "buffering" functions of associations emphasized in *Roberts*. But that very fact has helped to produce workplaces that are more integrated than most voluntary associations. The not-quite voluntary nature of workplace relations means that individuals who would not choose voluntarily to associate with others of different racial groups may nonetheless end up in integrated workplaces and in reasonably constructive workplace relations with those others. So the constraints that operate on the composition of workplaces are part of what allows the workplace to bring people together across lines of division.

So, too, with the constraints that operate within the workplace, and in particular the presence of hierarchical authority. Hierarchical authority, where it is brought to bear on the project of racial integration, can achieve impressive advances in racial relations. The success of integration in the military, and particularly in the Army, stands as a testament to the potentially democratic uses of hierarchy. Of course we cannot count on ordinary employers committing themselves to the project of integration to the extent the military leadership has done. Even if we could, it would be absurd to argue that the military model could or should be transported into ordinary workplaces. But the military model reminds us of the troubling but familiar tension between freedom and equality. It also reminds us that people can be compelled to get along with each other. The fact that there is less individual freedom within the workplace than, for example, in the public square may actually contribute to successful integration of workplaces, the experience of which can in turn spill outside the workplace and enrich democratic life.

But the successes seen in the "social capitalist" workplaces discussed in chapter 3—both the nonunion and the union versions—show that more hierarchy is not necessarily better when it comes to building cooperative social ties in a diverse workforce. We need to distinguish between the elements of unfreedom and constraint that are endemic to workplaces and those elements that are contingent on how a particular organization and its managers decide to motivate and direct production. Any workplace, whether it is based on hierarchical structures or on autonomous, self-managing teams of employees, is driven primarily by the instrumental imperative of getting a job done (and, typically, producing profits for the owners). Nearly every worker is driven by the economic compulsion to work for a living. The need for a paycheck keeps people in workplace relationships that they would not have chosen. So, too, the need to get a job done—whether it is enforced hierarchically by management or horizontally by teams of workers—entails constraints on human interaction, such as social norms or formal disciplinary rules against rudeness or fighting. Some of those constraints contribute to making workplace interactions more constructive, cooperative, and civil than interactions in more "free" and "voluntary" settings. Those constrained interactions provide an indispensable complement to the often raucous, uninhibited, and uncivil domain of public discourse, as well as to the often homogeneous, albeit autonomous, voluntary associations.

Keeping one's job and getting the job done both require workers to get along; and getting along requires constraints on conflict. Those constraints may be imposed by hierarchical and authoritarian means, by mutually agreed-upon social norms and informal sanctions, or by contract. But it is the presence of effective constraints on conflict and effective pressure toward cooperation, not hierarchy as such, that makes the workplace uniquely productive of cooperative bonds among diverse individuals. Economic power, coercion, and inequality still complicate this effort to make the workplace a more central institution in democratic society. But the problem is much less straightforward than it may initially appear.

Traces of Democracy in Undemocratic Workplaces: The Partial Constitution of the Workplace

So the mediating role of the workplace depends in part on the presence of constraints on individual freedom that are *incongruent* with liberal democratic principles. But that role also depends on some ways in which the principles governing the workplace are *congruent* with democratic principles. While the workplace is indeed pervaded by inequality on the basis of class and socioeconomic status, it is the most important place in the daily lives of most adults that is governed by legal norms of equality on the basis of race, ethnicity, religion, and sex. That limited version of equality, though it leaves untouched economic disparities and hierarchies, has a particular constitutional resonance, for it roughly parallels the limited form of "equal protection" that the Fourteenth Amendment affords as against the state. By virtue of its susceptibility to regulation, the workplace can claim some of the features of liberal democracy that many of the classic civic associations cannot.

But antidiscrimination law is not the only regulatory intervention that has sought to impose certain democratic principles on the internal governance of the workplace. Indeed, the Civil Rights Act must be seen as a crucial and belated amendment to the "constitution of the workplace" that originated in the New Deal. The Wagner Act of 1935 represented the historic apex of legislative support for industrial democracy in this country.[22] The leading proponents of the Wagner Act, and especially Senator Robert Wagner himself, often described their objectives in terms of bringing freedom and democracy to the American worker. Senator Wagner described his bill as "the next step in the logical unfolding of man's eternal quest for freedom," and as the "cornerstone of industrial liberty." Other supporters spoke of the vindication of "[t]he right of self-government through fairly chosen representatives [—] a right which is inherent in the American people," and of "the constitutional rights of employees to associate themselves."[23] The soaring rhetoric and noble aspirations of its sponsors, and particularly of Senator Wagner, were not fully borne out by the actual legislation and have been even more thoroughly undermined by subsequent events.[24] But the Wagner Act did establish a degree of legally enforceable (though still underenforced) freedom of expression and association and a form of democratic self-governance through majority rule, elections, and collective bargaining.

One might fairly describe the basic components of the Wagner Act as analogues to the First Amendment and the "Republican Form of Government" clause (without the Guarantee). It establishes a basic charter of civil liberties in the workplace—protecting freedom of association and peaceful concerted expression and action—and a form of workplace democracy available at the option of a majority of the workforce. Viewed from the vantage point of political democracy, collective bargaining—the right of a majority to form a union, negotiate for improvements in terms and conditions of employment, and exert collective economic power against them in support of collective demands—looks like a very pale version of democracy and nothing like a republic. But as compared to the baseline regime of unilateral employer governance, collective bargaining and the contracts that emerged from it represented the rule of law, the institution of due process, and the opportunity for a real collective voice in the determination of wages and working conditions. Collective bargaining thus emerged as the imperfect realization of workplace democracy within a system of private ownership of capital and employment of wage labor.

The political analogy places in sharp relief some of what was missing from the New Deal constitution of the workplace: It lacked an "equal protection clause" banning discrimination on the basis of group status, a void that was finally filled 30 years later with the 1964 Civil Rights Act. It lacked a "due process clause" to back up the law's ban on employer reprisals; due process—in the form of "just cause" for discipline and discharge and arbitration of disputes—was and still is left to be won by employees through collective bargaining or individual contract. The New Deal constitution of the workplace also lacked any "guarantee" of employee representation; it merely established a mechanism by which a majority of employees could choose collective representation, and enforced that choice. Failing an affirmative majority choice of union representation—and the hurdles that lie on the path to union representation are legion—the employer retains plenary power, constrained only by the minimal "civil liberties" imposed by the Act and by other regulatory requirements (and whatever constraints flow from the need to maintain worker morale and productivity). Some of what I will have to say in chapter 8 about how the law can better support the civic-ness of the workplace can be organized around those missing features.

Consider, however, what the original "constitution of the workplace" did, and still does, contain: Most importantly, it grants to employees a basic set of rights—in particular, freedom of expression and association—as against their employers. Section 7 of the Act guarantees to most private sector employees the right of "self-organization" and the right to engage in "concerted activity for . . . mutual aid or protection . . ."[25] This encompasses rights of association and expression: the rights to join with fellow workers in a labor union, to solicit and express support for work-related causes and organizations, to discuss shared grievances, to petition the employer, and to engage in other forms of peaceful protest.[26] It includes the right to engage in these activities on the employer's property—to solicit support for unions and discuss other matters of common concern in non-work areas of the workplace during nonwork hours.[27] Section 7—underenforced though it is—operates as a kind of First Amendment of the private sector workplace, complete with its own limited version of "public forum" law. Just as a municipality cannot invoke its "property rights" to limit citizens' rights to speak and solicit others on public streets and sidewalks, the employer cannot claim a property right to limit employees' statutory rights to discuss matters of shared concern with co-workers.[28]

The significance of the New Deal model is thus much greater than the faltering system of collective bargaining that it sought to promote. It gave workers—whether or not they secure or even seek union representation—a rudimentary regime of civil liberties against their employers. Moreover, it established the idea of the workplace as an appropriate domain of freedom and democracy, and the legislature's power to intervene into the internal workings of private firms and to limit employer property rights in order to further employees' freedom and self-determination.[29] That powerful idea was advanced dramatically in 1964, when the "constitution of the workplace" was amended by the addition of an "equal protection clause."

The idea of the workplace as a domain for the protection of liberty has continued to inspire legal reform. Federal and state legislation, as well as common law decisions, have taken that basic notion, given it a more individualistic spin, and extended it beyond labor relations, and beyond the law of group status rights, into some aspects of the individual employment contract.[30] Nothing in contemporary constitutional jurisprudence suggests that these enactments and doctrines have reached the limits of what is constitutionally permissible.[31] To the extent the society is persuaded that the workplace will work better—better for workers, better for the society as a whole—under a more encompassing and effective regime of civil liberties and democratic structures, there is a great deal of latitude to impose those reforms.

Having It Both Ways: Congruence and Incongruence in the Constitution of the Workplace

This much should be clear: The argument here is not that workplaces are democratic. Nor is it that workplaces need to be democratic in order to play a useful role in democratic society. There is a long and powerful, though recently subdued, line of argument to the effect that the workplace can play a role in democratic society if and only if the workplace itself is democratic. For the proponents of industrial democracy, self-determination at work is both a direct form of democratic participation and a kind of training for democratic participation in the public political process.[32] In particular, the idea of the workplace as a potential "school for democracy" may give a familiar ring to the proposition that the workplace has a role to play in democratic society. The case for democratization of the workplace is, in my view, powerful and appealing. But it is distinct from the case made here for the capacity of the workplace to foster connectedness in a diverse democracy.

According to Carole Pateman, a leading proponent of workplace democracy, "there is something paradoxical in calling socialisation inside existing organisations and associations, most of which, especially industrial ones, are oligarchical and hierarchical, a training explicitly in *democracy*."[33] But I am making something like that paradoxical claim: Even hierarchically organized, nonunion workplaces can foster social ties and civic skills that are essential in a diverse democratic society. In other words, the integrative function of the workplace in democratic society does not directly depend on the institution of democracy inside the workplace. Rather, the function of the workplace in democratic society is related in a more complex way to the existence of democratic principles and norms in the internal governance of workplaces.

I have argued that the external law governing the modern private sector workplace can be thought of as a kind of "constitution" for the workplace. That constitution includes principles of private property and contract that give managers a relatively free hand to "legislate" within it—to organize and manage the workplace using greater or lesser degrees of hierarchical control and of cooperation and trust. But the constitution of the workplace also includes employer obligations and employee rights that constrain management: It includes some basic civil rights and civil liberties, as well as a majoritarian mechanism by which the employees can play a more organic role in workplace governance.

The workplace as it is thus constituted—with rudimentary elements of democracy, liberty, and equality superimposed on a basically undemocratic foundation of private ownership and management—serves democracy in important ways. If we are persuaded that different organizing principles for the workplace will better serve democracy, then we the people can amend the "constitution" of the workplace, subject only to the limited constraints posed by the other Constitution on workplace legislation. Once again, we find that the regulability of the workplace, which disables it from performing some functions of associational life, plays a constructive role in this account. Here, the regulability of the workplace—what the law has done and what it could do to promote the democracy-enhancing role of workplace associations—enables us to transcend a debate over the importance of "congruence" between liberal democratic principles and the internal organizing principles of associations.

Commentators have sharply divided over the extent to which the value of associations, and of freedom of association, in liberal democratic society depends on associations themselves being organized along liberal democratic lines. Some commentators have questioned whether undemocratic, discriminatory, or exclusionary associations can make a positive contribution to democratic life.[34] On the other hand, Professor Nancy Rosenblum has been particularly cogent in her critique of the notion that only associations that operate in accordance with basic democratic principles—that are "congruent" in their internal governance with democratic institutions—can make an affirmative contribution to a free democratic society. Even "noncongruent" associations can express liberty and personal or social identity, temper self-interest, provide spaces for the accommodation of differences, help integrate otherwise isolated individuals into society, nurture trust, and resist the totalizing tendencies of state power.[35]

We can identify counterparts to these polar positions in discussions of the role of workplaces in a democracy. The underlying issue is the same: Can an organization that is not itself democratic play a valuable role in democratic society? Many proponents of industrial democracy, like Pateman, have taken the side of "congruence," and have called for the institution of democracy within the workplace in part to make the workplace a valuable "school for democracy." Other commentators, for example, Milton Friedman, argue quite the opposite: The system of free enterprise capitalism—in which principles of private property confer on owners of firms broad power to manage them in their own interests, autocratically if they choose, without state interference—plays a crucial role in supporting political freedom in a democracy, chiefly as a source of countervailing power as against the state.[36] They claim—contrary to the industrial democrats' call for "congruence"—that virtual autocracy within firms is entirely consistent with liberal democracy in the society.

My claim here straddles that divide, and stakes out a third way—albeit one with which both sides would probably disagree: Workplaces need not be democratic to play a valuable role in supporting political democracy; but neither need they or should they be insulated from regulations that promote democratization. Within broad limits, neither private property rights nor associational rights stand in the way of governmental efforts to make workplaces more democratic. In other words, we can have it both ways. That may not be possible in the case of voluntary associations, some of whose crucial functions depend on their autonomy from the state. But broad autonomy from the state is not critical—indeed, it would be counterproductive—to the role that workplace associations play in democratic society.

So we find that, contrary to the thrust of much of the growing literature on civil society, civic engagement, and associational life, workplace ties do many of the things that civil society is supposed to do. Those ties provide a medium for the cultivation of empathy and a sense of belongingness, of "social capital" and habits and norms of cooperation and reciprocity, of civic skills of participation, communication, and compromise, and of conversations that enrich public discourse. The fact that they cultivate all these qualities, skills, habits, and feelings in an environment of relative diversity and even compulsory integration makes the workplace a central and uniquely important component of civil society.

But even as we have explored the value of what does happen among co-workers, we have seen many ways in which reality falls far short of what seems possible. Let us now turn to the programmatic part of this project: If one is persuaded of the good things that workplace ties can and do bring to civic and political life, what can be done through law and public policy to better fulfill the only partially realized civic potential of those ties?

Part Three

BUILDING BETTER WORKPLACE BONDS

Preliminary Thoughts on What Law Can Do

The workplace has become a uniquely important site for the building of cooperative and constructive social ties across lines of group identity and social division. Workplace cooperation, sociability, and solidarity all play a role in promoting these ties, and all of those emerge out of basic features of human psychology and basic imperatives of human labor in a modern economy. The law, too, plays a role, both in promoting equal opportunity and demographic heterogeneity in the workplace and in imposing some rudimentary "constitutional" norms of freedom of association and communication and democracy on the workplace. But this basically optimistic assessment of the value of "working together" is qualified by the law's uneven success and the enormous variety of workplaces, some of which utterly mock the vision of cooperation and sociability that animates this book. Even as we have explored the value of what often happens among co-workers, we have seen many ways in which reality falls far short of what seems possible.

The "working together" thesis thus has both a descriptive and an aspirational dimension. It is both about what happens in workplaces and about what can and should happen there. And it suggests what is possible partly by showing what already exists. The analysis has thus far straddled the dichotomy between the descriptive and the prescriptive, bringing to the foreground the good things that can already be seen in workplace relations while acknowledging the serious flaws and gaps in the picture. But if one is persuaded of the good things that workplace ties can and do bring to civic and political life, one should be led to ask what can be done to better fulfill the only partially realized civic potential of those ties.

Before launching into even a preview of any particular aspects of workplace law reform, it is worth asking whether law and policy have any role left to play. Perhaps the forces that are already in motion—the demographic trends that are diversifying workplaces, the incentives of firms to promote collegiality and productivity, the human needs and proclivities that fuel sociability and solidarity—are enough and are best left alone. The civil rights laws, together with labor market demographics, have helped to make diversity a fact of life for many employers. At the same time, as we have seen, production in many workplaces has become increasingly cooperative, social, and interactive. Where both demographic diversity and the need for cooperation are seen as given, employers have their own reasons to find ways to facilitate productive and constructive interaction across group lines. Where these circumstances are present, we should expect employers themselves to organize work and exercise their authority in a way that promotes trust and communication, builds a sense of common purpose, and fosters effective cooperation across group lines. Might further social engineering to the end of enhancing the civic and integrative potential of the workplace be unnecessary or even counterproductive?

Consider the rise of corporate "diversity management." There are now legions of consultants urging employers to adopt training programs, new rules of conduct, and organizational changes in order to increase the ability of diverse groups to work together productively. Some of those techniques have proven effective in improving intergroup cooperation and in combating subtle forms of bias and discrimination; other techniques of diversity management may raise the salience of racial and ethnic identity and exacerbate divisions.[1] But over time, one would expect to find improvements in the practice of "diversity management." Managers are motivated to find what works and to reject what doesn't work in promoting effective intergroup cooperation. Indeed, this suggests the makings of a "market" for effective diversity management techniques. Programs that fail to overcome intergroup tensions, or that exacerbate them, will end up losing out, simply through market pressures and the demands of productivity- and profit-minded managers, to more effective methods for promoting intergroup cooperation.

This might suggest that public-minded lawyers and policymakers should not worry too much about intergroup relations at the workplace, for that is something employers have every reason to worry about and to address themselves. We might look for ways to make the employment discrimination laws and other elements of the "constitution" of the workplace—such as the freedom of association—more effective within their own terms. But those paths are well worn, and not worth taking here, if the quality of workplace relations lies beyond the purview of wise policymaking. I would suggest a few caveats, however, that underscore the value of reexamining the law of the workplace through the lens of "working together."

First, the ability of market pressures to induce the cultivation of more cooperation and better intergroup relations depends on the ability of managers to get good information about what works and what doesn't in this area. But it may be very hard to evaluate what works even within one's own firm; comparative information from other firms may be even harder to come by.

Take, for example, the idea of a "market" in effective diversity management. The "diversity management" profession itself has an interest in publicizing, but also in "puffing," their own accomplishments. Employers may have little reason to publicize their successes, much less their failures. Indeed, as Professor Susan Sturm has argued, the law itself might even discourage employers from disseminating information about the effects of diversity management techniques insofar as that information might seem to pose a potential threat in discrimination litigation down the line. At a minimum, we should seek ways to avoid squelching the flow of good information about what works in the diverse workplace; ideally we might seek ways to promote it. The law may, for example, be able to support the role of market actors by encouraging the production of information about what works in this arena.[2]

The possibility that the law may play a counterproductive role here points to a broader justification for reexamining the law of the workplace: We have focused thus far on the broad strokes of the law and the positive role it plays in constituting the workplace as a site for constructive interaction. But the law may sometimes play a corrosive role, undermining the potential of "working together" or even exacerbating social divisions. At a minimum, we should try to identify any counterproductive consequences of existing law and to look for ways to avoid them.

Recall, as well, the two "ifs" on which the happy market scenario is based: *If* demographic diversity is a given and *if* cooperation is a necessity, then we might well leave it to private firms themselves to improve the workplace as a site of intergroup and interpersonal connectedness. For some employers, demographic diversity is not a given but merely a prospect to be considered and possibly resisted. That raises questions about how well the law works to encourage the maintenance of a diverse and integrated workforce. For other employers, cooperation is not seen as a necessity. Some employers seek to secure profits by minimizing labor costs—breaking down and routinizing tasks, intensely monitoring performance, and disciplining through the threat of discharge—rather than by building productivity through greater trust, cooperation, and commitment. The problem in these workplaces is not usually employers' unwillingness to hire minorities, for these worst of all workplaces are disproportionately occupied by people of color and especially recent immigrants. The problems are different: payment of low (often illegally low) wages, the maintenance of unsafe and unhealthy conditions of work, and the suppression of workers' freedom to discuss and redress their grievances through self-organization. We will turn to these problems below in chapter 9. For now, the point is to qualify any undue confidence that employers themselves always have an interest in fostering cooperation among diverse workers.

Finally, we cannot assume that the cooperation and harmony that some employers seek to foster is the same sort of interaction that is valuable for the society as a whole. Most obviously, many employers suppress employees' expressions of shared grievances and of solidarity with each other. That may be one of the most powerful forces in the building of intergroup bonds and empathy, but it may look like an economic threat to employers. So, too, employers may seek to banish friction from the workplace. Friction among workers may impede productivity. Yet some friction, expressed within a constrained setting in which the work has to get done, may be socially valuable, or at least inevitable whenever workers have time, space, and freedom for informal social interaction. In other words, workplace cooperation, sociability, and solidarity may have "positive externalities" that employers have no economic reason to cultivate and may have reason to suppress.

Of course, not all firms and managers are driven exclusively by the bottom line. Some employers encourage charitable contributions and civic involvements by their employees without regard to any immediate economic return to the firm. Some pursue family-friendly policies partly out of a sense of moral and civic obligation. Many comply with costly legal obligations even where their failure to do so is unlikely to be detected or aspire to higher standards of safety and service than the market rewards.[3] Indeed, given the mixed evidence about the productivity effects of diversity and the spotty enforcement of Title VII, there is good reason to believe that many employers who actively pursue diversity in their workforces are doing so partly out of a sense of justice (and the wish to appear just). Those firms and managers who are committed to being good corporate citizens have good reason to take the lessons of this book to heart and to devote themselves to maintaining diverse workforces and friendly, constructive, and egalitarian relations within the workplace.

Still, it is fair to assume that most employers respond to incentives, positive and negative, of the sort that law can supply. All in all, it seems well worth undertaking a more particularized examination of the law of the workplace through the lens of the "working together" thesis: How might the law contribute to making the workplace a better environment for the cultivation of social capital, civic skills, democratic deliberation, and bonds of empathy and understanding across lines of social division? That question has two big components that are the subjects of chapters 8 and 9 respectively: How might the law better promote demographic diversity and more constructive and egalitarian intergroup relations within workplaces? And how might the law better promote cooperation, sociability, and the expression of shared concerns within workforces? Unfortunately, answering those questions with any degree of seriousness would quickly take us into a world of law and policy, and of cases and statutes, in which only some readers would be conversant and engaged. That is therefore a project that I undertake more fully elsewhere. What follows here is only a preview—a quick tour of some of the possible sites of interest and some of the pathways down which we might travel.

REFINING THE "EQUAL PROTECTION CLAUSE"

OF THE WORKPLACE

The law has a well-established role in securing equal opportunity in the workplace. By prohibiting discrimination in the composition and the treatment of a workforce, the law of equal employment tends to make workplaces more heterogeneous and less stratified on the basis of race, sex, and other traits that have historically shaped individuals' employment opportunities. It tends, in short, to produce workplaces that are more integrated and more likely to foster constructive intergroup bonds. So one important component of a strategy for building the civic potential of the workplace lies in the already well-developed legal effort to make workplaces more egalitarian, particularly along lines of race, ethnicity, and sex.

Yet the law's commitment to equal opportunity in the workplace, and its tendency to produce greater integration, does not always add up to an affirmative commitment to workplace integration. It should. We have seen that workplace integration—both more-than-token representation and genuine intergroup interaction—is a crucial social good. Moreover, as an empirical matter, workplace integration is closely linked, even essential to, real workplace equality.[1] So the common theme of this brief foray into the implications of the "working together" thesis for antidiscrimination law is this: Antidiscrimination law should be interpreted, applied, and if necessary reformed so as to affirmatively promote workplace integration. That makes sense within the conventional terms of antidiscrimination law, given strong empirical evidence that more-than-token representation of minority groups mitigates unconscious and subtle biases against members of those groups within the workplace. It also makes eminent sense for the reasons developed here: Workplace integration advances the compelling societal goals of mending and narrowing social (and especially racial) divisions and of promoting genuine equality on the basis of race, ethnicity, and gender.

The significance of linking the statutory goal of intergroup equality and the goal of integration can be seen in a rather obscure corner of Title VII doctrine:

the legal status of intergroup solidarity.[2] The intergroup amity and empathy that can grow up among co-workers sometimes leads to white support for black co-workers, or male support for female co-workers, in opposition to discrimination or harassment on the basis of race or sex. For example, several white male police officers in Richmond, Virginia, when faced with a racially and sexually abusive supervisor, "did the right thing: . . . they joined their black and female co-workers to demand that their supervisor be disciplined for undermining the cross-race, cross-gender teamwork that they asserted was essential to safe and effective policing." Their solidarity was met with employer harassment, threats of discharge, and other adverse actions. When the white male employees sued under Title VII, claiming a "hostile working environment" pervaded with sex and race discrimination, their suit was dismissed. The white male officers were held to have no cognizable interest in working in an environment that was free from divisive discrimination; indeed, the conditions they complained of were thought to render the workplace "biased in their favor."[3]

Nothing could be more at odds with the vision of workplace cooperation and solidarity delineated here. The open-textured provisions of Title VII can and clearly should be read to protect rather than disparage intergroup solidarity in the face of efforts to divide co-workers on the basis of race or sex. Indeed, the point can be made in more general terms: Where existing law can be fairly read and applied so as to promote integration as well as equality on the basis of group membership, it should be.

That may sound simple, but it is not. Antidiscrimination law can enhance or impair the capacity of the workplace to foster integration and intergroup ties, and it is not always a simple matter to sort out the law's effects or to discern the proper direction for reform. The "working together" thesis is infused with paradox: The paradoxical role that workplace hierarchy and employer authority can play in fostering constructive intergroup relations; the paradoxical role of state regulatory power in fostering some of the functions that are usually assigned to free and voluntary associations. These paradoxes reappear when we put the thesis to work—that is, when we explore its critical and prescriptive implications for the law of the workplace. The "working together" thesis proves to be a double-edged sword in many instances.

Some policies that might make workplaces more demographically integrated—for example, some forms of group preference—might also provoke intergroup tensions. Some policies that aim toward greater intergroup equality—for example, some versions of workplace harassment law—might inhibit sociability and solidarity across group lines. More broadly, some ways of promoting diversity within the workplace—to the extent that they highlight the fault-lines of group identity and intergroup differences—may be in tension with what I would submit is the more compelling goal of integration: the working together, getting along together, and connectedness that make workplace interaction so distinctively valuable in a diverse society. What follows points out some areas of concern and suggests some directions for reform.

Affirmative Action and Workplace Integration

The issue of affirmative action in employment illustrates both some prescriptive implications and the double-edged quality of the "working together" thesis.[4] On the one hand, the thesis offers an important and underappreciated argument in favor of a strong form of affirmative action: race- or sex-conscious hiring, promotion, or (more rarely) layoff preferences in favor of a grossly underrepresented group. After several decades of affirmative action under the dual banners of "remedying past discrimination" and "diversity," we are manifestly in need of a fresh perspective on what is at stake. What is at stake is the creation of a more integrated, less divided society, a goal that workplace integration can do much to advance.[5]

The goal of building an integrated society is, to begin with, forward-looking and pragmatic as compared to the most well-established remedial argument for affirmative action. While claims for remediation carry a powerful moral force for many proponents of affirmative action, those claims increasingly meet resistance from white Americans as the worst evils of de jure segregation fade from memory. Whether it is warranted or not, there is a widespread weariness with appeals based on guilt, entitlement, and victimhood that has surely contributed to the growing skepticism toward affirmative action programs. That skepticism has taken its greatest toll on affirmative action programs in education, especially in public institutions. But it is reflected as well in attitudes about workplace affirmative action.

Recall that, according to a recent survey, 63 percent of all workers, and 60 percent of white workers, agreed or strongly agreed that "the diversity of a company's employees should reflect the diversity of the city in which it is located," and that over half of all workers (56 percent), and nearly half of all white workers (49 percent) agreed that "employers should be *required by law* to maintain a certain level of diversity in the workplace." Yet this remarkably strong endorsement of demographic diversity at work—even, seemingly, of mandatory "quotas"—is coupled with overwhelming opposition to the proposition that "because of past discrimination, qualified African Americans should receive preferences over equally qualified whites in such matters as getting jobs."[6]

So the idea of preferences—even among "equally qualified" applicants—triggers negative reactions even as diversity has acquired largely positive connotations.[7] Of course, that leads one to wonder how respondents expect employers to reach and maintain the levels of workplace diversity that they support, at least in higher level jobs. Support for workplace diversity leaves open not only the question of means but also the question of ends: Why is diversity valued?[8]

The conventional diversity argument for affirmative action puts a particular spin on the value of demographic heterogeneity that is quite different from the value of integration elaborated here. In one sense, integration and diversity are two sides of the same coin. Both begin with the value of bringing together people from different identities and backgrounds.[9] But the standard diversity argument points to the salutary effects of *differences*—different backgrounds, experiences, and attitudes that are thought to correspond with demographic differences—within the particular institution. The integration argument emphasizes the benefits of *connectedness* and *common ground* (though not sameness) across lines of difference in the society at large. The integration argument does not use race as a proxy for distinct experiences or views—a premise that can itself verge into stereotyping. Rather, it recognizes that racial identity as such trigger stereotypes, biases, and divisions, and that intergroup cooperation can help to overcome those social ills.

The integration argument also differs from the diversity argument because it does not turn on enhancement of the employer's particular products or services. Many employers would be hard-pressed—if pressed beyond platitudes—to demonstrate the instrumental benefits of diversity within their operations. Indeed, we have noted an emerging consensus among researchers that diversity within work groups tends to produce some benefits—a diverse group may generate more ideas, for example—but is often associated with greater friction, turnover, and dissatisfaction among participants. Techniques for ameliorating these tensions are also emerging. The fact remains, however, that on the employers' yardstick of productivity a diverse workforce might well come up short as compared to a more homogeneous workforce.

The societal calculus is different: We have a diverse society, and we have to live in it and govern it together. More cooperative interracial contact in the workplace contributes to our ability to live together and govern our society together whether or not it contributes to an employer's bottom line. Indeed, given the limited occasions for cooperative interracial interaction outside the workplace, even interaction that produces some degree of friction is better than no interaction at all. So the societal interest in integration, while it does not give employers an economic motive for seeking workplace integration, offers a compelling societal justification for allowing employers to use affirmative group preferences—whatever is motivating their use—where they are necessary to achieve workplace integration.

On closer examination, however, further ambiguity and tension appear. To uphold affirmative action preferences is to empower employers to use race or gender as an explicit criterion in the allocation of jobs among co-workers and would-be co-workers. That creates not only a potential conflict with the antidiscrimination mandate itself—a conflict that has been exhaustively explored in legal doctrine and scholarship—but also a potential for counterproductive and divisive intergroup dynamics within the workplace. That potential is greatest when group advantages and disadvantages are dealt out not among job applicants but among the existing workforce. The potential for division is much less when preferences affect only the terms on which one enters the workplace community. So the societal value of integration both offers a powerful justification for affirmative action preferences and a reason for caution in the circumstances, manner, and extent of their use.

There remains the legal question whether the goal of integration is an adequate justification for affirmative action—whether it is sufficiently consistent with the goals of Title VII itself so as to pass legal muster. An adequate answer to that question would take us into more technical terrain than I mean to enter here. But one very helpful and important piece of the answer is supplied by the extensive empirical evidence that more-than-token representation of a group tends to reduce discrimination—conscious discrimination and harassment as well as unconscious prejudice—toward members of the group. Indeed, Professor Michael Yelnosky has argued on the basis of this evidence that affirmative action can be justified as a means of preventing discrimination—a goal that finds ample support from within the four corners of antidiscrimination law.[10]

The "prevention argument," like the "integration argument" and indeed any argument for affirmative action that is not strictly remedial, requires a forthright affirmation of the "asymmetry" of antidiscrimination law and a rejection of the equation between all forms of racial or gender preference. Employment discrimination *in favor of* racial groups (and women) that were long excluded and segregated and are still disadvantaged in the labor market is fundamentally different, morally and legally, from discrimination *against* those groups. The former still must be justified, but it sometimes can be; the latter cannot.

"Ordinary" Discrimination Law and Workplace Divisions

Let us turn from voluntary efforts to increase representation of women and minorities (and claims of "reverse discrimination" that might accompany such efforts) to the treatment of "ordinary" discrimination claims on behalf of women and people of color who are numerical minorities within the workforce or job category. I refer to both groups as "minorities" and as "protected groups." One might object to identifying women and nonwhites as "protected groups," for the law prohibits discrimination based on race, not just against nonwhites, and discrimination based on sex, not just against women. Still, "reverse" discrimination suits face special doctrinal obstacles and are relatively rare.[11] The common understanding that Title VII protects mainly women and people of color is thus true enough to justify calling them "protected groups." Moreover, these "protected groups" are still in need of protection, for they continue to experience discrimination in employment. Recall the audit and name studies, which show significant discrimination against black job applicants as compared to closely matched white applicants.[12]

Those studies focused solely on hiring discrimination. So, too, the original focus of the law's proponents, and the initial focus of enforcement efforts, was on the removal of barriers to the hiring of minority, especially black, workers.[13] But since the 1970s, hiring cases under Title VII have actually declined, while discharge cases have mushroomed. These days the large majority of Title VII actions challenge allegedly discriminatory terminations of employment—discharges and layoffs.[14] Professors Donohue and Siegelman estimated that, as of 1989, "the likelihood of suit if the employer fires a protected applicant is thirty times greater than the likelihood of suit if the employer simply fails to hire the worker."[15] Recent data follow a similar pattern.[16]

The overwhelming predominance of termination cases over hiring cases under Title VII is not hard to understand.[17] One who loses a job has much more information about the decision and much more at stake—psychologically, socially, and economically—than someone who doesn't get one of the often-several jobs that he or she has applied for.[18] But the wholesale shift from hiring challenges to termination litigation is still cause for concern, in part because there are reasons to believe that discrimination is more prevalent in hiring than in firing or layoffs. First, it seems fair to assume that the most discriminatory employers hire relatively few minorities, and have less occasion to discriminate in firing; minority employees are thus more likely to be employed, and exposed to the risk of discharge, by less discriminatory employers. Second, the evidence reviewed in chapters 4 and 5 suggests that unconscious biases and stereotypes tend to have a greater effect when one has little individuating information about a person and tend to be reduced by the experience of cooperative interaction in pursuit of common goals. Clearly employers have more information and more personal interaction to inform their judgment about current employees than about job applicants.[19]

So there is probably more discrimination against minorities in hiring, while there is much more discrimination *litigation* over terminations. At a minimum this suggests a mismatch between the nature of the problem and the remedy. But the predominance of exit-stage litigation under Title VII has serious ripple effects on the workplace and its denizens. Let us look first at what happens in a typical individual Title VII discharge lawsuit,[20] and then back up from there to the decisions that are made and the perceptions and relationships that are formed under the shadow of Title VII.

First of all, the growth of discrimination challenges to discharges should not mislead us about the difficulty of winning such cases. In the typical Title VII case, the plaintiff must prove not simply that the decision against him or her was not justified, but that it was motivated by race or sex.[21] He or she must prove the bad motive on the part of an employer who created and controls the relevant documents, who employs most potential witnesses, and who typically has law-yers on staff or on retainer. The problem looms larger as managers and supervisors become savvier about the law, more cautious in avoiding overt signs of bias, and more diligent in documenting employee shortcomings.[22] Whether or not such caution and diligence produces less discrimination, it certainly produces less *evidence* of discrimination. The liability-conscious employer has means, motive, and opportunity to create a plausible record in support of what may actually be an illegally motivated discharge. "Smoking guns" are scarce indeed.

The difficulty of proving a discriminatory motive, along with the limited damages most plaintiffs can hope to recover, make it difficult for many middle- and lower-income plaintiffs to find a lawyer. Many who believe themselves to have suffered discrimination never file suit.[23] On the other hand, for the aggrieved employee who is determined to challenge a discharge, it is usually all he or she has got. In the at-will workplace, a discharge that results from simple negligence, lack of notice or of warnings, personal favoritism, pique, or mistake is not ille-gal.[24] Employees who belong to a protected group, at least if they consult an at-torney, will quickly learn that a discrimination claim is probably their only ground for challenging a termination. They will be encouraged to look for bias, and may perceive it, even where there is simple garden-variety unfairness or bad management. That is likely to produce some marginal or nonmeritorious dis-crimination claims (even while some meritorious claims are not filed).

Given the difficulty of proving intentional discrimination without the prover-bial "smoking gun," employers can expect to win most litigated cases. But of course it is not just judgments, or even settlements, but litigation itself that is costly to the employer. Litigation entails legal fees, hours of lost work by managers and em-ployee witnesses, harm to the firm's reputation, upheaval within the workplace, and angry denials from accused individuals. Particularly if a claim of discrimina-tion is mistaken, or if management sincerely believes it to be mistaken (as is likely in cases of unconscious discrimination), management may feel obliged to defend aggressively the reputation of the firm and of the accused individuals. In light of all this, management will seek ways to avoid costly litigation.

What does "litigation avoidance" look like inside the workplace? Employers obviously seek to avoid overtly biased comments by managers and supervisors. They also engage in defensive documentation and process in hopes of heading off or defeating discrimination claims; they may even "sanitize" their files, purg-ing them of "misleading" references to race or sex.[25] (These efforts to minimize *evidence* of discrimination are not matched by efforts to uncover and avoid unconscious discrimination itself.) Finally, we might also expect a litigation-conscious employer to delay or avoid a termination that may be challenged as discriminatory, and to give more process and more leeway to employees in pro-tected groups. There is some evidence to that effect in an in-depth study of lay-off procedures in five major companies. In four of the five companies studied, managers reported giving special scrutiny to layoff recommendations affecting "protected employees" in light of the risk of discrimination litigation. At least where those employees would be disproportionately affected by layoffs, these recommendations triggered extra scrutiny and, in some cases, the layoff of a "nonprotected" employee who was viewed as marginally more qualified in place of a protected employee.[26] So it seems that some employers *believe* that, to avoid litigation, they are tipping the scales *in favor of* minority employees.

The likely presence of unconscious bias *against* minorities—bias that appears to be widespread but that cannot be pinned to particular decisions—complicates the picture. Those subtle biases against women and minorities may operate quite freely in "low-profile" judgments about employees: evaluations of work product, assignment of projects, team members' assessment of each others' contributions and interpersonal skills, and informal socializing and mentoring. Existing antidiscrimination law is extremely poor at policing unspoken bias in these informal interactions and judgments; yet those interactions and judgments increasingly determine employees' fates in the workplaces of today.[27]

There is no way to know what decisions an unbiased process would produce. The extra scrutiny triggered by fear of discrimination litigation may simply offset unconscious discrimination *against* the protected groups. But it appears that white or male managers often perceive some bias in favor of minorities or women in terminations and layoffs, while the latter often perceive (but may be unable to prove) the opposite bias. These counterproductive and contradictory dynamics may help to explain the highly divergent perceptions of white and nonwhite employees about the extent of employment discrimination against (or in favor of) minorities. They are also likely to contribute to intergroup friction and resentment, to which we will return shortly.

All this has repercussions on entry-stage, or hiring, decisions. For the uncertain but threatening prospect of discriminatory discharge litigation operates as a kind of tax on minority hiring, paradoxically *encouraging* discrimination against minorities in hiring. Of course hiring discrimination is illegal; but the risk of a challenge is very low. On the other hand, hiring a minority applicant entails some risk that he or she will eventually be discharged or laid off, which is much more likely to trigger a discrimination charge. Professors Donohue and Siegelman have calculated that an employer may actually reduce the risk of costly Title VII litigation by discriminating, at the margin, against minority applicants.[28]

In particular, the employer may avoid hiring minority applicants regarded as "risky." Suppose two applicants present similarly uncertain productivity prospects, and thus a significant risk of termination after an initial trial period. The white employee, if he proves to be a bad bet, can be costlessly fired under the employment at will rule; the black employee's discharge might provoke a costly Title VII suit. In that situation, it may be rational for the employer to prefer the white employee.[29] We need not imagine elaborate calculations by the employer to produce this result. An ephemeral anxiety about discharge litigation, together with other unconscious biases, may cloud the comparison of candidates and make an employer unwilling to "take a chance" on a marginal minority applicant without any conscious discrimination.

So Title VII—given current patterns of litigation—may generate some incentive to favor minorities in terminations, but to disfavor them in hiring. A purely individualistic conception of the interests served by Title VII might deem that trade-off acceptable, for it reflects in part the much greater impact of a discharge on an individual's life. But from the societal standpoint of promoting workplace integration, a discriminatory nonhiring is just as harmful as a discriminatory discharge, for it may undermine minority representation in workplaces in which minorities are currently most underrepresented.

More than numbers are at stake, for these same dynamics may infect co-worker relations. It appears that minority employees continue to perceive discrimination against themselves, while white managers themselves believe that they marginally favor minority employees at the exit stage. If managers believe that, then white employees are likely to believe it, too. These beliefs may be exaggerated as they are filtered through the employees' own unconscious biases. The perception that employers are applying racial preferences, in particular, taps into widespread resentment and opposition among whites.[30] A perception that minority preferences are operating in layoffs is especially likely to be divisive, for layoff preferences, unlike hiring preferences, pit co-workers against each other just when the stakes are highest.

In short, antidiscrimination law as it currently operates may contribute to perverse employer incentives and to divisive intergroup tensions. For while majority employees have no recourse against an unfair employment action, including discharge, the former may have a potential remedy *if* they plausibly claim discrimination. That contrast may lead employers to discriminate against minorities in hiring, but to be more lenient, at least superficially, in their treatment of minorities who are hired; it may lead minorities to look for discrimination where there may only be supervisory sloppiness or a personality conflict; and it may lead other employees to see "special treatment" of minorities where there may in fact be lots of undetected and effectively unremediable discrimination against minorities coupled with superficial efforts by the employer to avoid litigation.

The starkly paradoxical picture drawn thus far ignores three important developments within firms. The first is the rather remarkable embrace of workforce diversity in many corporate quarters.[31] Many organizations—especially large and visible public corporations—have not merely accepted diversity as a fact of life, but have embraced it as a shield against discrimination liability, as a manifestation of good corporate citizenship, as a tool for reaching an increasingly diverse customer base, or as a way of improving group decisionmaking and organizational performance. That development may refute or at least counteract the supposed tendency of the law to encourage hiring discrimination (though the best available evidence suggests that hiring discrimination against minorities still predominates). Whatever the motivations behind this development, it should be encouraged. In addition to multiplying the sheer frequency of intergroup interactions at work, organizations that accept or embrace diversity in their workforces have a strong incentive and prodigious resources to develop better ways of working together.

The other two important developments are closely linked: the proliferation of internal grievance and dispute resolution procedures and the rise of mandatory arbitration of employees' legal claims, including discrimination claims. Both reflect the efforts of firms to ameliorate the tension between outside legal norms and internal organizational needs by bringing the organization into closer conformance with outside norms, as well as by "domesticating" those outside norms and the means of their enforcement. The consequence may be to reduce the gap between the process afforded antidiscrimination claimants and the process afforded others who believe they have been unfairly treated. This, in itself, would count as a good thing for intergroup relations at the workplace *if* it does not come at the cost of undermining statutory protections against discrimination. The unsettled state of the law governing arbitration agreements makes it difficult to resolve this last question. Both internal grievance procedures and arbitration of statutory claims deserve closer attention than this preview permits. For the moment, it will suffice to note that these trends probably mitigate but do not eliminate the counterproductive dynamics reviewed above.

All this suggests that Title VII law as it stands is doing too little to promote the hiring of women and minorities, and thus too little to promote the integration of workplaces. It is doing a poor job of policing the bias that operates in the low-profile decisions that end up determining an employee's workplace stature and success. And it is contributing to contradictory and corrosive perceptions and resentments among co-workers. Antidiscrimination law has been essential and at least partly effective in promoting equal opportunity and integration in employment. But like a river running over a rocky and uneven streambed, the main current of Title VII enforcement produces unexpected and perilous countercurrents along the way. The question for policymakers is how to make Title VII a more effective guarantor of equal employment opportunity and of workplace integration while minimizing the counterproductive dynamics that current Title VII litigation appears to produce.

The foregoing analysis of the problem points toward two general strategies for reform. First, it would support a shift away from the increasingly problematic if not pointless inquiry into motive and toward greater emphasis on results—the hiring and maintenance of a reasonably integrated workforce. For the existence of an integrated workforce is both probative evidence of a lack of bias against women and minorities and a prophylactic mechanism for preventing or reducing bias in judgments about those employees.[32] Second, the analysis supports efforts to shift the weight of Title VII enforcement toward the entry—or hiring—point.

There is peril as well as promise in shifting the focus to results, and especially to numbers. Such a shift carries some of the same risks of divisiveness and resentment as does the use of affirmative preferences for women and minorities. I would judge those risks to be outweighed by the importance of making antidiscrimination law an effective tool for advancing workplace equality and integration in the modern era. But those risks can also be minimized by placing the legal pressure for results primarily at the hiring stage, where they have no direct impact on current employees. It must be recalled, too, that where employers are faced with the fact of an integrated workforce, they have their own good reasons to seek ways to minimize tensions and foster productive intergroup relations.

Here are three simple suggestions for reform that follow one or both of these strategies: First, public enforcement resources—the investigative and litigation resources of the EEOC and state agencies—should be shifted toward hiring challenges as a counterweight to the forces that tip the bulk of private litigation toward exit discrimination. In particular, agencies should focus on large-scale hiring cases, where the aggregate impact on the public is large and the evidence is not readily available to individuals.[33] Second, government agencies and advocacy groups should be proactive in identifying workplaces that are not integrated and investigating the possibility of discrimination. The use of "auditors" is an especially promising investigative tactic.[34] Indeed, if duly publicized, the mere deployment of auditors should deter hiring discrimination. Third, the law should make available exemplary damages of some kind—say, treble damages—for hiring discrimination in light of the low probability of detection. The extra compensation would deter wrongdoing as well as attract the private bar to cases of public significance that may require significant up-front investments in information. These are all ways to encourage the hiring of minorities and to discourage hiring discrimination against them. Some would require a change in existing law; all require further elaboration that I leave for another day.

Another approach is to reduce the cost of discharging minorities, and thus the "tax" on hiring minorities that Title VII appears to create, if that can be done in a manner that is consistent with the basic commitment to remedy discrimination. One suggestion, offered by Professors Ayres and Siegelman, is to recognize a statutory "probationary period" during which an employee can be freely fired without any Title VII liability. The proposal sounds counterintuitive, but the idea is this: Many discharges occur during this early try-out period for perfectly legitimate reasons; employers learn a lot about employees' productivity that they cannot learn prior to employment.[35] A statutory probationary period should induce employers to take greater risks with minority applicants, giving them a chance to prove themselves to be productive (and unlikely to be discharged in the future). Some meritorious claims of discrimination would be barred, but the net effect might be to reduce the overall incidence of discrimination and to promote the hiring of minorities and the integration of workforces.

This proposal begins to confront the other side of the equation: One way to encourage the hiring of minorities is to reduce the cost or probability of exit-stage litigation. More precisely, reducing the *gap* between the expected cost of exit-stage litigation by minorities and that of litigation by nonminorities will reduce the "tax" on the hiring of minority applicants. We have already discussed two measures that employers themselves have taken that tend in this direction: the creation of internal grievance procedures and a workforce-wide promise of "some kind of hearing" for nonlegal as well as legal claims; and the imposition of mandatory arbitration of discrimination and other employment claims. The first slightly increases the cost and process associated with firing members of nonprotected groups, and at least aims to reduce the incidence of litigation by protected groups. The second reduces the cost and process associated with firing members of protected groups (while possibly expanding access to "some kind of hearing"). These two procedural developments, if properly channeled, may be the beginnings of a fair system of publicly "regulated self-regulation."[36]

A much more drastic step toward narrowing the "at-will gap" would be to reverse the presumption of employment at will and replace it with some kind of just cause principle. Just cause protection, together with a prompt and accessible procedure for adjudicating it, would give all employees the right to fair treatment. It would give employees a common stake in the principle and the process by which it is administered and would tend to mitigate the potentially divisive pressures exerted by some aspects of antidiscrimination law. And a just cause principle could do all these things without reducing the substantive protection of minorities against discrimination, for a requirement that the employer show just cause for discharge is in substance more protective than a rule that overturns discipline only upon a showing of discriminatory motive. Of course, the issue of legally imposed job security also poses some vexing practical and economic questions, given the growing pressures of competition and the increasing need for flexibility and agility in the organization of work. I will return to those questions briefly in chapter 9.

The operation of the employment discrimination laws in ordinary hiring and firing cases is both essential to and, in some of its current manifestations, corrosive of the conditions for productive intergroup relations in an integrated workplace. As it stands, Title VII does too little to bring minority employees into workplaces in which they are underrepresented, partly because it may do too much to deter the discharge or layoff of minority employees. It is important that we find ways to make the employment discrimination laws—one of the watershed accomplishments of the civil rights era—into a more effective vehicle for the promotion of both equality and integration at work.

Harassment Law, Freedom, and Equality

Countercurrents appear, too, when we examine the law of discriminatory harassment.[37] To begin with, the volume and cost of harassment litigation exacerbates the exit–entry gap, for harassment claims necessarily involve current employees rather than job candidates, and most of those claims arise in connection with an employee's departure. Fear of harassment litigation may, for example, discourage the hiring of women into overwhelmingly male workplaces where they are likely to experience harassment. Once again, we find that antidiscrimination law—where it is not a real threat at the hiring phase—may have the perverse effect of encouraging hiring discrimination.

But harassment law poses a distinctive dilemma: On the one hand, it provides crucial legal support for constructive and egalitarian intergroup relations in the workplace. At the same time, however, the law of discriminatory harassment has pushed some employers toward policies that threaten both workplace sociability and equality. Some employment lawyers and management consultants advise employers to adopt censorious "zero tolerance" policies banning "[s]uggestive joking of any kind," "anything that can be remotely interpreted as sexual/sexist in nature," or "[a]ny disparaging comments or joking references concerning an employee's age, sex, race, religion or national origin." Some employers follow this advice to the letter, prohibiting, for example, "[v]ulgar, inappropriate or sexual comments, jokes, stories or innuendoes." Professor Vicki Schultz has documented the particular fixation on banning sexual comments or conduct, without regard to whether they are sexist or conducive to gender-based discrimination, segregation, or exclusion.[38] The ban on sexual harassment has become unmoored from the antidiscrimination norm from which it arose.

Defenders of harassment law point out that these policies go further than the law requires employers to go in preventing harassment. It is true that employment discrimination law does not directly punish isolated "sexual comments" or "suggestive joking"; harassment must be "severe or pervasive" to be actionable. But neither does the law establish any clear limits on what "counts" in showing a pervasively hostile environment: a series of incidents, none of them "severe or pervasive" by themselves, can create a hostile environment. That being the case, the liability-conscious employer—and especially the employer who seeks to avoid litigation altogether—is well advised to ban anything that could *contribute* to a harassment claim. As the law stands, that is just about anything that might offend any employee who hears it on the basis of race, sex, religion, national origin, age, disability, or other protected trait. And that is just what many employers are doing. Harassment law has thus become a powerful engine of censorship in the workplace.[39]

The law's role in encouraging employer censorship raises serious First Amendment questions about the shape of harassment doctrine. That is certainly not to say that everything that the First Amendment protects in the public square or the broadcast media should be protected in the workplace against Title VII liability. The workplace context matters a great deal to the appropriate resolution of the First Amendment challenge to harassment law. The presence of economic compulsion, the importance of workplace equality, and the power of even verbal harassment to enforce racial and gender segregation are crucial factors that tilt toward giving broader scope to speech restrictions. But not everything about the workplace context cuts in favor of suppressing speech. The presence of economic compulsion, for example, magnifies the power of employer censorship as well as the power of harassment. Moreover, it is far from self-evident that workplace equality or intergroup sociability and solidarity is advanced by inducing employers to suppress any mention of sex, race, or ethnicity.

Apart from the constitutional issues raised by the law that spawns these policies, let us consider the impact of these policies—especially sexual harassment policies—on workplace interaction. A workplace that is purged, on pain of discipline, of any "vulgar, inappropriate or sexual comments, jokes, stories, or innuendos" is surely better, and more conducive to equality for women, than one that is "permeated with 'discriminatory intimidation, ridicule, and insult.'"[40] But that is a false choice. To begin with, the notion that any "sexual comments, jokes, stories, or innuendos" are offensive and discriminatory toward women is implausible; institutionalizing that notion is a highly dubious contribution to gender equality. A ban on "[s]uggestive joking of any kind," "anything that can be remotely interpreted as sexual/sexist in nature," or "[a]ny disparaging comments or joking references concerning an employee's . . . sex" arguably imposes on the whole workforce the sensibilities and sensitivities of its most easily offended denizens. Insofar as these policies may punish some workers (mainly men) at the behest of others (mainly women), they are rife with potential for division and resentment.[41] At a minimum these workplace "speech codes" create a rather sterile environment for the growth of friendly and cooperative peer relations between men and women.

Given all we have learned about the importance of workplace conversations in civic and social life, it is deeply troubling that the law encourages employers to be so censorious and so vigilant in policing co-worker conversations and interactions. It is no answer to say—as defenders of harassment law sometimes do—that "the workplace is for work."[42] As we have seen, the workplace is for much more than work, both in the lives of individual workers and in the society as a whole. The law should not adopt as its motto a proposition that would so impoverish social life.

Even beyond the realm of expression, the fear of harassment liability has led in some potentially counterproductive directions. One construction manager told a reporter that, in light of concerns about harassment liability, "You have to be more reserved. I'm treating women in the office less like friends. It means the workplace is less fun now. You can't kid around as much."[43] Fear of harassment liability has led some employers to regulate or prohibit dating and romance between co-workers (though most of the outright prohibitions sensibly apply only to relations between employees and those they supervise).[44]

Fear of the mere accusation of harassment or of inappropriate "fraternization" has led some senior male managers and professionals to avoid closed-door and late-night meetings, social outings, and travel—typical earmarks of close mentoring relationships—with young female subordinates. So found Cynthia Fuchs Epstein in her report on New York law firms:

> Several male lawyers we talked to admitted that they avoid all informal contact with younger women attorneys because they fear that their behavior may be misinterpreted as sexist when it is merely friendly. Thus, they reported that they make it a blanket rule not to dine or have drinks with women associates after late night work sessions or while working on a case.[45]

That cannot be good news for women who aspire to positions of leadership within organizations currently dominated by men.

The law of discriminatory harassment, which contributes to these tendencies, bears a closer look to see whether it is possible to promote workplace equality at a lower cost to sociability and freedom of interaction among co-workers. With respect to the policing of sexual conduct and expression in particular, Professor Schultz argues for repudiating the false equation of sexuality and sexism, and for shifting the focus of legal scrutiny from particular comments and incidents to the broader workplace context in which they take place: Sexual comments, jokes, flirting, and even sexual relationships among co-workers have an entirely different meaning in a genuinely integrated workplace in which women and men interact as equals than they have in a workplace in which women are a small and embattled minority.[46] This approach to the problem of discriminatory harassment, if it can be made workable, would help to direct employers' attention to the real issues of workplace integration and equality—to the numbers and the authority of minority employees in the workplace.

Some Issues on the Frontiers of Antidiscrimination Law

I have chosen three large but still limited components of antidiscrimination law to illustrate some of the implications of the "working together" thesis. I have neglected other broad swaths of antidiscrimination law that merit a closer look. Just to name two: disparate impact doctrine, which allows the challenge of some workplace practices that adversely affect protected groups without proof of discriminatory motive, and the beginnings of a legal framework for encouraging firms' own efforts to prevent discrimination and harassment and to promote equality.[47] Both issues open interesting vistas for reform, but I reserve those topics for another day.

It is also true that the law's pursuit of workplace integration and equality does not proceed solely under antidiscrimination law as conventionally understood. In particular, women's pursuit of economic equality has generated numerous proposals that warrant closer consideration—closer than is possible here—from the perspective of promoting gender integration of workplaces. For the goals of promoting women's economic advancement and promoting gender integration do not invariably point in the same direction.

For example, laws that mandate parental leave, paid or unpaid, aim to allow women to maintain workforce continuity during a crucial career-building phase of their work lives. But insofar as these benefits shift some of the cost of child-bearing from parents—and overwhelmingly from women—to employers, they have implications for employers' willingness to hire and promote women.[48] More generally, proposals that would compel employers to accommodate the child-bearing and early childrearing roles that are still predominantly borne by women have ambiguous implications for workplace integration as well as for women's economic advancement. In part they pose the same dilemma explored above: Legal obligations and legal remedies that impose significant costs on employers only with respect to current employees, and overwhelmingly with respect to employees from underrepresented groups, may lead employers to avoid hiring such employees. Antidiscrimination law, because it is rarely invoked against hiring decisions, does not effectively counteract that tendency. So those added obligations may have counterproductive side effects unless they are accompanied by effective pressures to hire women, or unless they are made to operate relatively neutrally as between male and female employees.[49]

The tension between the goal of economic advancement for women and the goal of gender integration is more direct in the case of calls for "pay equity" or "comparable worth." The persistence of occupational segregation on the basis of gender, together with the striking pay disparities between occupations dominated by women and those dominated by men, has led to calls for "equal pay for work of equal value."[50] Advocates contend that these pay disparities reflect gender discrimination, and an undervaluing of jobs performed mainly by women, and they call for objective evaluations of the skills, knowledge, and effort that different jobs demand. Others have criticized the theory as a radical departure from the principle of nondiscrimination and a misguided effort to displace the market as a mechanism for setting wages.[51] But it is not the tension with the market that I wish to highlight; it is the tension with the goal of occupational desegregation.[52]

The call for pay equity is based partly on the assumption that occupational segregation is extremely resilient and should be taken, at least for the foreseeable future, as a "given." But there is a risk that the pursuit of pay equity may undermine the further pursuit of occupational desegregation. If successful, it would diminish the economic incentive for women themselves to enter predominantly male (and more highly paid) occupations; that economic incentive has driven much of the progress toward occupational desegregation that has occurred so far. Of course, pay equity would also tend to draw men into predominantly female occupations; occupational desegregation has thus far been slowed by the very limited movement in that direction.[53] The net effect on occupational segregation is uncertain but worth examining. For occupational desegregation has important noneconomic advantages in the overall pursuit of gender equality.

The society's pursuit of workplace equality has proceeded almost entirely under the aegis of antidiscrimination law and largely through the condemnation of particular decisions that are demonstrably infected with conscious bias. To the extent that antidiscrimination law and the pursuit of equal opportunity has also helped to bring about the *integration* of workplaces on the basis of race, ethnicity, and sex, that has been somewhat incidental. But workplace integration must be more than an incidental benefit of workplace equity. It is both a crucial condition for genuine equality within the workplace and an extraordinary medium for intergroup connectedness within and beyond the workplace. Antidiscrimination law and its allied doctrines should embrace the promotion of workplace integration as a central objective.

PROTECTING COLLECTIVE VOICE AND PROMOTING

COOPERATION IN THE WORKPLACE

We have seen that the law that governs the demographics of the workplace and that aims to promote intergroup equality—what I have called "the equal protection clause" of the workplace—produces both intended and unintended effects on intergroup relations and the quality of workplace interactions. Let us now extend our inquiry to the law that affects workplace interactions and relationships among co-workers generally. What could the law do to enrich the capacity of workplaces to foster constructive co-worker interactions and relations within what we hope will be demographically integrated workforces?

What follows skips across the surface of a vast landscape of labor and employment law. Even more than my foray into the law of intergroup equality, this is offered as a quick tour of some sites of interest and a glance down some of the possible pathways of reform. We will begin by looking for some footholds in existing law for the promotion of informal sociability, cooperation in the work itself, and the sharing of workplace concerns among co-workers.

Associational Rights as Leverage for Securing Sociability and Cooperation

Viewed through the lens of existing law, the three kinds of social interaction we wish to foster begin to diverge. For example, it is hard to find a foothold in existing law for the project of affirmatively promoting informal sociability among co-workers. There is a whisper of support in the emerging law—mostly state common law—recognizing individual employee "privacy" rights, for privacy rights, where they extend beyond the protection of bodily integrity, have always been mostly about the protection of relationships.[1] However, the emerging law of employee privacy rights is largely confined to the protection of *off-duty* activities and relationships.[2] That law bears a closer look, but it does not provide an especially sturdy platform from which to launch an affirmative effort to protect sociability *within* the workplace.

With respect to cooperation in the work itself, it seems similarly quixotic and potentially counterproductive to set about directly regulating the organization of production—requiring collaboration over Tayloristic production methods, for example. The law might play a useful supporting role, for example, by encouraging the production of information among employers about what works—what sorts of participatory mechanisms or team structures best tap the productive potential of cooperation. And it might play, as we will see, an indirect role in fostering both sociability and cooperation as a by-product of seeking other objectives. But it is hard to envision a direct and purposeful role for law in encouraging either cooperation in the work itself or informal sociability.

This does not mean, however, that the law has no impact on workplace cooperation and sociability. It may play a negative role. We should be alert to points at which the law, in pursuit of other goals, may get in the way of cooperative forms of production and informal sociability. For example, we have seen that the law of harassment, while aiming to promote equality, has contributed to employer policies that squelch workplace sociability. In such cases we should seek ways to achieve the law's legitimate goals without incidentally inhibiting productive forms of workplace interaction. But there is no need for law to serve as a driving force here, for both cooperation and sociability emerge quite naturally—albeit not inevitably—from the mix of economic and psychological forces that operate within modern production. Once we recognize the societal value of those impulses, one thing the law can do is simply get out of the way.

By contrast, under the modern "constitution of the workplace," the law has a longstanding affirmative role in protecting and promoting workers' rights to associate for shared aims: to communicate among themselves and with management about terms and conditions of employment, to organize a collective voice if they so choose, and to pursue shared workplace objectives. The protection of collective voice is a sensible starting point for building workplace connectedness.

It is a sensible starting point not only because the law already has a foothold in that area, but also because collective voice can serve as the opening wedge in expanding both informal sociability and cooperation in the work itself. Employees, given a viable collective voice and the time and space to associate and discuss shared workplace issues, will secure for themselves outlets for sociability. Recall, for example, that the NLRA gives employees the right to discuss work-related issues in nonwork areas of the workplace during nonwork hours.[3] That right is violated by employer rules against "solicitation," rules against discussion of wages or other terms and conditions of employment, or surveillance of employees in such times and places.[4] If that right were fully enforced, employees would incidentally gain time and space for informal sociability. Moreover, in a competitive economy in which persistent labor–management conflict spells economic disaster, the empowerment of employees should nudge managers toward greater reliance on trust and cooperation and away from intensive monitoring and management-by-threat. At least that is true if the alternative strategy of disempowering employees is not readily available. So one linchpin of a legal strategy for enhancing the civic potential of the workplace must be to provide stronger and broader legal support for employees' efforts to associate with each other in pursuit of shared workplace objectives.

Even in connection with the possibilities for collective employee voice, there are points at which "getting out of the way" may be a useful starting point for law reform. For those unfamiliar with labor law, the law takes what may seem to be a puzzling posture toward some mechanisms for employee voice. The NLRA prohibits employers from supporting or dominating "labor organizations," which the statute defines broadly to include virtually any employee representation mechanism that deals with terms and conditions of employment.[5] Aimed primarily at the "company unions" that flourished in the early New Deal as mechanisms for evading independent union representation, the NLRA's broadly written ban casts a shadow over current trends toward greater employee involvement and more collaborative workplace structures. It is hard to know how much and what kind of experimentation these provisions actually inhibit; it is, like many of the NLRA's prohibitions, a bit of a paper tiger. But the law's explicit prohibition of some potentially valuable mechanisms for workplace interchange and participation cries out for a closer look.[6]

Still, perhaps the most important contribution the law could make to social connectedness and solidarity in the workplace would be to fulfill its commitment to enabling employees to associate and to form their own independent collective voice. We will return to that commitment below in connection with the "constitution of the workplace" and its missing provisions. But note that, insofar as a basic tenet of the low-wage system of production is the suppression of workers' collective voice and power, one consequence of protecting and promoting employees' collective voice would be to put pressure on the low-wage model. Putting pressure on low-wage workplaces—both by enforcing and improving minimum material conditions of work and by supporting employees' ability to exercise a collective voice—could help steer employers toward other ways of organizing work that cultivate and capitalize on human skill, experience, goodwill, and cooperative impulses.

Targeting the Low-Wage and High-Contingency Models

That strategy suggests another way of approaching the question of what the law can do to promote civic-ness at work. Chapter 3 identified four models of workplace organization with staying power in the modern economy, two of them basically hospitable and two of them basically inhospitable to socially productive workplace relationships. The "social capitalist" human relations model in the nonunion setting and the joint-team-based model in the union setting both depend on and build connectedness and trust among co-workers. By contrast, the high-contingency, market-infused workplace—though it may foster agility in the formation of usable human ties—also fosters an extreme individualism and a ready resort to exit over voice or loyalty, both of which undercut the civic potential of the workplace. The low-wage workplace is simply civic hell. So one way to think about what the law can do is to consider ways in which the law can push employers away from the last two models and toward the first two.

Amplifying Employee Voice in the Low-Wage Workplace

Enforcing employee rights that are chronically violated in the low-wage workplace—economic rights, occupational safety standards, and rights of association and expression among co-workers—is one such strategy. Happily, there is good reason to believe that these rights are mutually reinforcing. In other words, a promising strategy for improving the enforcement of minimum material standards in the low-wage workplace lies precisely in empowering employees themselves to help enforce such standards.[7] Of course, workers' right to speak among and for themselves is perhaps the most systematically abused and underenforced legal right in the low-wage setting. That presents a conundrum of sorts, but it also suggests some promising regulatory strategies.

The link between employees' ability to voice shared concerns and the enforcement of minimum material standards points most obviously to the value of targeting the low-wage workplace for more intensive and proactive enforcement of existing associational rights. An example of how *not* to approach the problem of associational rights in the low-wage workplace may be found in the Supreme Court's recent decision in *Hoffman Plastic Compounds, Inc. v. NLRB*, in which the Court held that it was beyond the power of the NLRB to award meaningful individual remedies to undocumented workers who were fired for seeking to form a union in a plastics factory.[8] The decision may give committedly antiunion employers another reason to hire and exploit undocumented workers. The inability of union organizers to promise those workers even the inadequate remedies available under the NLRA will inevitably undermine the ability to organize a union in those workplaces in which undocumented workers make up a significant part of the workforce.

Vigorous enforcement of associational rights for all "citizens" of the workplace would have an extra payoff in the enforcement of material rights. But the link between collective voice and material conditions in the workplace may suggest a different and novel strategy for responding to the repeated or egregious violations of the law's minimum material standards that typify the low-wage workplace: government-backed employee representation. Given such a pattern of violations, the government would oversee the election of independent employee representatives with powers to monitor and seek improvement in the regulated conditions of work, with protection against reprisals, and with active government sponsorship and support. The remedial logic of such a "representation remedy" is clear: The presence of an independent collective employee voice enhances the enforcement of regulatory standards.[9] Under current law, that means a union. But that evidence suggests that a more limited form of independent employee representation—one tailored to the particular regulatory failing—could be part of an appropriate and effective prospective remedy for serious material violations. At the same time, independent employee representation—independent of the employer, that is—is perceived by low-wage employers as a danger assiduously to be avoided. That gives the "representation remedy" a valuable deterrent effect beyond what ordinary fines and make-whole remedies might have.

Of course, the idea of a "representation remedy" leaves much to the imagination in terms of implementation. In particular, it would be challenging to make employee representatives secure against employer reprisals in an organization that is governed by threats and whose workers see few labor market options. But the idea is in keeping with contemporary interest among policymakers in the potential for "self-regulation." Witness the Republican administration's withdrawal of ergonomics standards promulgated by OSHA under President Clinton, and its advocacy of "voluntary self-regulation" and the development of ergonomics standards by industry itself.[10] Without worker representation in the formulation and implementation of standards, self-regulation might become a disguised form of deregulation. But the existence of institutions of employee representation, with rights and resources for aiding in the enforcement of standards, and with the protection of regulatory officials, has the potential for making the "self" that is doing the regulating more responsive to the "selves" on whose behalf the regulations exist. In other words, democracy, writ small, has an important role to play in transforming centralized "command-and-control" regulations into something that works in the modern economy.

At the same time, institutions of employee representation may deliver benefits that are incidental to the regulatory agenda but central to the thesis developed here: Securing a collective voice for employees, beyond enabling employees to address common workplace concerns and to better enforce workplace standards, should also secure for employees some space for informal sociability; and it should push employers in the direction of more collaborative ways of working that make use of employee engagement and experience.

However challenging this agenda already sounds, it is further confounded by the workings of the labor market in a global economy. In sectors of the economy in which American producers compete directly with producers in the developing world, enforcing a decent floor on working conditions and ensuring a voice for workers may drive some employers and some capital across increasingly porous national borders in search of cheaper labor. In some parts of the economy, higher domestic labor costs may be offset by productivity gains from improved skills, experience, and collaboration. In other sectors those costs may be buffered by the high cost of transporting goods from abroad. In much of the service sector, higher labor costs may be simply absorbed by necessarily local consumers. In other parts of the economy, however, especially in much manufacturing, international low-wage competition appears inescapable.

The problem of regulating labor conditions in markets that spill across jurisdictional boundaries—the dilemma of the "race to the bottom" and of runaway capital and jobs—is familiar. Unfortunately, nothing here promises to resolve the dilemma; it only casts a different light on what is at stake on both sides. The importance of workplace sociability, cooperation, and solidarity underscores *both* the social costs of the low-wage pattern of workplace organization *and* the social costs of unemployment, which economic theory predicts would follow from stronger enforcement of minimum standards and of the right to unionize. For one clear implication of the "working together" thesis is that unemployment is anathema from a societal standpoint, even if its economic impact on individuals can be cushioned.

Combatting Contingency, Supporting Job Stability and Security

When we turn from the low-wage model to the high-contingency model, we confront another similar set of knotty questions: What kind of legal intervention, if any, could nudge employers away from the high-contingency, market-infused model toward models that capitalize on a connected, committed, and relatively stable workforce? Job security, stability, and internal labor markets appear in this account as the friends of sociability and connectedness in the workplace, while insecurity, turnover, and contingency have appeared as their foes. That leads toward some familiar debates within employment law over the relative merits of employment at will and just cause as the basic rule for discharges,[11] and, more recently, over the problems of the contingent workforce and the possibilities for law reform.[12] Typically these two debates are carried on separately. Yet the issues are intimately related, both in what is at stake and in what is possible given the "hydraulics" of the labor market—the ability of employers to change their usage of labor in response to legal constraints.[13]

So, for example, mandating job security for some class of workers—say, "regular non-probationary employees"—inevitably creates some incentive for employers to shift toward using other classes of workers—"temporary" employees, contract employees, or independent contractors—that are not covered by that mandate.[14] Mandating job security might thus backfire by fueling the growth of the contingent workforce, producing greater fragmentation, transience, and segmentation of workplace relationships. At the same time, clamping down more directly on the use of contingent workers, or greatly increasing its cost, could itself backfire, and yield not more permanent employment but less employment altogether.[15] High unemployment is surely the worst case from the standpoint of encouraging workplace connectedness.

Before despairing of the possibilities of reform, we need to thicken the mix of incentives and alternatives that employers face when deciding whether to offer job security and whether to use regular or contingent workers. For job security may appear to cost more than employment at will, and regular employees may appear to cost more than contingent workers, but appearances may be deceiving. The cost disparities may be exaggerated and may be outweighed by productivity gains. Clearly some employers have concluded that a cohesive and committed workplace community, supported by generous benefits and a reconstructed internal labor market, fosters greater productivity, creativity, and dedication, and helps attract and retain talented workers. These employers have decided that investments in human and social capital pay off.

It may be that these employers have discovered what other employers have not—that the cost of training new and temporary workers, and of their limited commitment and experience, wash out the apparent savings from lower wages and benefits. If that is true, we should see firms shift away from contingency and toward security and stability in their workforces without any societal intervention. A just cause mandate might then be a relatively innocuous way of nudging this development along and disciplining the laggards. Or it might simply be unnecessary. The law might be better cast in a supporting role, for example, by promoting the exchange of information about "best practices" and the advantages and disadvantages of flexible staffing arrangements.

Alternatively, it may be that the cost of training and the value of experience are greater in some sectors and in some jobs than in others. In that case we should expect to see different patterns gaining dominance within particular occupations or product-market sectors. And in that case the law may play distinctive roles in each. An across-the-board just cause law, for example, might be counterproductive in some sectors, constructive in others, and superfluous in still others.

It seems likely, however, that both of the foregoing scenarios underestimate the degree to which firms make choices about how to organize and manage labor, and that, in many sectors and in many parts of their operations, employers can choose to pursue either a low-cost, low-wage strategy or a high-commitment-and-cooperation strategy. If that is true, then law might play not just the modest supporting role of enabling firms to pursue their chosen strategy, but the broader and more challenging role of steering firms, when they do have a choice, toward a strategy that has spillover benefits for the society as a whole. All this suggests that there is no simple response to problems of job insecurity and instability. At a minimum it demonstrates that proposals for protection against unjustified dismissal and proposals to address the growth and vulnerability of the contingent workforce must be examined together with an eye toward employers' likely labor market responses.

Amending the Partial Constitution of the Workplace

A final way of framing the search for reform strategies is in terms of the missing provisions of the existing "constitution of the workplace," the outlines of which were sketched in chapter 7. That existing constitution, with its New Deal origins and its Great Society amendments, undertakes to enable employees to discuss shared concerns, make common cause, and form associations for the purpose of improving their conditions. Apart from the commitments of antidiscrimination law, the law's even more longstanding commitment to protecting employees' freedom of expression and association, and their efforts to democratize the workplace through unionization, is the firmest foothold in existing law for improving civic-ness and connectedness in the workplace.

The right of employees to associate and form organizations for mutual aid is widely flouted by employers, who perceive too great an economic threat in the rumblings of union talk, and too easy and cheap a response in the discharge of union adherents. Yet that right has become recognized internationally as the foundation of any civilized system of labor relations.[16] It is hard to see how we could do without it. As for collective bargaining, what could be more in sync with the current mood of working with rather than against market forces than a reliance on private ordering through contract? Assuming that we are not on our way back to pure individual liberty of contract, some form of collective bargaining seems to respond well to the modern discontent with "command and control" regulation.[17] It is decentralized, tailored to particular circumstances, flexible, and democratic. Collective bargaining in its essence—if not always in its particulars—suits the current disposition toward flexible and market-sensitive alternatives to traditional regulation.

The model of union organizing and collective bargaining is useful, too, for the fear and the inventiveness it seems to inspire in management, especially management in firms that face a highly competitive environment. The existing framework of "optional democracy" through union representation and collective bargaining does not make union *avoidance* unlawful. It seeks to close off the path of union *suppression* and to steer employers toward either acceptance of unions or competition with them for their employees' support—toward union *substitution*. Nonunion firms seeking to remain nonunion, if they are foreclosed from repressing union sentiment, must offer competitive wages and benefits, some sense of job security, and at least a semblance of fair dispute resolution procedures, lest they lose the best employees and applicants to union firms. So a viable threat of unionization, as long as it cannot be fought off with "sticks," has an impact on wages and working conditions that extends beyond the domain of collective bargaining itself. If the law did what it promised to do, and closed off the strategy of union suppression, we would see more union substitution as well as more union representation.

But existing law has proven inadequate to the task, leaving the low-cost, low-wage, antiunion alternative all too readily available. The law's failure to enforce basic associational rights of workers is traceable partly to the procedures and remedies it authorizes for the enforcement of those rights: remedies for antiunion discrimination are notoriously tardy and inadequate. It is also traceable to the very partial nature of its animating vision of workplace democracy. The basic components of the Wagner Act may be seen as rough analogues to the First Amendment and the "Republican Form of Government" clause (without the Guarantee): a basic charter of civil liberties and a form of workplace democracy available at the option of a majority of the workforce. The political analogy suggests some of the elements that are still missing from the workplace constitution, even after the 1964 "amendments." In particular, it lacks any "guarantee" of employee representation, and it lacks a "due process clause" to back up the ban on employer reprisals. Those missing elements go a long way toward explaining the weakness of the structure of rights that does exist.

While the NLRA was seen by many employers as "revolutionary" in the constraints it imposed on employer power within the workplace, it was to some extent the very partiality of the NLRA's revolution and of its version of workplace democracy that made union organizing itself a revolutionary threat in the eyes of employers. For the law did not condemn employers' chosen autocratic form of workplace governance or require democratization; it merely protected employees' efforts to secure a form of democracy by convincing a majority of their co-workers to demand it. Employees themselves—dependent on employers for their livelihood—had to campaign for what appeared to those employers to be an overthrow of the existing form of government. And they had to do so one firm at a time, each of which was in competition with others that continued to operate autocratically, and that did not face the constraints and costs associated with unionization.

Returning to the federal constitutional analogy, it is as if the states in 1787 were run by absolute monarchs, without any popular representation, and the federal Constitution left to the citizens of each state the right to agitate among themselves, under the noses of their autocratic governors, for majority support for a republican form of government. By resting on employee "free choice" and majority rule in the matter of whether to have any collective voice in workplace governance, the Act thus laid the ground for the continual refighting of the battle over the establishment of workplace democracy.

None of this means that it would have been conceivable in the 1930s, or that it would make sense today, to impose a regime of mandatory workplace democracy. Thus far I have sought simply to highlight some of what is present and some of what is missing in the constitution of the workplace; for some of what is missing may undermine some of what is present. The missing guarantee of collective representation in the NLRA means that employees have to battle for representation from a position of economic dependence on a "government" that is zealously opposed to it. Not surprisingly, the civil liberties that the law promises to employees afford rather flimsy support in that battle, as would the civil liberties of any citizenry that has no powers of self-governance.

Missing, too, is a requirement of "due process." The typical private sector nonunion employee is terminable at will, for any reason or no reason at all, without notice of whatever reasons there are, and without any opportunity to contest those reasons. Unlike nearly every advanced industrial nation in the world, there is no requirement in the United States that the employer demonstrate a legitimate reason for discharge. In the private sector, it is mainly through unionization and collective bargaining that employees can secure these just cause rights. But the lack of just cause rights makes the effort to organize a union riskier because it makes it easier for the employer to get rid of a union supporter. Of course, the employee can bring an unfair labor practice charge and overturn the discharge if the unlawful antiunion motive can be proven.[18] But that can be notoriously difficult to do, and it can take many years to get any relief. The background rule of employment at will casts a heavy burden of proof and procedural fortitude on the employee who claims unlawful retaliation or discrimination. The lack of just cause rights thus undermines the liberty rights, as well as the equality rights, that employees do have in the workplace.[19]

Turning again to the governmental analogy, it is as if the Constitution prohibited the state from punishing citizens based on their political activities or associations (or their race or sex), but allowed the state to jail them or banish them without any reason, any explanation, or any opportunity to contest that explanation. A moment's reflection shows that both liberty and equality rights would be extremely insecure in the absence of constraints on arbitrary and summary punishment. Due process requirements function as indispensable prophylactic support for any other limitations that the law imposes on the reasons for which the government may take adverse action against a citizen. Due process within the workplace, where it exists, functions much the same way.

Of course it is possible to have too much job security—too much for the efficient operation of an enterprise and too much for the cohesiveness of the workforce. Few organizations could survive in a competitive environment if it were impossible to fire anyone. Moreover, few people would want to work in a place where it is impossible to fire anyone for serious misconduct or poor performance. But "just cause" does no such thing. It recognizes the employee's stake in the job by placing a burden of justification and procedural fairness on the employer. As such, it protects employees against arbitrary and summary dismissal and incidentally supplements the protection of other employees rights.

So it is quite easy to see how due process—a just cause requirement along with a reasonable enforcement procedure—can bolster the civil rights and civil liberties that are part of the workplace constitution. It is much harder to figure out whether and how those protections should be extended to workers generally. Given the hydraulics of the labor market, an effort to legislate job security might have unintended and undesirable consequences.

So the partial constitution of the workplace—the prevailing regime of limited civil liberties and optional unionization—is an inherently unstable vehicle of even the rights that it does contain. Speaking architecturally, it lacks crucial structural components and is vulnerable to collapse under conditions of stress, such as those that prevail in a low-wage workplace in which the employer vehemently opposes unionization. So one important question for reformers is how to fortify workers' basic civil liberties and, more broadly, how to revive the possibilities for collective voice that the moribund New Deal model has failed to secure.

We may find some useful tools and resources in the mechanisms of workplace governance that have grown up as the collective bargaining model has receded: (1) the tort-like model of judicially enforced individual rights that has proven a potent vehicle of civil rights enforcement; (2) the administrative enforcement of minimum standards; and (3) the background regime of contract and private ordering, which can itself be a powerful engine of innovation. Each of those competing models captures some dimension of what is needed in a system of workplace governance, and each taps the energies of actors and institutions—aggrieved private parties and their lawyers, public agencies, judges, and market actors—that could be channeled into the task of supplying the missing dimension of collective employee participation.

So, for example, we might explore the implications of enforcing existing statutory rights of free expression, association, and self-organization with a tort-like cause of action along the lines of antidiscrimination law. Private employment litigation, especially under the antidiscrimination laws, has dramatically altered the incentives faced by employers and transformed organizational practices. So, too, in seeking to make workplace regulatory regimes more effective, especially in the low-wage workplace, I have suggested the possibility of a "representation remedy"—a government-backed form of employee representation—as part of the regulatory response to chronic or willful violations of workplace standards. Such a move would be well in sync with the movement toward decentralization and greater flexibility and responsiveness in regulation.[20] Finally, as suggested above, we should look for ways to expand the freedom of firms to put in place alternative mechanisms of employee representation without impeding employee efforts to secure independent representation. The "all-or-nothing" model of employee representation first enacted nearly 70 years ago has become increasingly untenable as the system of mass production on which it was based has been largely supplanted by more fluid and agile organizational forms, and as more and more of the labor force has ended up with "nothing" by way of collective representation.

Each of these suggestions for reform raises hard questions of justification, efficacy, and implementation that I leave unanswered here. But it should at least be clear that, once having recognized the unique power and value of workplace bonds in holding together a diverse society, we have before us a wide array of public policy tools and resources by which to cultivate those bonds. Some of those tools and resources, such as those of antidiscrimination law, are well developed, though in need of refinement; others have yet to be invented. Some possible reforms are well grounded in the more conventional terms of discussion in labor and employment law, which focus on labor productivity, economic vitality, and worker well-being; others build more directly on the societal value of workplace connectedness.

A Plea for Public Sector Leadership

Thus far this account has largely ignored the particularities of public sector workplaces, which, putting aside the military branches, employed 19 million workers, or roughly 14 percent of the civilian workforce in 2001.[21] Some of those particularities are of special interest here. Perhaps most importantly, the public sector has historically offered greater employment opportunities, and especially white-collar, managerial, and professional opportunities, to African Americans and others who have encountered resistance and discrimination in the private sector. Public sector workplaces, even apart from the military, are generally more racially integrated than private sector workplaces.[22] The public sector has also defied trends toward deunionization. Unionization levels in the private sector have fallen to less than 10 percent. However, operating under state and federal public sector bargaining laws, unions have maintained a fairly steady 37 percent of the public sector workforce.[23]

Public sector employees also, and perhaps not coincidentally, enjoy a more complete workplace "constitution" than do most of their private sector counterparts. In large part that is because their "constitution" draws on the federal Constitution itself, which applies to state action and thus to the actions of government employers toward their employees. All public employees thus enjoy the protections of the First Amendment; they cannot be fired or otherwise penalized for speaking out on matters of public concern so long as they do not unduly interfere with their employer's legitimate interest in getting the public's business done. So, too, public employees enjoy associational rights and the right to petition their government employer under the First Amendment, as well as privacy rights under the Fourth Amendment.[24] Many public employees are protected as well against arbitrary discipline and discharge, and are entitled to a hearing before a neutral decisionmaker, under state and federal civil service laws. Those employees enjoy "due process" rights that few private sector nonunion employees enjoy.[25]

All this suggests that the experience of "working together" should be especially well realized in the public sector. Or at least that the law supplies a relatively strong framework for that experience. Undoubtedly there are public sector workplaces in which job security and longevity, a collective voice in workplace governance, and norms of fair and equal treatment combine with a shared sense of public mission to produce rich and multifaceted bonds among diverse co-workers. Undoubtedly, too, there are public sector workplaces in which indolent or unimaginative management—which may be more likely to survive in a non-competitive setting—and a highly bureaucratic structure has fostered an ethos of marking time and marking territory. The legal constitution of the workplace—the legal standards of equal protection, due process, free speech and free association, and "democracy on demand"—merely establishes a skeletal framework for workplace governance. That framework still leaves a great deal up to the actors themselves. The relative absence of competitive pressures on public sector managers may work for or against their inclination and ability to cultivate productive and cooperative workplace relationships. That brings us to the point I wish to stress here.

The burden of this book has been to show that much that is valuable, even indispensable, to democratic life in a diverse society can be cultivated within even nondemocratic (but especially within more democratic) workplaces. We the people enjoy rich rewards from the cumulative experience of citizens cooperating, socializing, and sharing workplace concerns with a diverse set of co-workers. One challenge is to enlist employers and managers in the project of cultivating those valuable "externalities" of connectedness across social cleavages. Sometimes—and according to some observers, increasingly—connectedness and diversity within the workforce both go hand in hand with productivity. Sometimes, however, employers organize work in ways that subvert the preconditions of connectedness; and sometimes, as in the case of the antiunion, low-wage model, they assiduously suppress connectedness. So, too, some employers value or at least accept demographic diversity in their ranks; others resist it. Recognizing that employers do not always find it in their own private interests to build connectedness within a diverse workforce, I have looked for ways to deploy the law to compel or induce employers to contribute directly or indirectly to that project.

But we the people have more immediate means of shaping the organizational practices of the public sector workplace. Moreover, government managers with a broad understanding of their public mission have the ability to exercise their own discretion to make their workplaces more productive of valuable connections among employees. The brief review of emerging workplace practices above suggests that there is no unavoidable conflict between that legitimate goal and what must be the primary objective of implementing public policy and the agency's assigned mission effectively and efficiently.

So those workplaces that are under more-or-less democratic control—in which the public stands in the shoes of the owners or "shareholders"—can be enlisted directly in the project of building workplace connectedness and diversity. To some extent, the Constitution already does that by subjecting government employers to many of the "constitutional" elements that had to be legislated, or that remain unlegislated, for the private sector. To some extent, public sector labor laws do that, too; for they express a commitment to collective participation and collective voice within the government workplace. So, too, the early commitment of the federal government to expanding the employment opportunities and promoting the integration of black workers was based on broader societal objectives, not just each agency's accomplishment of its own assigned mission.

The distinctive features of public employment do not cut in only one direction, for there are some things that private employers can do to promote workplace integration and connectedness that public employers cannot. In particular, the Constitution's equal protection clause may place tighter restraints on affirmative action and race- or sex-based preferences by government than Title VII places on private employers.[26] Still, there is little doubt that more could be done within the public sector workplace by elected and appointed officials at all levels of government who are persuaded of the importance of "working together."

Nor does the public sector employers' role end with their own workplace practices. For those employers often—too often, say many observers—contract out aspects of their work to private employers. This practice potentially subverts all of the virtues of public employment catalogued above: It substitutes employees and workplaces that are much less likely to be represented by a union, that may have won their contract by pursuing a lower labor cost strategy, and that usually do not enjoy the more generous constitutional protections of public employment.[27] Indeed, perversely, "state action" doctrine insures that the more completely the government disengages itself from the supervision of work and working conditions, the more surely the contractor escapes the strictures of the Constitution.[28]

On the other hand, responsible public agencies can condition the award of public contracts on compliance not only with public law but with some standards and some procedures that are stricter and more far-reaching than what public law otherwise requires of private employers. The federal government and many states already do that with respect to the equal employment laws. Expanding on its own pioneering role in the direct employment of black workers beginning in World War II, federal contract compliance requirements instituted in the 1960s provided a crucial impetus for expanding employment opportunities for women, racial minorities, and others protected by the antidiscrimination laws in the private sector.[29] Many states have followed suit. To the extent that these governments can impose other conditions that incidentally or directly foster workplace connectedness, they should do so.

Many questions remain here. Just to point out one complication in existing law, the NLRA, the foundation of the "constitution" of the private sector workplace, has been construed to sharply limit the power of federal, state, and local governments to use their market power to effectively regulate labor relations; that task is committed to the exclusive jurisdiction of the National Labor Relations Board under the NLRA. On the one hand, the government may attach labor-friendly conditions to public projects that might otherwise be disrupted by labor disputes.[30] On the other hand, government agencies may not leverage their spending power into a regulatory role. The Supreme Court has thus struck down both federal and state strictures on the award of government contracts to private employers who have permanently replaced strikers, which federal labor law permits them to do, or who have repeatedly violated the federal labor laws, which federal law obviously does not permit but does not effectively deter either.[31]

This short detour into the intricacies of labor law shows that the strategy outlined here is not a simple one. Even freeing the government to act in its nonregulatory capacity may sometimes require legislative action. But the present point is to suggest some of what might follow from a public embrace of the propositions contended for here. For the public acts through many institutional vehicles: It can act through legislation, through regulatory bodies and the interpretation and enforcement of existing law, or through courts and their articulation of public policy, their interpretation of statutes, and constitutional doctrine. The public can act through federal institutions or through state or local bodies. Many of these actions face lower political hurdles than does, for example, federal legislation covering all private sector workplaces. Moreover, the prospect of different government entities trying out different approaches to cultivating connectedness within their own workplaces or within those of their own contractors has positive virtues: It is more decentralized, flexible, and experimental, and might lead toward a better set of outcomes than any one legislative standard or rule could possibly do.[32]

A public that is persuaded of the value of connectedness in the workplace can cultivate that connectedness in its own workplaces. Public sector managers that are so persuaded can lead the way.

CONCLUSION

Recall Tocqueville's most profound observation about the virtues of association: "Feelings and ideas are renewed, the heart enlarged, and the understanding developed only by the reciprocal action of men one upon another."[1] "Reciprocal action" through collective activity not only fosters particular relationships and usable ties but also more diffuse and generalized feelings of empathy and understanding, of connectedness and being-in-this-togetherness among citizens. This diffuse sense of connectedness operates as a soft form of social capital, for it fosters the ability and willingness to support and carry out projects for the common good. It also contributes to the quality of public discourse and democratic deliberation, for deliberation among citizens who care about each others' well-being is more likely to produce understanding, compromise, and progress toward solutions to social problems. But the value of connectedness as such, and especially the role of economic associations in fostering connectedness, hearkens to an older tradition in social theory—one that has mostly receded from public view and that deserves to be refurbished and updated in light of more recent commitments to intergroup equality and integration in the workplace. That has been my objective here.

I do not mean to claim too much for the role of the workplace in democratic society. The workplace is far from an oasis of equality and harmony. Even the unionized workplace is not a site of genuine democracy and collective self-determination. The workplace cannot replace the voluntary civic associations at the center of the prevailing conception of civil society. Freely chosen, autonomous, self-governing associations organized around shared values and objectives serve many individual, group, and societal interests that the workplace cannot, especially for the millions of adults who are retired, unemployed, or otherwise outside of the paid labor market.

But for those who do spend much of their lives there, the workplace cultivates some of the same qualities of social life that voluntary civic groups do, as well as other qualities that those groups often do not. Workplace relationships and conversations alone—without the intermediate step of something like unionization—seem unlikely to spawn a renaissance of popular engagement and democratization of political power. Yet those relationships and conversations help to build up the diffuse resources of empathy and connectedness on which any democratic social movement must draw and build. For ordinary citizens, workplace interactions and relationships with co-workers—former strangers from diverse families, neighborhoods, backgrounds—can help to foster that ephemeral but essential sense of connectedness, of "being in this together." The daily experience of working together, multiplied across the legions of working adult citizens, can strengthen the social foundations for collective self-governance in a complex and heterogeneous society.

That brings us to a troubling question: If I am right about the civic value of workplace connections, then why are other forms of social capital declining? Why, for example, are Americans expressing less "generalized social trust"—less inclination to believe that "most people can be trusted"? We must consider the troubling possibility that the increasing diversity, and even the desegregation, of American society is part of the explanation.

I am not suggesting that the erosion of social trust is a product of racial intolerance or "white flight" in any simple sense.[2] On the contrary, declining levels of generalized trust and civic involvement have coincided with a rise in tolerant and egalitarian racial attitudes.[3] The claim is rather that greater diversity, and the friction that goes with it, may take a toll on social trust and civic engagement without regard to conscious racial attitudes. This hypothesis is suggested by the geographic as well as the generational distribution of social capital. Consider that the most civic and socially trusting generation, by Putnam's reckoning, came of age in comparatively homogeneous communities and neighborhoods in which "most people" were more like themselves.[4] Consider, too, the unsettling fact that, by Putnam's measures, social capital is highest in some of the most racially homogeneous—that is, the whitest—parts of the country. North and South Dakota are at the top of the scale, followed by Vermont, Minnesota, Montana, Nebraska, Iowa, New Hampshire, and several other overwhelmingly white states in New England, the Upper Midwest, and the West.[5] Other studies confirm that individuals in more heterogeneous communities have a lower rate of participation in civic associations, politics, and even informal social networks, as well as less generalized social trust.[6]

It would not be surprising to find that people tend to have more trust in people whom they see as being like themselves. And in much of the country, the people we see around us in our daily lives—in stores and malls, in streets and public buildings, and at work, though not in our homes and neighborhoods—are a much more diverse group than they were 40 or 50 years ago. These changes have produced friction within the workplace as well. In the days when workplaces were mostly segregated on the basis of race and gender, and co-workers often shared ethnic and even neighborhood ties as well, common working conditions and common grievances led readily—albeit often against employer opposition—to feelings of solidarity and demands for a collective voice. White-collar workplaces were at least as segregated; shared loyalty to the organization rather than solidarity among co-workers was the order of the day. But for both blue-collar and white-collar workers, bonds of sameness reinforced the "ties formed by sharing in common work." Indeed, bonds of sameness within every part of the more segregated society of the mid-twentieth century may have underwritten much of the civic and fraternal activity and generalized social trust that Putnam chronicles and celebrates. By the same token, the troubled and tortuous process of desegregation may have something to do with the concomitant erosion of associational life and generalized trust.

So it seems quite possible that the desegregation and diversification of American society has contributed to the decline of "generalized social trust" and of some forms of community involvement. But what does this suggest about my own claim that working together in integrated workplaces helps to produce cooperation and connectedness across racial lines? Shouldn't there be more connectedness and a greater sense of inclusiveness in the most integrated environments? Doesn't evidence to the contrary undermine the thesis of this entire book? It does not.

Recall that the social science of intergroup relations led to a complex conclusion about the effects of diversity within working groups. If the question is whether more diverse work groups function better or worse than homogeneous groups, the answer appears to be discouraging: On balance, diverse groups tend to perform somewhat less well. But if the question is whether working together in diverse groups improves intergroup relations over time, the answer is quite clearly affirmative. We may face a similar dichotomy in the case of connectedness and trust within communities and societies: It may be that diverse communities, whatever their other great advantages, tend to foster less civic involvement and less social trust than do homogeneous communities. But if the diversity of a community is a given and the question is whether such a community will function better with or without close and cooperative interaction across lines of social division, the evidence strongly supports the value of that interaction.

Demographic diversity and integration are increasingly facts of life in American communities and in American society as a whole. Indeed, insofar as integration is inextricably linked to improving the life chances of groups long subordinated in this society, it is a moral imperative. All that being the case, American society is much better off with spheres of real social integration in which people learn to deal more constructively and to feel more affinity with people who are different from themselves. Modern commitments to intergroup equality and integration render both more difficult and more important the task of building social bonds and feelings of connectedness in the workplace.

These concerns can be reframed in terms of the distinction between bonding and bridging ties. Many of the social ties that have suffered the most in recent decades brought together fairly homogeneous groups and drew them closer together. Consider organizations like the Elks, Kiwanis, and Jaycees.[7] Such "bonding ties," especially among people who live their lives in relatively homogeneous environments, may be especially productive of the kind of generalized social trust that social surveys uncover. There was, after all, a much higher level of "generalized social trust" in 1955, in a society that was sharply segregated and in which segregation and inequality was widely tolerated (if not actively defended) by whites, than there is now. But that underscores the trade-off between these two kinds of connectedness. A rich network of bonding ties among homogeneous groups is not merely consistent with exclusion, intolerance, and prejudice toward outsiders; it may even promote those vices.[8]

Bridging ties—connections across lines of social identity that normally divide people—are harder to cultivate. People may not form those ties spontaneously or voluntarily; left to their own devices, they may prefer to associate with others like themselves, or maybe just to watch TV. Once people do find themselves in contact with diverse others, differences in background and identity may produce conflict and friction. Overcoming those differences to accomplish things together can be hard work—much harder than learning and expressing liberal and tolerant beliefs within a relatively homogeneous environment. It may require an element of external control or even compulsion. And the process may take a toll in terms of one's sense that "most people can be trusted." Yet the resulting proliferation of bridging ties—and even the resulting weakening of bonding ties—may promote a more genuine tolerance for difference and dissidence and a greater capacity to cooperate and to empathize with diverse others.

That is what can happen in the workplace. In today's world, workplace ties tend to be thinner and weaker than the multistrand ties among people who share several aspects of their background and identity, and who choose to associate with each other on the basis of what they share. They also are more likely to bridge fractious group lines. As workplace ties come to make up a larger share of our social connections—and that has clearly happened with the erosion of many of those other ties—we find ourselves linked more weakly to a more diverse group of people, and through them to a broader segment of the community. Those weaker ties may not generate as strong a sense that "most people can be trusted"; but they help to generate a crucial sense of "being in this together." We may have traded a small-town kind of trust for a thinner but more inclusive and more cosmopolitan sense of connectedness.

One can hope—and the social science evidence reviewed above would encourage this hope—that, over time, the proliferation of ties across social divisions would tend not only to bridge but to narrow those divisions, making them less fractious, less fraught, and less conflict-ridden. "Bridging ties" would then have to span less social distance. They would function more like "bonding ties," thickening and warming up and generating a broader and more inclusive sense of social trust and empathy. If that is to happen, the workplace will have to play a leading role.

In the workplace, and often only there, individuals have to find ways of cooperating on an ongoing basis, over weeks or years, with others who have distinct cultural backgrounds, life trajectories, opinions, and experiences, and racial and ethnic identities. That makes the workplace a uniquely important institution in a diverse democratic society and a central component of any reasonably capacious account of "civil society." Moreover, the workplace is, by constitutional design and by its nature, more tractable and more amenable to regulation than other components of civil society. It is one site of associational life where the law has both leverage and legitimacy. The potential contribution of workplace relations to democratic life is decidedly different than the contribution of civic engagement through voluntary associations. But the unique potential that does lie in working together is more readily realized through the deliberate interventions of public policy. We should not neglect that opportunity.

NOTES

Chapter 1

1. ROBERT D. PUTNAM, BOWLING ALONE: THE COLLAPSE AND REVIVAL OF AMERICAN COMMUNITY (New York: Simon & Schuster 2000) [hereinafter BOWLING ALONE]; Robert D. Putnam, *Bowling Alone: America's Declining Social Capital,* 6 J. DEMOCRACY 65 (1995) [hereinafter *Declining Social Capital*].

2. Robert D. Putnam, *The Strange Disappearance of Civic America,* 24 AM. PROSPECT 34 (1996) [hereinafter Putnam, *Strange Disappearance*].

3. *See, e.g.,* Andrew Greeley, *The Other Civic America: Religion and Social Capital,* 32 AM. PROSPECT 68 (1997); Alejandro Portes & Patricia Landolt, *The Downside of Social Capital,* 26 AM. PROSPECT 18 (1996); Theda Skocpol, *Unravelling from Above,* 25 AM. PROSPECT 20 (1996); Sidney Verba et al., *The Big Tilt: Participatory Inequality in America,* 32 AM. PROSPECT 74 (1997).

4. In Putnam's early accounts, the workplace appears only as a possible culprit in the decline of America's social capital. *See* Putnam, *Strange Disappearance, supra* note 2, at 35. But later accounts recognize it as a potential source of social capital. *See* PUTNAM, BOWLING ALONE, *supra* note 1, at 85–92; *Better Together: Report of the Saguaro Seminar: Civic Engagement in America* (Kennedy School of Government, Harvard Univ. 2001).

5. *See* ERNEST GELLNER, CONDITIONS OF LIBERTY: CIVIL SOCIETY AND ITS RIVALS (London: Hamish Hamilton 1992).

6. *See, e.g.,* JÜRGEN HABERMAS, BETWEEN FACTS AND NORMS 366–67 (Cambridge: Polity Press 1996); JEAN L. COHEN & ANDREW ARATO, CIVIL SOCIETY AND POLITICAL THEORY ix (Cambridge, Mass.: MIT Press 1992); JOHN EHRENBERG, CIVIL SOCIETY: THE CRITICAL HISTORY OF AN IDEA 235 (New York: NYU Press 1999).

7. Other contemporary theorists maintain a broader definition of civil society that includes corporations—*see, e.g.,* Neil MacCormick, *Institutions and Laws Again,* 77 TEX. L. REV. 1429, 1435 (1999)—and some workplace ties. *See* FRANCIS FUKUYAMA, TRUST: THE SOCIAL VIRTUES AND THE CREATION OF PROSPERITY 4 (New York: Free Press 1995); ALAN WOLFE, WHOSE KEEPER? SOCIAL SCIENCE AND MORAL OBLIGATION 20 (Berkeley: U. of Cal. Press 1989).

8. JULIET B. SCHOR, THE OVERWORKED AMERICAN: THE UNEXPECTED DECLINE OF LEISURE (New York: Basic Books 1991).

9. The average American from 18 to 64 years of age spends about 26 hours per week working and about 2 hours in religious and other organizations, while employed adults spend more time at work (about 35 hours), *id.* at 95, and less in voluntary organizations. JOHN P. ROBINSON & GEOFFREY GODBEY, TIME FOR LIFE: THE SURPRISING WAYS AMERICANS USE THEIR TIME 94–95, 170–74 (University Park: Penn. State U.P. 1997).

10. *See* Robert Huckfeldt et al., *Political Environments, Cohesive Social Groups, and the Communication of Public Opinion,* 39 AM. J. POL. SCI. 1025, 1031–32 (1995); Bruce C. Straits,

Bringing Strong Ties Back In: Interpersonal Gateways to Political Information and Influence, 55 PUBL. OP. Q. 432, 446–47 (1991).

11. PUTNAM, BOWLING ALONE, *supra* note 1, at 275.

12. *Compare* STEPHAN THERNSTROM & ABIGAIL M. THERNSTROM, AMERICA IN BLACK AND WHITE: ONE NATION INDIVISIBLE 493–529 (New York: Simon & Schuster 1997), *with* ANDREW HACKER, TWO NATIONS: BLACK AND WHITE, SEPARATE, HOSTILE, UNEQUAL (New York: Scribner's 1992).

13. From 1987 to 1994, approval of dating between blacks and whites rose from 72% to 88% among black respondents and from 43% to 65% among white respondents; between 1968 and 1994, approval of marriages between blacks and whites rose from 48% to 68% among blacks, and from 17% to 45% among whites. *See* THERNSTROM & THERNSTROM, *supra* note 12, at 524–25 (reporting data from GEORGE GALLUP, JR., THE GALLUP POLL: PUBLIC OPINION, 1991 171 (Wilmington, Del.: Scholarly Resources 1992) and THE GALLUP POLL: 1994 142 (Wilmington, Del.: Scholarly Resources 1994)). More recent data show that 22% of whites would oppose a close relative's marrying a black person, while just 10% of blacks would oppose a close relative's marrying a white person. *Saguaro Seminar on Civic Engagement in America, Social Capital Community Benchmark Survey, Executive Summary* 4-5 (Cambridge, Mass.: John F. Kennedy School of Government, Harvard U. 2001), *available at* http://www. cfsv.org/communitysurvey/results3.html [hereinafter *Saguaro Executive Summary*]. For a wide-ranging and provocative exploration of the issues, see RANDALL KENNEDY, INTERRACIAL INTIMACIES: SEX, MARRIAGE, IDENTITY, AND ADOPTION (New York: Pantheon 2003).

14. From 1975 to 1994, the percentage who reported having a "good friend" of the other race—someone with whom they get together at least once a month and keep in close touch with—rose from 21% to 78% among black respondents and from 9% to 73% among whites. *See* THERNSTROM & THERNSTROM, *supra* note 12, at 521. In a 2000 survey, 71% of black respondents and 57% of white respondents reported having a personal friend of the other race. *Saguaro Seminar on Civic Engagement in America, Social Capital Community Benchmark Survey, National Survey Results* 19 (Cambridge, Mass.: John F. Kennedy School of Government, Harvard U. 2001), *available at* http://www.cfsv.org/communitysurvey/docs/marginals. pdf [hereinafter *Saguaro Survey Results*].

15. The percentage of new marriages by African Americans to a spouse of a different race rose from 0.7% in 1963 to 12.1% in 1993. *See* THERNSTROM & THERNSTROM, *supra* note 12, at 526. On the rising incidence and societal significance of black-white marriages, see KENNEDY, *supra* note 13, at 123-61.

16. Census data show high levels of segregation of black residents, with modest declines since the 1960s. *See* DOUGLAS S. MASSEY & NANCY A. DENTON, AMERICAN APARTHEID: SEGREGATION AND THE MAKING OF THE UNDERCLASS 64 (Cambridge, Mass.: Harvard U.P. 1993). *See also* Reynolds Farley & William H. Frey, *Changes in the Segregation of Whites from Blacks during the 1980s: Small Steps Toward a More Integrated Society,* 59 AM. SOC. REV. 23, 30–32 (1994). Levels of segregation for other large minority groups, such as Hispanics and Asians, have consistently been lower. *See id.* at 32. In nationwide polls, the share of respondents reporting that people of another race live in their neighborhood rose for blacks from 66% in 1964 to 83% in 1994, and for whites from 20% to 61%. THERNSTROM & THERNSTROM, *supra* note 12, at 218. More recently, in June 2000, 45% of black respondents reported that almost all of their nearby neighbors were black; 52% reported that a few (21%) or about half (31%) were black; 85% of white respondents reported that none (25%) or a few (60%) of their nearby neighbors were black. Kevin Sack, *Poll Finds Optimistic Outlook but Enduring Racial Division,* N.Y. TIMES, July 11, 2000, at A23.

17. *See* Xavier de Souza Briggs, Social Capital and Segregation: Race, Connections, and

Inequality in America, John F. Kennedy School of Government, Harvard University, Faculty Research Working Paper Series, RWP02-011 (2002).

18. In a 1992 Detroit poll, 66% of whites and 57% of blacks who had neighbors of the other race "hardly knew" those neighbors. Lee Sigelman et al., *Making Contact? Black–White Social Interaction in an Urban Setting*, 101 AM. J. SOC. 1306, 1311–12 (1996).

19. *See* Nancy A. Denton, *The Persistence of Segregation: Links between Residential Segregation and School Segregation*, 80 MINN. L. REV. 795 (1996); John A. Powell, *Living and Learning: Linking Housing and Education*, 80 MINN. L. REV. 749, 755–56 (1996).

20. *See* GARY ORFIELD ET AL., DISMANTLING DESEGREGATION: THE QUIET REVERSAL OF BROWN V. BOARD OF EDUCATION 53–71 (New York: New Press 1996); Davison M. Douglas, *The End of Busing?*, 95 MICH. L. REV. 1715, 1722–24 (1997) (reviewing ORFIELD ET AL., *supra*).

21. In the June 2000 *New York Times* survey, 73% of black respondents reported that almost all of their congregation were black; 90% of white respondents reported that none (34%) or a few (56%) of their congregation were black. *See* Sack, *supra* note 16, at A23.

22. *Saguaro Survey Results* at 12.

23. *See Saguaro Executive Summary* at 4–5; Alberto Alesina & Eliana La Ferrara, Participation in Heterogeneous Communities, National Bureau of Econ. Research Working Paper No. 7155 (1999).

24. *See* WILLIAM G. BOWEN & DEREK BOK, THE SHAPE OF THE RIVER: LONG-TERM CONSEQUENCES OF CONSIDERING RACE IN COLLEGE AND UNIVERSITY ADMISSIONS (Princeton, N.J.: Princeton U.P. 1998).

25. *See* Steven A. Holmes, *Survey Finds Race-Relations Gap in Armed Services, Despite Gains*, N.Y. TIMES, Nov. 23, 1999, at A-1; Steven A. Holmes, *Which Man's Army, in* THE NEW YORK TIMES, HOW RACE IS LIVED IN AMERICA 41–55 (New York: Times Books 2001).

26. *See* CHARLES C. MOSKOS & JOHN SIBLEY BUTLER, ALL THAT WE CAN BE: BLACK LEADERSHIP AND RACIAL INTEGRATION THE ARMY WAY (New York: Basic Books 1996). Indeed, the presence of integrated Army bases appears to be associated with greater racial integration in surrounding communities. *See* Farley & Frey, *supra* note 16, at 33.

27. In the *New York Times* poll from June 2000, 31% of white respondents said none of the people they worked with were black; 52% said "a few," 17% said "about half" or more." Among black respondents, 5% said "none" of their co-workers were black; 48% said a "few," 29% said "about half," and 17% said "almost all." *See* Sack, *supra* note 16, at A23. *See also* Mark Whitaker, *A Crisis of Shattered Dreams*, NEWSWEEK, May 6, 1991, at 30.

28. JOHN J. HELDRICH CENTER FOR WORKFORCE DEVELOPMENT, A WORKPLACE DIVIDED: HOW AMERICANS VIEW DISCRIMINATION AND RACE ON THE JOB 8–9, 34 (New Brunswick, N.J.: Rutgers U. 2002).

29. *See* Sigelman et al., *supra* note 18, at 1314–17; *Gallup Poll Social Audit on Black/White Relations in the United States, Executive Summary* (1999), *available at* http://www.gallup.com/poll/socialaudits/sa970610.asp.

30. Anna Byrd Davis, *Racial Boundaries Softening Here among the Middle-Class*, Com. Appeal, Mar. 29, 1998, at A1.

31. Jo Mannies, *Area Study Illuminates Gulf Separating Races; Status Quo Saddens Many Blacks and Whites Here*, ST. LOUIS POST-DISPATCH, Sept. 10, 1995, at C-1.

32. *See* Sack, *supra* note 16, at A23.

33. *See* Mannies, *supra* note 31.

34. *See* Mary R. Jackman & Marie Crane, *"Some of My Best Friends Are Black . . .": Interracial Friendship and Whites' Racial Attitudes*, 50 PUB. OPINION Q. 459, 483–84 (1986).

35. *See* Briggs, *supra* note 17, at 52–53.

36. WILLIAM KORNBLUM, BLUE COLLAR COMMUNITY 36–67 (Chicago: U. of Chicago Press 1974).

37. *Id.* at 36.

38. *Id.* at 66. Some black workers rose to positions of leadership in unions operating within the plant, often with widespread white support. *Id.*

39. *See* PUTNAM, BOWLING ALONE, *supra* note 1, at 22–24.

40. Kenneth L. Karst, *The Coming Crisis of Work in Constitutional Perspective*, 82 CORNELL L. REV. 523, 550 (1997); Kenneth L. Karst, *Private Discrimination and Public Responsibility: Patterson in Context*, 1989 SUP. CT. REV. 1, 10–11.

41. Sometimes legal actors are directly engaged with an organization—for example, in the remedial or settlement phase of a large-scale lawsuit—and are in a position to help restructure work processes and reshape workplace dynamics so as to overcome intergroup tensions and biases. Mapping and shaping those innovative possibilities is a challenging and important project that I do not undertake here. For valuable work along those lines, see Susan Sturm, *Second Generation Employment Discrimination: A Structural Approach*, 101 COLUM. L. REV. 458 (2001).

Part I

1. *See* ROBERT D. PUTNAM, BOWLING ALONE: THE COLLAPSE AND REVIVAL OF AMERICAN COMMUNITY (New York: Simon & Schuster 2000).

2. *Id.* at 275.

Chapter 2

1. *See* JOHN P. ROBINSON & GEOFFREY GODBEY, TIME FOR LIFE: THE SURPRISING WAYS AMERICANS USE THEIR TIME 94–95 (University Park: Penn. State U.P. 1997).

2. *See* Robert Huckfeldt et al., *Political Environments, Cohesive Social Groups, and the Communication of Public Opinion*, 39 AM. J. POL. SCI. 1025, 1031–32 (1995); Bruce C. Straits, *Bringing Strong Ties Back In: Interpersonal Gateways to Political Information and Influence*, 55 PUBL. OP. Q. 432, 446–47 (1991).

3. Stephen R. Marks, *Intimacy in the Public Realm: The Case of Co-workers*, 72 SOCIAL FORCES 843–58 (1994) (citing data from 1985 General Social Survey).

4. STEPHEN L. CARTER, CIVILITY: MANNERS, MORALS, AND THE ETIQUETTE OF DEMOCRACY 12–13 (New York: Basic Books 1998) (emphasis added). Only a few pages of this sweeping exploration of the wellsprings and modern significance of civility are devoted to the workplace. *See id.* at 181–84.

5. *See* ALAN FOX, BEYOND CONTRACT: WORK, POWER, AND TRUST RELATIONS 76–77 (London: Faber 1974); Charles F. Sabel, *Constitutional Ordering in Historical Context, in* GAMES IN HIERARCHIES AND NETWORKS 114 (Fritz Scharpf ed., Boulder, Colo.: Westview Press 1993); Mark Barenberg, *Democracy and Domination in the Law of Workplace Cooperation: From Bureaucratic to Flexible Production*, 94 COLUM. L. REV. 753, 894–96 (1994).

6. *See* JAMES T. BOND ET AL., FAMILIES AND WORK INSTITUTE: THE 1997 NATIONAL STUDY OF THE CHANGING WORKFORCE 78–79 (1997). Most agreed that they had freedom to decide what they do on the job (74% in 1997 vs. 56% in 1977), that it is basically their own responsibility to decide how the job gets done (86% vs. 80%), and that they have a lot of say about what happens on their job (71% vs. 59%).

7. *See* Fox, *supra* note 5, at 77.

8. Maria T. Poarch, *Ties that Bind: US Suburban Residents on the Social and Civic Dimensions of Work*, 1 *Community, Work, & Family* 125, 132–34 (1998).

9. *See* Fox, *supra* note 5, at 80–81.

10. On the mediating potential of unions, *see* Thomas C. Kohler, *Civic Virtue at Work: Unions as Seedbeds of the Civic Virtues*, 36 B.C. L. Rev. 279 (1995); Thomas C. Kohler, *Individualism and Communitarianism at Work*, 1993 BYU L. Rev. 727, 731–40; Molly S. McUsic & Michael Selmi, *Postmodern Unions: Identity Politics in the Workplace (An Essay)*, 82 Iowa L. Rev. 1339 (1997).

11. For some legal analyses of identity-based associations and their usefulness within the workplace, *see* Marion Crain, *Colorblind Unionism*, 49 UCLA L. Rev. 1313 (2002); Alan Hyde, *Employee Caucus: A Key Institution in the Emerging System of Employment Law*, 69 Chi.-Kent L. Rev. 149 (1993); Michael J. Yelnosky, *Title VII, Mediation, and Collective Action*, 1999 U. Ill. L. Rev. 583 (1999).

12. *See* Mark Barenberg, *The Political Economy of the Wagner Act: Power, Symbol, and Workplace Cooperation*, 106 Harv. L. Rev. 1379, 1461–89 (1993).

13. Lizabeth Cohen, Making a New Deal: Industrial Workers in Chicago, 1919–1939 204 (New York: Cambridge U.P. 1990).

14. Barbara Ehrenreich, Nickel and Dimed: On (Not) Getting By in America 21, 34, 37, 97–98 (New York: Henry Holt & Co. 2001).

15. *Id.* at 37.

16. George A. Akerlof, *Labor Contracts as Partial Gift Exchange*, 97 Q. J. Econ. 543, 546–50 (1982).

17. *See* Jon Elster, The Cement of Society: A Study of Social Order 121–22 (New York: Cambridge U.P. 1989).

18. *See* Arlie Russell Hochschild, The Time Bind: When Work Becomes Home and Home Becomes Work 35–52 (New York: Metropolitan Books 1997).

19. Poarch, *supra* note 8, at 130.

20. Maggie Jackson, *Is Your Company Your Hometown?*, Ass'd Press, Sept. 29, 1998, *available in* 1998 WL 6730663.

21. *Id.*

22. A website about Celebration, U.S.A., a Disney designed town puts it plainly: "Live by the rules, and you are living in paradise. Break the rules, and you are living in a totalitarian state." *Available at* http://www.themagicalmouse.com/celebration/index.php.

23. *See* Juliet B. Schor, The Overworked American: The Unexpected Decline of Leisure 139–65 (New York: Basic Books 1991).

24. *See* Hochschild, *supra* note 18, at 163–74, 280.

25. *See* Robert D. Putnam, Bowling Alone: The Collapse and Revival of American Community 191 (New York: Simon & Schuster 2000) (emphasis in original).

26. *Id.* at 195–201.

27. *See* Marie Jahoda, Paul Lazarsfeld & Hans Zeisel, Marienthal: The Sociography of an Unemployed Community (Chicago: Aldine-Atherton, 1933 [1971]); Eli Ginzberg, The Unemployed (New York: Harper & Bros. 1943).

28. Putnam, Bowling Alone, *supra* note 25, at 195.

29. *See* Sidney Verba et al., Voice and Equality: Civic Voluntarism in American Politics 312–16, 319, 378 (Cambridge, Mass.: Harvard U.P. 1993).

30. *See* Vicki Smith, Crossing the Great Divide: Worker Risk and Opportunity in the New Economy 48–50, 70–71 (Ithaca, N.Y.: ILR Press 2001).

31. Robert Lane, The Market Experience 237–59 (Cambridge: Cambridge U.P. 1991).

32. *Id.* at 249.

33. *Id.* at 252 (citing Melvin L. Kohn & Carmi Schooler, Work and Personality: An Inquiry into the Impact of Social Stratification (Norwood, N.J.: Ablex Pub. Corp. 1983)).

34. *Id.* at 252 (citing ALEX INKELES & DAVID H. SMITH, BECOMING MODERN 24 (Cambridge, Mass.: Harvard U.P. 1974)).

35. *See* Samuel Bowles, *Endogeneous Preferences: The Cultural Consequences of Markets and Other Economic Institutions*, 36 J. ECON. LIT. 75, 99 (1998); Joseph Henrich et al., *In Search of Homo Economicus: Behavioral Experiments in 15 Small-Scale Societies*, 91 AMER. ECON. REV. 73–78 (2001); Margaret M. Blair & Lynn A. Stout, *Trust, Trustworthiness, and the Behavioral Foundations of Corporate Law*, 149 U. PA. L. REV. 1735 (2001).

36. Henrich et al., *supra* note 35, at 75.

37. Blair & Stout, *supra* note 35, at 1751 n. 30. Of course, the "other-regarding" preference reflected in the rejection of offers perceived as too low is not an altruistic one; and, to the extent the offeror anticipates the rejection of low offers, a "fair" offer may be entirely rational (in light of the anticipated "other-regarding" preferences of the offeree).

38. *Id.*

39. Bowles, *supra* note 35, at 80.

40. Henrich et al., *supra* note 35, at 74.

41. *Id.* at 76–77.

42. Bowles, *supra* note 35, at 89.

43. *Id.* (emphasis added).

Chapter 3

1. The focus here is on the private sector. Public sector workplaces have some distinctive features and are discussed briefly in chapter 9.

2. Some observers see rising "virtuality" as a major threat to "social capital" within firms. DON COHEN & LAURENCE PRUSAK, IN GOOD COMPANY: HOW SOCIAL CAPITAL MAKES ORGANIZATIONS WORK 155–81 (Boston: Harvard Bus. School Press 2001).

3. *See* SUE SHELLENBARGER, WORK AND FAMILY: ESSAYS FROM THE "WORK AND FAMILY" COLUMN OF THE WALL STREET JOURNAL 54, 55 (Ballentine 1999).

4. *See* ROBERT D. PUTNAM, BOWLING ALONE: THE COLLAPSE AND REVIVAL OF AMERICAN COMMUNITY 172–73 (New York: Simon & Schuster 2000) [hereinafter PUTNAM, BOWLING ALONE].

5. *See, e.g.,* Shira J. Boss, *Face-to-Face Won't Soon Bow to Technology*, CHRISTIAN SCIENCE MONITOR (Dec. 20, 1999); Frances Reel, *Telecommuting Not for Everyone*, DENVER POST (Oct. 12, 1997). That seems especially true for women. *See* Boss, *supra* (reporting research by National Foundation for Women Business Owners).

6. Quoted in Amy Goldwasser, *Building Dilbert's Dream House*, NEW YORK TIMES MAGAZINE, Mar. 5, 2000, at 68.

7. *See* COHEN & PRUSAK, *supra* note 2, at 170.

8. Boss, *supra* note 5.

9. *See* THOMAS KOCHAN & PAUL OSTERMAN, THE MUTUAL GAINS ENTERPRISE (Boston: Harvard Bus. School Press 1994). *See also* Peter Cappelli & Nikolai Rogovsky, *Employee Involvement and Organizational Citizenship: Implications for Labor Law Reform and "Lean Production,"* 51 INDUS. & LAB. REL. REV. 633 (1998).

10. *See, e.g.,* KIM MOODY, WORKERS IN A LEAN WORLD: UNIONS IN THE INTERNATIONAL ECONOMY (New York: Verso 1997); Mike Parker & Jane Slaughter, *Unions and Management by Stress, in* LEAN WORK: EMPOWERMENT AND EXPLOITATION IN THE GLOBAL AUTO INDUSTRY (Steve Babson ed., Detroit: Wayne State U.P. 1995).

11. *See, e.g.,* Cappelli & Rogovsky, *supra* note 9, at 636–37; Toby D. Wall et al., *Outcomes of Autonomous Workgroups: A Long-Term Field Experiment*, 29 ACAD. OF MGMT. J. 280, 299 (1986).

12. John Godard, *High Performance and the Transformation of Work: The Implications of Alternative Work Practices for the Experience and Outcomes of Work*, 54 INDUS. & LAB. REL. REV. 776, 777–78 (2001).

13. The questions making up the "belongingness" variable asked about feeling "well-accepted by your co-workers," and "like you belong," and about "fitting in" and not feeling "isolated." *Id.* at 787. The questions on "citizenship behavior" asked whether employees "help others with work-related problems," "volunteer to help others with their work," are courteous and "mindful of the concerns of others," "take an active interest in what goes on at work," and "participat[e] in meetings and in social events related to work." *Id.*

14. *Id.* at 795–98.

15. *Id.* at 798–99.

16. WILLIAM KORNBLUM, BLUE COLLAR COMMUNITY 36–67 (Chicago: U. of Chicago Press 1974).

17. *See* RICHARD B. FREEMAN & JAMES MEDOFF, WHAT DO UNIONS DO? 21 (New York: Basic Books 1984); THOMAS A. KOCHAN, HARRY C. KATZ, & ROBERT B. MCKERSIE, THE TRANSFORMATION OF AMERICAN INDUSTRIAL RELATIONS 27–29 (New York: Basic Books 1986).

18. Freeman & Medoff, *supra* note 17, at 104–07.

19. *See* PETER CAPPELLI, THE NEW DEAL AT WORK: MANAGING THE MARKET-DRIVEN WORKFORCE 63 (Boston: Harvard Bus. School Press 1999); HARRY C. KATZ & OWEN DARBISHIRE, CONVERGING DIVERGENCES: WORLDWIDE CHANGES IN EMPLOYMENT SYSTEMS 25–26 (Ithaca, N.Y.: Cornell U. Press 2000). These rigidities stem partly from the unions' having ceded to management the continuing right to make strategic and entrepreneurial decisions. Having conceded so much to managerial discretion, unions had no choice but to tightly circumscribe discretion over the terms and conditions over which they had gained a say. *See* KOCHAN, KATZ, & MCKERSIE, *supra* note 17, at 27–28.

20. *See, e.g.*, Michael L. Wachter & George M. Cohen, *The Law and Economics of Collective Bargaining: An Introduction and Application to the Problems of Subcontracting, Partial Closure, and Relocation*, 136 U. PA. L. REV. 1349, 1362 (1988).

21. For one compelling narrative of strike-induced solidarity (and bitterness), *see* JULIUS GETMAN, THE BETRAYAL OF LOCAL 14: PAPERWORKERS, POLITICS, AND PERMANENT REPLACEMENTS (Ithaca, N.Y.: Cornell U. Press 1998).

22. On unions as intermediate institutions, *see* Thomas C. Kohler, *Civic Virtue at Work: Unions as Seedbeds of the Civic Virtues*, 36 B.C. L. REV. 279 (1995); Thomas C. Kohler, *Individualism and Communitarianism at Work*, 1993 BYU L. REV. 727; on unions as sites for the development of common ground among diverse workers, *see* Molly S. McUsic & Michael Selmi, *Postmodern Unions: Identity Politics in the Workplace (An Essay)*, 82 IOWA L. REV. 1339 (1997).

23. *See* F. RAY MARSHALL, THE NEGRO AND ORGANIZED LABOR 113, 128–29 (New York: Wiley 1965); F. Ray Marshall, *The Negro in Southern Unions, in* THE NEGRO AND THE AMERICAN LABOR MOVEMENT 128, 145 (Julius Jacobson ed., Garden City, N.Y.: Anchor Books 1968).

24. LIZABETH COHEN, MAKING A NEW DEAL: INDUSTRIAL WORKERS IN CHICAGO, 1919–1939 333–36 (New York: Cambridge U.P. 1990).

25. Indeed, union seniority practices, in conjunction with employer discrimination, often operated to lock in the subordinate status of black workers. *See* Alfred W. Blumrosen, *The Law Transmission System and the Southern Jurisprudence of Employment Discrimination*, 6 INDUS. REL. L.J. 313 (1984).

26. *Id.* at 317–20, 233–24.

27. KATZ & DARBISHIRE, *supra* note 19, describe the evolution of the traditional New Deal pattern into either high conflict (often on the way to deunionization) or "joint team-based production." *Id.* at 26–27.

28. For a lively and tendentious telling of this tale, *see* WILLIAM H. WHYTE, JR., THE ORGANIZATION MAN 23–38 (New York: Simon & Schuster 1956).

29. *Id.* For an updated version of the bureaucratic model, *see* ROSABETH MOSS KANTOR, MEN AND WOMEN OF THE CORPORATION (2d ed., New York: Basic Books 1993).

30. KATZ & DARBISHIRE, *supra* note 19, at 22; KOCHAN, KATZ, & McKERSIE, *supra* note 17, at 30, 35.

31. *See* STEVEN L. WILLBORN, STEWART J. SCHWAB & JOHN F. BURTON, JR., EMPLOYMENT LAW: CASES & MATERIALS 49–68 (2d ed., Charlottesville, Va.: Lexis 1998).

32. Ronald Gilson and Mark Roe make this point about the even stronger "lifetime employment" model that prevailed in the core of the Japanese labor market. Ronald Gilson & Mark Roe, *Lifetime Employment and the Evolution of Japanese Corporate Governance*, 99 COLUM. L. REV. 508 (1999).

33. *See* Lauren B. Edelman, *Legal Environments and Organizational Governance: The Expansion of Due Process in the American Workplace*, 95 AM. J. OF SOC. 1401, 1408–13, 1435–36 (1990).

34. *See* Lawrence E. Blades, *Employment at Will vs. Individual Freedom: Limiting the Abusive Exercise of Employer Power*, 67 COLUM. L. REV. 1404 (1967); Stewart Schwab, *Life-Cycle Justice: Accommodating Just Cause and Employment at Will*, 92 U. MICH. L. REV. 8, 32–38 (1993); Clyde W. Summers, *Individual Protection against Unjust Dismissal: Time for a Statute*, 62 VA. L. REV. 481 (1976).

35. MICHAEL PIORE & CHARLES SABEL, THE SECOND INDUSTRIAL DIVIDE: POSSIBILITIES FOR PROSPERITY (New York: Basic Books 1984); Charles Sabel, *Flexible Specialization and the Re-Emergence of Regional Economies*, in REVERSING INDUSTRIAL DECLINE? INDUSTRIAL STRUCTURE AND POLICY IN BRITAIN AND HER COMPETITORS 17–70 (Paul Hirst & Jonathan Zeitlin eds., New York: St. Martin's Press 1989).

36. Katz and Darbishire see a pattern of "converging divergences": the demise of distinctive national patterns of industrial organizations in favor of greater divergence within each nation, but along lines and toward models that are increasingly common across national boundaries. KATZ & DARBISHIRE, *supra* note 19, at 9–12. *See also* David Soskice, *Divergent Production Regimes; Coordinated and Uncoordinated Market Economies*, in CONTINUITY AND CHANGE IN CONTEMPORARY CAPITALISM (H. Kitscheldt, P. Lange & G Marks eds., New York: Cambridge U.P. 1999).

37. *See* CAPPELLI, *supra* note 19, at 136–44. Some observers emphasize the size and growth of the contingent workforce, *e.g.*, Richard S. Belous, *The Rise of the Contingent Work Force: The Key Challenges and Opportunities*, 52 WASH. & LEE L. REV. 863 (1995); others emphasize its heterogeneity, *e.g.*, Gillian Lester, *Careers and Contingency*, 51 STAN. L. REV. 73 (1998); *and* Stewart Schwab, *The Diversity of Contingent Workers and the Need for Nuanced Policy*, 52 WASH. & LEE L. REV. 915 (1995).

38. *But see* COHEN & PRUSAK, *supra* note 2, at 133–54.

39. CAPPELLI, *supra* note 19, at 1.

40. *Id.* at 22–37. *See also* Katherine Van Wezel Stone, *The New Psychological Contract: Implications of the Changing Workplace for Labor and Employment Law*, 48 UCLA L. REV. 519 (2001).

41. Robert Drago, *New Systems of Work and New Workers*, in CONTINGENT WORK: AMERICAN EMPLOYMENT RELATIONS IN TRANSITION 144, 151–53, 167–78 (Kathleen Barker & Kathleen Christensen eds., Ithaca, N.Y.: ILR Press 1998).

42. ALAN HYDE, WORKING IN SILICON VALLEY (Armonk, N.Y.: M. E. Sharpe 2003).

43. *See* ALBERT HIRSCHMAN, EXIT, VOICE, AND LOYALTY (Cambridge, Mass.: Harvard U.P. 1970).

44. *See* Sanford M. Jacoby, *Melting into Air? Downsizing, Job Stability, and the Future of Work*, 76 CHI.-KENT L. REV. 1195 (2000) [hereinafter Jacoby, *Melting into Air*].

45. *Id.* at 1219–20.

46. *Id.* at 1209, 1215–16.

47. *See* Mary Williams Walsh, *Luring the Best in an Unsettled Time*, N.Y. TIMES, Jan. 30, 2001, at G1; Jonathan Glater, *Business Students Do an About-Face; Recruiters for Banks and Consultants Have Regained the Upper Hand*, N.Y. TIMES, Feb. 14, 2001, at C1.

48. Jacoby, *Melting into Air*, *supra* note 44, at 1227.

49. *See* HYDE, *supra* note 12.

50. VICKI SMITH, CROSSING THE GREAT DIVIDE: WORKER RISK AND OPPORTUNITY IN THE NEW ECONOMY 54–59 (Ithaca, N.Y.: ILR Press 2001).

51. *Id.* at 70–72.

52. Jacoby, *Melting into Air*, *supra*, note 44, at 1222. *See also* TRUMAN BEWLEY, WHY WAGES DON'T FALL DURING A RECESSION (Cambridge, Mass.: Harvard U.P. 1999).

53. Jacoby, *Melting into Air*, *supra* note 44, at 1230 (citing Martha Groves, *In Tight Job Market, Software Firm Develops Programs to Keep Employees*, L.A. TIMES, June 14, 1998, at D-5 (quoting a vice president for human resources at SAS Institute)).

54. COHEN & PRUSAK, *supra* note 2.

55. *Id.* at 4.

56. *Id.*

57. *Id.*

58. They identify UPS, Aventis (a pharmaceutical firm), 3M, Hewlett-Packard, Russell Reynolds Associates (an executive recruitment firm), SAS Institute (a software company), and Viant (an internet-business consulting firm), among others. *Id.*

59. *Id.* at 22.

60. Adrian Wooldridge, *Come Back, Company Man!*, N.Y. TIMES MAGAZINE, Mar. 5, 2000, at 82. SAS is one of Cohen and Prusak's favorite companies. *See supra* note 58.

61. Professor Jacoby thus foresees that "as some companies [like SAS] accelerate the internalization process, others will follow suit as a defensive necessity." Sanford Jacoby, *Are Career Jobs Headed for Extinction*, 42 CAL. MGMT. REV. 123, at 137 (1999).

62. Peter Cappelli, *A Market-Driven Approach to Retaining Talent*, HARV. BUS. REV., Jan.–Feb. 2000, at 108.

63. COHEN & PRUSAK, *supra* note 2, at 82.

64. *Id.*

65. *Id.* at 2–3.

66. *Id.* at 22.

67. The UAW's dispute with Caterpillar exemplifies the destructive dynamics of these conflicts:

> The dispute started in November of 1991, when the company insisted on concessions in medical-care benefits and an overall wage package that was less generous than settlements that had been negotiated at other agricultural implement companies . . . The dispute escalated into a more severe conflict . . . when the company began to hire what it declared would be permanent replacements for workers who remained on strike in the spring of 1992. Although workers then returned to work in response to fears that they would be permanently replaced, an acrimonious series of strikes and job actions followed.

KATZ & DARBISHIRE, *supra* note 19, at 26. On the bitter International Paper strike, *see* GETMAN, *supra* note 21.

68. Katz & Darbishire, *supra* note 19, at 27.

69. *Id.* at 41.

70. *Id.*

71. *Id. See also* Drago, *supra* note 41, at 146–49.

72. Katz & Darbishire, *supra* note 19, at 41.

73. *See generally* U.S. Gen. Accounting Office, HRD-88–130BR, *"Sweatshops" in the U.S: Opinions on Their Extent and Possible Enforcement Options* (Aug. 1988), *available at* http://archive.gao.gov/d17t6/136973.pdf; U.S. Gen. Accounting Office, HRD-89-1-1BR, *"Sweatshops" in New York City: A Local Example of a Nationwide Problem* (June 1989), *available at* http://archive.gao.gov/d25t7/138958.pdf. For accounts of low-wage employment in food service, discount retail, and housekeeping, *see* Barbara Ehrenreich, Nickel and Dimed: On (Not) Getting by in America (New York: Henry Holt & Co. 2001); in fast-food service and meat-processing industries, Eric Schlosser, Fast Food Nation: The Dark Side of the All-American Meal (Boston: Houghton Mifflin 2001); and in clothing and textiles, Edna Bonacich & Richard P. Appelbaum, Behind the Label: Inequality in the Los Angeles Apparel Industry (Berkeley: U. of Cal. Press 2000).

74. Katz & Darbishire, *supra* note 19, at 21–22.

75. Charlie Leduff, *At a Slaughterhouse, Some Things Never Die, in* New York Times, How Race is Lived in America 103 (New York: Times Books 2001).

76. *Id.* at 109.

77. Ehrenreich, *supra* note 73, at 209.

78. *Id.* at 209–10.

79. *See* Wal-Mart Stores, Inc., 2002 NLRB LEXIS 462 (Sept. 24, 2002); Wal-Mart Stores, Inc., 2001 NLRB 634 (Aug. 27, 2001); Wal-Mart Stores, Inc., 1999 NLRB LEXIS 870 (12/14/99). *See* also Sam's Club (A division of Wal-Mart), 2001 NLRB LEXIS 959 (Dec. 6, 2001).

80. Leduff, *supra* note 75, at 98.

81. *Id.* at 102–03.

82. For a sampling of cases from one recent week, *see, e.g.,* John W. Hancock, Jr., Inc., 337 NLRB No. 183 (Aug. 1, 2002); Shamrock Foods Co., 337 NLRB No. 138 (July 30, 2002); Michael's Painting, Inc., 337 NLRB No. 140 (July 26, 2002).

Chapter 4

1. *See* Lani Guinier & Gerald Torres, The Miner's Canary: Enlisting Race, Resisting Power, Transforming Democracy 43–44 (Cambridge, Mass.: Harvard U.P. 2002).

2. *See* chapter 1.

3. *See, e.g.,* T. Alexander Aleinikoff, *The Constitution in Context: The Continuing Significance of Racism,* 63 U. Colo. L. Rev. 325, 325–26, 339–44 (1992); Charles R. Lawrence III, *The Id, the Ego, and Equal Protection: Reckoning with Unconscious Racism,* 39 Stan. L. Rev. 317 (1987).

4. Margery A. Turner et al., Opportunities Denied, Opportunities Diminished: Racial Discrimination in Hiring (Wash., D.C.: Urban Institute Press 1991). For a skeptical view of such audits, *see* Stephan Thernstrom & Abigail M. Thernstrom, America in Black and White: One Nation, Indivisible 447–49 (New York: Simon & Schuster 1997).

5. Marianne Bertrand & Sendhil Mullainathan, *Are Emily and Brendan More Employable than Lakisha and Jamal? A Field Experiment on Labor Market Discrimination* (Working paper, Nov. 18, 2002, on file with author).

6. For example, minorities are severely underrepresented, relative to their presence in both the population and the profession as a whole, in major law firms. *See* David B. Wilkins

& G. Mitu Gulati, *Reconceiving the Tournament of Lawyers: Tracking, Seeding, and Information Control in the Internal Labor Markets of Elite Law Firms*, 84 VA. L. REV. 1581 (1998); Alex M. Johnson, Jr., *The Underrepresentation of Minorities in the Legal Profession: A Critical Race Theorist's Perspective*, 95 MICH. L. REV. 1005, 1007–21 (1997).

7. *See* FEDERAL GLASS CEILING COMM'N, U.S. DEP'T OF LABOR, GOOD FOR BUSINESS: MAKING FULL USE OF THE NATION'S HUMAN CAPITAL 12 (1995). For example, black workers are significantly overrepresented, relative to their share of the workforce (10.7%), in service occupations (17.2%), particularly nurses' aides and orderlies (33.2%) and cleaning and building services (22.8%). *See* STATISTICAL ABSTRACT OF THE UNITED STATES 1997 412 (Washington, D.C.: U.S. Dep't of Commerce 1998). Hispanic workers are significantly overrepresented among service occupations (13.7%), especially private household workers (26.2%), janitors (19.7%), and farm workers (37.3%).

8. For an overview of the employment status of black workers from 1940 to 1990, *see* THERNSTROM & THERNSTROM, *supra* note 4, at 184–89; *see also* John J. Donohue III & Peter Siegelman, *The Changing Nature of Employment Discrimination Litigation*, 43 STAN. L. REV. 983, 1010–11 (1991).

9. For 1975, *see* U.S. Equal Employment Opportunity Commission, Occupational Employment in Private Industry by Race/Ethnic Group and Sex and by Industry, United States, 1975 (Participation Rate). For 2001, *see* U.S. Equal Employment Opportunity Commission, Occupational Employment in Private Industry by Race/Ethnic Group and Sex and by Industry, United States, 2000 (Participation Rate) *available at* http://www.eeoc.gov/stats/ jobpat/2001/national/html. These figures cover all private sector employers required to file reports with the Equal Employment Opportunity Commission, including all those with 100 or more employees. See U.S. Equal Employment Opportunity Commission, Job Patterns for Minorities and Women in Private Industry, 1998: Technical Notes, *available at* http://www.eeoc.gov/stats/jobpat/technotes.html (last visited 6/1/2003).

10. *See* WILLIAM JULIUS WILSON, WHEN WORK DISAPPEARS: THE WORLD OF THE NEW URBAN POOR (New York: Alfred A. Knopf 1996) [hereinafter WILSON, WHEN WORK DISAPPEARS].

11. See chapter 1.

12. *See* John J. Donohue III & James J. Heckman, *The Law and Economics of Racial Discrimination in Employment: Re-Evaluating Federal Civil Rights Policy*, 79 GEO. L.J. 1713 (1991) [hereinafter Donohue & Heckman, *Law & Economics*]; John J. Donohue III & James J. Heckman, *Continuous Versus Episodic Change: The Impact of Civil Rights Policy on the Economic Status of Blacks*, 29 J. ECON. LITERATURE 1603 (1991) [hereinafter Donohue & Heckman, *Continuous vs. Episodic*]; James J. Heckman & J. Hoult Verkerke, *Racial Disparity and Employment Discrimination Law: An Economic Perspective*, 8 YALE L. & POL'Y REV. 276 (1990).

13. *See* WILSON, WHEN WORK DISAPPEARS, *supra* note 10; WILLIAM JULIUS WILSON, THE BRIDGE OVER THE RACIAL DIVIDE: RISING INEQUALITY AND COALITION POLITICS 46–50 (Berkeley: U. Cal. Press 1999) [hereinafter WILSON, BRIDGE].

14. John O. Calmore, *Race/ism Lost and Found: The Fair Housing Act at Thirty*, 52 U. MIAMI L. REV. 1067, 1071 (1998).

15. *See* GARY ORFIELD ET AL., DISMANTLING DESEGREGATION: THE QUIET REVERSAL OF BROWN V. BOARD OF EDUCATION 53–71 (New York: New Press 1996).

16. *See* DOUGLAS S. MASSEY & NANCY A. DENTON, AMERICAN APARTHEID: SEGREGATION AND THE MAKING OF THE UNDERCLASS 83–113 (Cambridge, Mass.: Harvard U.P. 1993). Studies, including those using "testers"—matched pairs of black and white applicants—still find high levels of discrimination in the housing market. *See* Aleinikoff, *supra* note 3, at 336–37. On the low visibility of most modern housing discrimination, see Richard H. Sander,

Comment, *Individual Rights and Demographic Realities: The Problem of Fair Housing*, 82 Nw. U. L. Rev. 874, 892 (1988).

17. While both black and white people express a growing preference for living in "integrated" neighborhoods, whites tend to prefer, and to define as "integrated," a neighborhood that is about 20% black, while blacks tend to prefer about a 50–50 mix. *See* Massey & Denton, *supra* note 16, at 93; Thernstrom & Thernstrom, *supra* note 4, at 229. Whites thus tend to move out of neighborhoods as black families move in well before the 50% threshold and in spite of their expressed preference for an "integrated" neighborhood, thus contributing to neighborhoods that are more segregated than either group prefers. *See* Abraham Bell & Gideon Parchomovsky, *The Integration Game*, 100 Colum. L. Rev. 1965 (2000). On the premium paid for white neighborhoods, *see* Calmore, *supra* note 14, at 1101.

18. John J. Heldrich Center for Workforce Development, A Workplace Divided: How Americans View Discrimination and Race on the Job, at 17, 33 (New Brunswick, N.J.: Rutgers U. 2002) (hereinafter Heldrich Report).

19. On the difficulty of eliciting white attitudes on racial issues through surveys, *see* Paul M. Sniderman & Edward G. Carmines, Reaching beyond Race (Cambridge, Mass.: Harvard U.P. 1997).

20. Heldrich Report, *supra* note 18, at 37.

21. *See, e.g.,* Roy L. Brooks, Integration or Separation? A Strategy for Racial Equality (Cambridge, Mass.: Harvard U.P. 1996).

22. Derrick Bell, *Serving Two Masters: Integration Ideals and Client Interests in School Desegregation Litigation*, 85 Yale L.J. 470 (1976).

23. Missouri v. Jenkins, 515 U.S. 70, 114 (1995) (Thomas, J., concurring). *See also* Alex M. Johnson, Bid Whist, Tonk, *and* United States v. Fordice: *Why Integrationism Fails African-Americans Again*, 81 Cal. L. Rev. 1401 (1993).

24. They may choose to remain in black urban neighborhoods, *see* Calmore, *supra* note 14, at 1105–08, or to join a small exodus to majority-black suburbs, *see* Sheryll D. Cashin, *Middle-Class Black Suburbs and the State of Integration: A Post-Integrationist Vision for Metropolitan America*, 86 Cornell L. Rev. 729 (2001).

25. Calmore, *supra* note 14, at 1107.

26. Regina Austin, *"Not Just for the Fun of It": Governmental Restraints on Black Leisure, Social Inequality, and the Privatization of Public Space*, 71 S. Cal. L. Rev. 667 (1998).

27. Professors John Powell and John Calmore, for example, have called for a recommitment to genuine integration of schools and neighborhoods. *See* Calmore, *supra* note 14; John A. Powell, *Living and Learning: Linking Housing and Education*, 80 Minn. L. Rev. 749 (1996).

28. *See generally* Scott L. Cummings, *Community Economic Development as a Progressive Politics: Toward a Grassroots Movement for Economic Justice*, 54 Stan. L. Rev. 399, 410–13 (2001); Harold Cruse, The Crisis of the Negro Intellectual 19, 175–76 (New York: Morrow 1967).

29. Sam Fulwood III, Waking from the Dream: My Life in the Black Middle Class 204–05 (New York: Anchor 1996) (quoting a resident of Brook Glen, a predominantly black suburb of Atlanta).

30. *See* Calmore, *supra* note 14, at 1106–08. *See also* Cashin, *supra* note 24, at 747–50.

31. One commentator argues that this "false harmony" is invidious in its reassuring quality. Paul Farhi, *TV's Skin-Deep Take on Race; False Harmony, Not Lack of Black Shows, Called Problem*, Wash. Post, Feb. 13, 2000, at G-1.

32. William Kornblum, Blue Collar Community 36–67 (Chicago: U. Chicago Press 1974).

33. *Id.* at 66.

34. "'Whites' included Poles, Italians, Irish, Portuguese, and white Southerners; 'Hispanics' consisted of Argentinian, Puerto Rican, and Dominican workers; 'blacks' included Haitians and Jamaicans as well as native-born Americans from both the South and the North." RICK FANTASIA, CULTURES OF SOLIDARITY: CONSCIOUSNESS, ACTION, AND CONTEMPORARY AMERICAN WORKERS 77 (Berkeley: U. Cal. Press 1988).

35. *Id.* at 77.

36. *Id.* at 79.

37. Although there was rarely overt racial tension in mixed groups of workers, even white "workers who had worked closely with, been on friendly terms with, and . . . staunchly defended black workers in the plant" sometimes expressed racial animosity or used racial epithets among white co-workers. *Id.*

38. *Id.* at 92.

39. LIZABETH COHEN, MAKING A NEW DEAL (New York: Cambridge U.P. 1990).

40. *Id.* at 337.

41. *Id.* at 340–41.

42. *Id.* at 337.

43. For an analysis of the legal constraints such efforts face, *see* Marion Crain, *Whitewashed Labor Law, Skinwalking Unions,* 23 BERKELEY J. EMP. & LAB. L. 211 (2002).

44. GUINIER & TORRES, *supra* note 1, at 131–35.

45. *Id.* at 132.

46. *Id.* at 133.

47. *Id.* at 133.

48. *Id.* at 101 (citing Martha Mahoney, The Anti-Transformation Cases, September 16, 1999 (unpublished manuscript) (on file with author).

49. *See* GORDON W. ALLPORT, THE NATURE OF PREJUDICE (2d ed., Garden City, N.J.: Doubleday 1958); GUNNAR MYRDAL, AN AMERICAN DILEMMA: THE NEGRO PROBLEM AND MODERN DEMOCRACY (New York: Harper & Brothers 1944).

50. ALLPORT, *supra* note 49, at 264.

51. *Id.* at 267.

52. *See* Norman Miller & Marilynn B. Brewer, *The Social Psychology of Desegregation: An Introduction, in* GROUPS IN CONTACT: THE PSYCHOLOGY OF DESEGREGATION 1, 3 (Norman Miller & Marilynn Brewer eds., Orlando: Academic Press 1984).

53. *See* H. D. FORBES, ETHNIC CONFLICT: COMMERCE, CULTURE, AND THE CONTACT HYPOTHESIS 27, 48–51, 132 (New Haven: Yale U.P. 1997); Mary R. Jackman & Marie Crane, *"Some of My Best Friends Are Black . . .": Interracial Friendship and Whites' Racial Attitudes,* 50 PUB. OPINION Q. 459 (1986). Sigelman and Welch acknowledge that prior empirical results had been mixed; some involved situations of forced or limited interaction, artificially induced antagonisms, or other conditions that departed from the desiderata of the contact hypothesis. *See* Lee Sigelman & Susan Welch, *The Contact Hypothesis Revisited: Black–White Interaction and Positive Racial Attitudes,* 71 SOC. FORCES 781, 781–82 (1993).

54. Calmore, *supra* note 14, at 1121.

55. See Thomas F. Pettigrew, *Intergroup Contact Theory,* 49 ANN. REV. PSYCH. 65, 68–69 (1998) [hereinafter Pettigrew, *Intergroup*]; Lee Sigelman et al., *Making Contact? Black–White Social Interaction in an Urban Setting,* 101 AM. J. SOC. 1306, 1307 (1996) [hereinafter *Making Contact*].

56. FORBES, *supra* note 53, at 111.

57. *See id.* at 115; *cf.* THOMAS F. PETTIGREW, RACIALLY SEPARATE OR TOGETHER? 275 (New York: McGraw-Hill 1971) [hereinafter Pettigrew, SEPARATE]; Jackman & Crane, *supra* note 53, at 461; Forbes, *supra* note 53, at 22–24; David W. Johnson, Roger Johnson, &

Geoffrey Maruyama, *Goal Interdependence and Interpersonal Attraction in Heterogeneous Classrooms: A Metanalysis, in* GROUPS IN CONTACT, *supra* note 52, at 187.

58. *See* Pettigrew, *Intergroup, supra* note 55, at 76. According to Pettigrew, "[m]ost studies report positive contact effects, even in situations lacking key conditions." *Id.* at 68. One major study, for example,

> consistently found that interracial friendships decrease blacks' perceptions of racial hostility and that interracial neighborhood contacts decrease whites' perceptions of hostility. Both interracial friendships and neighborhood contacts increase whites' desire for racial integration. . . . In some instances, the positive effects of interracial contact are modest, but even these modest effects, aggregated over millions of black and white Americans, have the potential to ease the prevailing climate of race relations. And in some instances, the positive effects of interracial contact are substantial.

Sigelman & Welch, *supra* note 53, at 793; *see also* Daniel A. Powers & Christopher G. Ellison, *Interracial Contact and Black Racial Attitudes: The Contact Hypothesis and Selectivity Bias*, 74 SOC. FORCES 205, 213, 220–21 (1995); Christopher G. Ellison & Daniel A. Powers, *The Contact Hypothesis and Racial Attitudes among Black Americans*, 75 SOC. SCI. Q. 385, 395–96 (1994); Jackman & Crane, *supra* note 53, at 470 (1986).

59. *See, e.g.*, RUPERT BROWN, PREJUDICE: ITS SOCIAL PSYCHOLOGY 245 (Cambridge, Mass.: Blackwell 1995); B. Ann Bettencourt et al., *Cooperation and the Reduction of Intergroup Bias: The Role of Reward Structure and Social Orientation*, 28 J. EXPERIM. SOC. PSYCH. 301, 302 (1992); Marilynn B. Brewer & Norman Miller, *Beyond the Contact Hypothesis: Theoretical Perspectives on Desegregation, in* GROUPS IN CONTACT, *supra* note 52; S. W. Cook, *Cooperative Interaction in Multiethnic Contexts, in* GROUPS IN CONTACT, *supra* note 52, at 159.

60. Sigelman et al., *Making Contact, supra* note 55, at 1317.

61. *See* CHARLES C. MOSKOS & JOHN SIBLEY BUTLER, ALL THAT WE CAN BE: BLACK LEADERSHIP AND RACIAL INTEGRATION THE ARMY WAY (New York: Basic Books 1996).

62. Pettigrew, *Intergroup, supra* note 55, at 79. The study is reported in Cook, *supra* note 59.

63. Forty percent of the subjects (as compared to 12% of controls) showed "impressive change of potential practical significance." Cook, *supra* note 59, at 156–60.

64. *See generally* Linda H. Krieger, *Civil Rights Perestroika: Intergroup Relations after Affirmative Action*, 86 CAL. L. REV. 1251 (1998) [hereinafter Krieger, *Civil Rights Perestroika*]; Linda H. Krieger, *The Content of Our Categories: A Cognitive Bias Approach to Discrimination and Equal Employment Opportunity*, 47 STAN. L. REV. 1161, 1186–1211 (1995) [hereinafter Krieger, *Content of Our Categories*] (collecting and analyzing studies).

65. Malcolm Gladwell, *The Subtler Shades of Racism: Private Emotions Lag Behind Public Discourse*, WASH. POST, July 15, 1991, at A3; Calmore, *supra* note 14, at 1087–92. *See generally* Samuel L. Gaertner & John F. Dovidio, *The Aversive Form of Racism, in* PREJUDICE, DISCRIMINATION, AND RACISM 61 (John F. Dovidio & Samuel L. Gaertner eds., Orlando: Academic Press 1986).

66. Cited in Gladwell, *supra* note 65.

67. *See* Gary Blasi, *Advocacy against the Stereotype: Lessons from Cognitive Social Psychology*, 49 UCLA L. REV. 1241 (2002); Krieger, *Content of Our Categories, supra* note 64; Krieger, *Civil Rights Perestroika, supra* note 64; Charles R. Lawrence III, *The Id, the Ego, and Equal Protection: Reckoning with Unconscious Racism*, 39 STAN. L. REV. 317 (1987).

68. Krieger, *Content of Our Categories, supra* note 64, at 1198. "Social cognition theory" is closely related to theories of "social identification" and "social categorization," which posit that individuals seek to maintain high self-esteem in part by comparing themselves, and the

groups to which they see themselves as belonging ("in-groups"), to others ("out-groups"); and that they tend to perceive the in-group as more attractive than the out-group, and to perceive behaviors of in-group and out-group members as fitting those preconceptions. *See* Katherine Y. Williams & Charles A. O'Reilly III, *Demography and Diversity in Organizations: A Review of 40 Years of Research*, 20 RESEARCH IN ORG. BEHAVIOR 77, 83–84 (1998).

69. Krieger, *Content of Our Categories, supra* note 64, at 1188.

70. *Id.* at 1192–93. Most striking is the operation of these biases between artificially formed groups to which subjects are arbitrarily assigned. In these "minimal group" experiments, pioneered by Henri Tajfel, individuals may be grouped according to a supposed (but nonexistent) tendency to overestimate or underestimate the size of dots, for example. *See, e.g.*, Henri Tajfel et al., *Social Categorization and Intergroup Behaviour*, 1 EUR. J. SOC. PSYCHOL. 149, 154–55 (1971). Obviously, social groups that are further burdened with long-standing, learned cultural stereotypes suffer from more powerful biases. *See* Krieger, *Content of Our Categories, supra* note 64, at 1199–1211.

71. *See* Williams & O'Reilly, *supra* note 68, at 85.

72. *See* Krieger, *Content of Our Categories, supra* note 64; Susan Sturm, *Race, Gender, and the Law in the Twenty-first Century Workplace: Some Preliminary Observations*, 1 U. PA. J. OF LAB. & EMPL. L. 639, 646–50 (1998).

73. For an argument that they do not, *see* Amy L. Wax, *Discrimination as Accident*, 74 IND. L.J. 1129 (1999).

74. The Supreme Court recognized the problem of unconscious bias in subjective employment decisions in Watson v. Fort Worth Bank & Trust, 487 U.S. 977 (1988), and at the same time underscored the high threshold for what counts for courts as "conscious" and intentional discrimination:

> [E]ven if one assumed that [intentional] discrimination can be adequately policed through disparate treatment analysis, the problem of subconscious stereotypes and prejudices would remain. In this case, for example, petitioner was apparently told at one point that the teller position [which petitioner had sought and been denied several times] was a big responsibility with "a lot of money . . . for blacks to have to count." . . . Such remarks may not prove discriminatory intent, but they do suggest a lingering form of the problem that Title VII was enacted to combat.

Id. At 990. The characterization of this overtly biased comment as an example of "subconscious stereotypes and prejudices" suggests the difficulty of proving discriminatory intent.

75. Title VII reaches mainly "intentional discrimination"—decisions that are motivated in part by the prohibited trait. The law reaches some practices with a "disparate impact" on minorities. However, the doctrine makes it extremely difficult to challenge subjective decision-making processes without proof of discriminatory motive.

76. *See* Williams & O'Reilly, *supra* note 68, at 116.

77. *Id.* at 120.

78. *Id.*

79. For an overview of this research, see Irene Blair, *The Malleability of Automatic Stereotypes and Prejudice*, 6 PERS. SOC. PSYCH. REV. 242 (2002).

80. Williams & O'Reilly, *supra* note 68, at 119.

81. On the role of "salience," *see, e.g.*, Bettencourt et al., *supra* note 59, at 302–03; Marilynn B. Brewer, *Managing Diversity: The Role of Social Identities, in* DIVERSITY IN WORK TEAMS: RESEARCH PARADIGMS FOR A CHANGING WORKPLACE 47, 56 (Susan E. Jackson & Marian N. Rudman eds., Washington, D.C.: American Psychological Ass'n. 1995). For a summary of evidence concerning biases toward "token" group members, see Krieger, *Content of Our Categories, supra* note 64, at 1193–95. On the other hand, research on the effects of *proportional* representation has reached mixed results. *See* David A. Thomas & Robin D.

Ely, *Cultural Diversity at Work: The Effects of Diversity Perspectives on Work Group Processes and Outcomes*, 46 ADMIN. SCI. Q. 229 (2001).

82. *See, e.g.*, Brewer, *Managing Diversity, supra* note 80, at 60–62, 65; Amy Marcus-Newhall et al., *Cross-cutting Category Membership with Role Assignment: A Means of Reducing Intergroup Bias*, 32 BRIT. J. OF SOC. PSYCH. 125 (1993).

83. C. P. Alderfer, *An Intergroup Perspective on Group Dynamics, in* HANDBOOK OF ORGANIZATIONAL BEHAVIOR 190–219 (Jay William Lorsch ed., Englewood Cliffs, N.J.: Prentice-Hall, 1987).

84. *See* Thomas & Ely, *supra* note 81. Thomas and Ely refer to this as the "integration-and-learning perspective" on diversity and distinguish that from the "discrimination-and-fairness perspective" in which diversity is valued as evidence of fair and equal treatment, and the "access-and-legitimacy perspective," in which diversity is a tool in reaching diverse client and customer groups. *See* David A. Thomas & Robin D. Ely, *Making Differences Matter: A New Paradigm for Managing Diversity*, HARV. BUS. REV. 79–90 (Sept.–Oct. 1996).

85. *See* Karen A. Jehn, *Managing Workteam Diversity, Conflict, and Productivity: A New Form of Organizing in the Twenty-first Century Workplace*, 1 U. PA. J. LAB. & EMPL. L. 473 (1998).

86. *See* Sturm, *supra* note 72, at 644, 659–76.

87. *See, e.g.*, ROY L. BROOKS, INTEGRATION OR SEPARATION? A STATEGY FOR RACIAL EQUALITY (Cambridge, Mass.: Harvard U.P. 1996); ALPHONSO PINKNEY, THE MYTH OF BLACK PROGRESS (New York: Cambridge U.P. 1984); ELLIS COSE, THE RAGE OF A PRIVILEGED CLASS (New York: Harper Collins 1993); JOE R. GEAGIN & MELVIN P. SIKES, LIVING WITH RACISM: THE BLACK MIDDLE-CLASS EXPERIENCE (Boston: Beacon Press 1994).

88. *See* John O. Calmore, *Random Notes of an Integration Warrior*, 81 MINN. L. REV. 1441 (1997).

89. For a series of illuminating articles exploring the relationship between these tensions, and the extra "work" of performing or denying one's identity, and antidiscrimination law, *see, e.g.*, Devon W. Carbado & Mitu Gulati, *Conversations at Work*, 79 OR. L. REV. 103 (2000); Devon W. Carbado & Mitu Gulati, *Working Identity*, 85 CORNELL L. REV. 1259 (2000); Devon W. Carbado & Mitu Gulati, *Interactions at Work: Remembering David Charney*, 17 HARV. BLACK LETTER L.J. 13 (2001).

90. This point was made decades ago by Karl Llewellyn, *What Law Cannot Do for Inter-Racial Peace*, 3 VILL. L. REV. 30 (1957), in which he recognized the law's limited capacity to "'legislate' a change of heart or . . . friendship or even tolerance," but saw great potential in the law's ability to integrate institutions—in particular, workplaces—in which people learn, in spite of their prejudices, to appreciate each other as individuals. *Id.* at 32.

Chapter 5

1. "Families," of course, come in many configurations. Given the focus here on the consequences of workplace relations between men and women, I have in mind primarily heterosexual cohabiting couples, married or not (though most of the data is on married couples).

2. *See* Francine Blau, Trends in the Well-Being of American Women, 1970–1995, National Bureau of Economic Research Working Paper No. 6206, 6–9 (1995); Claudia Goldin, *Monitoring Costs and Occupational Segregation by Sex: A Historical Analysis*, 4 J. LAB. ECON. 1, 24–25 (1986).

3. *See* BUREAU OF LABOR STATISTICS, U.S. Dep't of Labor, *Employment and Earnings*, Table 3 (2001), *available at* www.bls.gov/cps/cpsaat.3.pdf; BUREAU OF LABOR STATISTICS,

U.S. Dep't of Labor, *Employment Characteristics of Families*, Table 5 (2001), *available at* www.bls.gov/news.release/famee.t05.htm.

4. *See* David Leonhardt, *Gap Between Pay of Men and Women Smallest on Record*, N.Y. TIMES, Feb. 7, 2003, at A1 (reporting on Bureau of Labor Statistics report on 2002 wage differentials). *See also* Blau, *supra* note 2, at 18; Goldin, *supra* note 2, at 58–59; Jane Friesen, *Alternative Economic Perspectives on the Use of Labor Market Policies to Redress the Gender Gap in Compensation*, 82 GEO. L.J. 31, 31 n. 1 (1994); Sharon M. Oster, *Is There a Policy Problem?: The Gender Wage Gap*, 82 GEO. L.J. 109, 111 (1994).

5. *See* FRANCINE D. BLAU & MARIANNE A. FERBER, THE ECONOMICS OF WOMEN, MEN AND WORK 134–37 (Englewood Cliffs, N.J.: Prentice-Hall 1986); Oster, *supra* note 4, at 111. The greater continuity of workforce participation of men appears to stem largely from childbearing and related responsibilities that fall predominantly on women, along with employer policies that make it difficult to reconcile these responsibilities with continuing advancement at work. *See* Samuel Issacharoff & Elyse Rosenblum, *Women and the Workplace: Accommodating the Demands of Pregnancy*, 91 COLUM. L. REV. 2154 (1994).

6. Kristin McCue & Manuelita Ureta, *Women in the Workplace: Recent Economic Trends*, 4 TEX. J. OF WOMEN & L. 125 (1995).

7. U.S. DEP'T OF LABOR, GOOD FOR BUSINESS: MAKING FULL USE OF THE NATION'S HUMAN CAPITAL: A FACT-FINDING REPORT OF THE FEDERAL GLASS CEILING COMMISSION, DAILY LAB. REP., Mar. 17, 1995 (Special Supp. DLR No. 52). *See also* Christine Jolls, *Is There a Glass Ceiling?*, 25 HARV. WOMEN'S L.J. 1 (2002).

8. *See generally* BARBARA GUTEK, SEX AND THE WORKPLACE: THE IMPACT OF SEXUAL BEHAVIOR AND HARASSMENT ON WOMEN, MEN AND ORGANIZATIONS 42–60 (San Francisco, Cal.: Jossey-Bass 1985); CATHARINE MACKINNON, SEXUAL HARASSMENT OF WORKING WOMEN: A CASE OF SEX DISCRIMINATION (San Francisco: Jossey-Bass 1979); James E. Gruber, *The Impact of Male Work Environments and Organizational Policies on Women's Experiences of Sexual Harassment*, 12 GENDER & SOC'Y 301, 306 (1998).

9. *See, e.g.*, MARY LINDENSTEIN WALSHOK, BLUE-COLLAR WOMEN: PIONEERS ON THE MALE FRONTIER 158, 168–70, 186, 204 (Garden City, N.Y.: Anchor Books 1981); Elvia R. Arriola, "*What's the Big Deal?" Women in the New York City Construction Industry and Sexual Harassment Law, 1970–85*, 22 COLUM. HUM. RTS. L. REV. 21 (1990); Vicki Schultz, *Reconceptualizing Sexual Harassment*, 107 YALE L.J. 1683 (1998) [hereinafter Schultz, *Reconceptualizing*].

10. Jane Gross, *Girls' Schools Teach Dollars and Sense*, N.Y. TIMES, Mar. 17, 2003, at A1.

11. *See* Francine D. Blau, Patricia Simpson, & Deborah Anderson, *Continuing Progress? Trends in the Occupational Segregation in the United States over the 1970s and 1980s*, 4 FEMINIST ECONOMICS 29, 34 (1998).

12. *Id.* at 53, 61–63.

13. *See* ROSABETH MOSS KANTOR, MEN AND WOMEN OF THE CORPORATION (2d ed., New York: Basic Books 1993); Elizabeth Chambliss & Christopher Uggen, *Men and Women of Elite Law Firms: Reevaluating Kanter's Legacy*, 25 LAW & SOC. INQUIRY 41 (2000).

14. Blau et al., *supra* note 10.

15. *See* Anne E. Winkler, *Earnings of Husbands and Wives in Dual-Earner Families*, 121 MONTHLY LAB. REV., Apr. 1998 at 42–44 (presenting data from Current Population Survey (CPS)).

16. A recent survey of the literature finds scant empirical research on the economic consequences of sex discrimination laws. David Neumark & Wendy A. Stock, The Effects of Race and Sex Discrimination Laws, NBER Working Paper Series, Working Paper 8215, at 4–5 (2001), *available at* http://www.nber.org/papers/w8215. Their own study illustrates the

difficulties of research on this question. They compare women's progress in each state based on the timing of the state's enactment of equal pay legislation; they cannot test for the effects of broader antidiscrimination laws because almost no states had such laws before Title VII was enacted. Equal pay laws alone raise the cost of female workers, yet leave employers free to discriminate in hiring, job placement, and promotions. *Id.* at 26. Not surprisingly, they find that equal pay laws alone had a negative effect on women's employment. *Id.* at 30.

17. *See* Blau, *supra* note 2, at 13–14, 26.

18. Note, though, that the Family and Medical Leave Act was meant partly to allow mothers to maintain continuity and career advancement over the period of childbirth. Some data suggests that it has had this effect. *See id.* at 49.

19. As of 1990 women still made up less than 5% of nearly all occupations within the construction trades. *See* Blau et al., *supra* note 10, at 67–68.

20. SUSAN EISENBERG, WE'LL CALL YOU IF WE NEED YOU: EXPERIENCES OF WOMEN WORKING CONSTRUCTION 16–17 (Ithaca, N.Y.: Cornell U. Press 1998). *See also id.* at 87–107. Quote used by permission of the publisher.

21. JULIUS GETMAN, THE BETRAYAL OF LOCAL 14: PAPERWORKERS, POLITICS, AND PERMANENT REPLACEMENTS 8 (Ithaca, N.Y.: Cornell U. Press 1998).

22. Suzanne E. Tallichet, *Gendered Relations in the Mines and the Division of Labor Underground,* 9 GENDER & SOC. 697, 709 (1995).

23. Such tales are indeed too numerous to recount. But samples can be found in EISENBERG, *supra* note 20; Schultz, *Reconceptualizing, supra* note 9; Tallichet, *supra* note 22, at 701–09.

24. *See* Schultz, *Reconceptualizing, supra* note 9, at 1690; Vicki Schultz, *Telling Stories about Women and Work: Judicial Interpretations of Sex Segregation in the Workplace in Title VII Cases Raising the Lack of Interest Argument,* 103 HARV. L. REV. 1750, 1832–39 (1990) [hereinafter Schultz, *Telling Stories*].

25. *See* GUTEK, *supra* note 8.

26. *See* Vicki Schultz, *The Sanitized Workplace,* 112 YALE L.J.—(2003) [hereinafter *Sanitized Workplace*].

27. *See* Cynthia L. Estlund, *Work and Family: How Women's Progress at Work (and Employment Discrimination Law) May Be Transforming the Family,* 21 COMP. LAB. L. & POL'Y J. 467–500 (2000).

28. *See* ROBERT D. PUTNAM, BOWLING ALONE: THE COLLAPSE AND REVIVAL OF AMERICAN COMMUNITY 195 (New York: Simon & Schuster 2000) [hereinafter PUTNAM, BOWLING ALONE]; Nancy Burns, Kay Lehman Schlozman & Sidney Verba, *The Public Consequences of Private Inequality: Family Life and Citizen Participation,* 91 AM. POL. SCI. REV. 373 (1997).

29. *See, e.g.,* KAY DEAUX, THE BEHAVIOR OF WOMEN AND MEN 24–34 (Monterey, Cal.: Brooks/Cole Pub. Co. 1976); Randi L. Hagen & Arnold Kahn, *Discrimination against Competent Women,* 5 J. APP. SOC. PSYCH. 362, 371–74 (1975); David Hamilton, *Some Thoughts on the Cognitive Approach, in* COGNITIVE PROCESSES IN STEREOTYPING AND INTERGROUP BEHAVIOR 333, 340 (D. Hamilton ed., Hillsdale, N.J.: L. Erlbaum Associates 1981).

30. *See, e.g.,* Helen T. Palmer & Jo Ann Lee, *Female Workers' Acceptance in Traditionally Male-Dominated Blue-Collar Jobs,* 22 SEX ROLES 607, 623 (1990); Deepti Bhatnagar & Ranjini Swamy, *Attitudes toward Women as Managers: Does Interaction Make a Difference?,* 48 HUM. RELA. 1285, 1297 (1995).

31. *See, e.g.,* Patrice Rosenthal, *Gender and Managers' Causal Attributions for Subordinate Performance: A Field Story,* 34 SEX ROLES 1, 11 (1996); Jerome Adams, Robert W. Rice & Debra Instone, *Follower Attitudes toward Women and Judgments Concerning Performance by Female and Male Leaders,* 27 ACAD. OF MGMT. J. 636, 640–41 (1984).

32. Rosenthal, *supra* note 31, at 5.

33. Richard N. Osborn & William M. Vickers, *Sex Stereotypes: An Artifact in Leader Behavior and Subordinate Satisfaction Analyses,* 19 ACAD. OF MGMT. J. 439, 447 (1976). *See also* Rosenthal, *supra* note 31, at 12; Adams et al., *supra* note 31, at 641–42.

34. *See* MARY R. JACKMAN, THE VELVET GLOVE: PATERNALISM AND CONFLICT IN GENDER, CLASS, AND RACE RELATIONS 142–46 (Berkeley: U. Cal. Press 1994).

35. This observation and some of its implications were suggested by Professor Catharine MacKinnon.

36. *See* H. D. FORBES, ETHNIC CONFLICT: COMMERCE, CULTURE, AND THE CONTACT HYPOTHESIS 120 (New Haven: Yale U.P. 1997).

37. *See* Schultz, *Sanitized Workplace, supra* note 26; Schultz, *Reconceptualizing, supra* note 9.

38. Oncale v. Sundowner Offshore Services, Inc., 523 U.S. 75 (1998).

39. On the dynamics that lead employers to ban much more activity than Title VII would reach, *see* Eugene Volokh, *How Harassment Law Restricts Free Speech,* 47 RUTGERS L.J. 561 (1995). On how sexual expression in particular has come to be targetted, *see* Schultz, *Sanitized Workplace, supra* note 26.

40. Schultz, *Sanitized Workplace, supra* note 26.

41. The inclusion of "sex" in Title VII was proposed by Southern opponents of the bill hoping to insure its defeat. But the ploy's failure was partly due to earlier legislative moves in the direction of sex equality in employment. *See* Katherine M. Franke, *The Central Mistake of Sex Discrimination Law: The Disaggregation of Sex from Gender,* 144 U. PA. L. REV. 1, 12–25 (1995).

42. That is the view of, for example, Orlando Patterson. *See* ORLANDO PATTERSON, THE ORDEAL OF INTEGRATION: PROGRESS AND RESENTMENT IN AMERICA'S "RACIAL" CRISIS x–xi (Wash., D.C.: Civitas/Counterpoint 1997).

43. *See* John O. Calmore, *Race/ism Lost and Found: The Fair Housing Act at Thirty,* 52 U. MIAMI L. REV. 1067, 1108–17 (1998); Reynolds Farley & William H. Frey, *Changes in the Segregation of Whites from Blacks During the 1980s: Small Steps toward a More Integrated Society,* 59 Am. Soc. Rev. 23, 32 (1994).

44. *See* Xavier de Souza Briggs, Social Capital and Segregation: Race, Connections, and Inequality in America, John F. Kennedy School of Government, Harvard University, Faculty Research Working Paper Series, RWP02-011 (2002). *See also* ALEJANDRO PORTES & RUBÉN G. RUMBAUT, LEGACIES: THE STORY OF THE IMMIGRANT SECOND GENERATION 19–20 (Berkeley: U. Cal. Press 2001).

45. Regina Austin, *"Bad for Business": Contextual Analysis, Race Discrimination, and Fast Food,* 34 J. MARSHALL L. REV. 207, 218–19 (2000) (citing Carol B. Stack, *Beyond What Are Given as Givens: Ethnography and Critical Policy Analysis,* 25 ETHOS 191, 191 (1997)).

46. EEOC Guidelines provide that the existence of an English-only policy establishes a prima facie case of "disparate impact" under Title VII. *See* 29 C.F.R. § 1606.7(a) & (b) (1991). Some courts have required proof of disparate impact in the particular case, at least as to rules that cover work time only. *See, e.g.,* Garcia v. Spun Steak Co., 998 F.2d 1480 (9th Cir. 1993); Garcia v. Gloor, 618 F.2d 264 (5th Cir. 1980), *cert. denied,* 449 U.S. 1113 (1981). Such rules are in any event suspect under Title VII.

47. Some critics claim that bilingual education programs stall children's development of English-language skills and impede their full-fledged integration into economic and civic life as adults. Research has reached conflicting results. One recent nationwide study of bilingual education programs found that some such programs produced significantly better results than mainstream English-only immersion. *See* Wayne P. Thomas & Virginia P. Collier, A National Study of School Effectiveness for Language Minority Students' Long-

Term Academic Achievement (Center for Research on Education, Diversity, & Excellence, 2002), *available at* www.crede.ucsc.edu/research/llaa/1.1_es.html.

48. *See* Briggs, *supra* note 92. *See also* PORTES & RUMBAUT, *supra* note 92, at 19–20.

49. Thus, for example, employers may have to make room under their dress codes for religiously prescribed attire, head coverings, or facial hair. On the scope of the duty to accommodate, *see* Kent Greenawalt, *Title VII and Religious Liberty*, 33 LOY. U. CHI. L.J. 1, 16–29 (2001).

50. *See id.* at 31–32.

51. *See id.* at 21–22; Karen Engle, *The Persistence of Neutrality: The Failure of the Religious Accommodation Provision to Redeem Title VII*, 76 TEX. L. REV. 317, 392–406 (1997).

52. *See* Kenji Yoshino, *Covering*, 111 YALE L.J. 769 (2002); Kenji Yoshino, *Assimilationist Bias in Equal Protection: The Visibility Presumption and the Case of "Don't Ask, Don't Tell,"* 108 YALE L.J. 485 (1998).

53. *See* Yoshino, *Covering*, *supra* note 51, for a vivid story of "passing" on the job.

54. On state and municipal legislation, see Thomas H. Barnard & Timothy J. Downing, *Emerging Law on Sexual Orientation and Employment*, 29 U. MEM. L. REV. 555, 557–59 & nn. 5–8 (1999); Josia N. Drew, Note, *Caught Between the Scylla and Charybdis: Ameliorating the Course of Sexual Orientation Anti-discrimination Rights and Religious Free Exercise Rights in the Workplace*, 16 BYU J. PUB. L. 287, 292–93 & nn. 21–23 (2002). The proposed federal statute, The Employment Non-Discrimination Act of 2001 (S. 1284, 107th Cong. (2001); H.R. 2692, 107th Cong. (2001)), has gained substantial support in Congress. As of 2002, it had the support of 45 Senate co-sponsors and 193 House co-sponsors. See Jeremy S. Barber, *Re-orienting Sexual Harassment: Why Federal Legislation is Needed to Cure Same-Sex Sexual Harassment Law*, 52 AM. U. L. REV. 493 (2002).

55. In Professor Yoshino's terms, gays are less often required to "pass" as heterosexual, though they are still often required to "cover"—to "act straight" and to avoid overt assertion of homosexual identity—in order to gain acceptance. The demand to "cover" remains powerful and largely immune from moral and legal condemnation. This is a barrier faced by sexual and racial minorities alike. Black workers, for example, may be penalized for not "acting white" without this being recognized as a form of discrimination. See Yoshino, *Covering*, *supra* note 51. Some of these pressures are discussed in Chapter 4 above.

56. *See* Gregory M. Herek & John P. Capitanio, *Some of My Best Friends: Intergroup Contact, Concealable Stigma, and Heterosexuals' Attitudes Toward Gay Men and Lesbians*, 22 PERSONALITY & SOC. PSYCHOL. BULL. 412 (1996); Gregory M. Herek & Eric K. Glunt, *Interpersonal Contact and Heterosexuals' Attitudes Toward Gay Men: Results from a National Survey*, 30 J. SEX RES. 239 (1993).

57. In a May 2002 Gallup poll, 51% of respondents said that "homosexuality should be considered an accepted alternative lifestyle," compared to 34% in 1982, and that 52% said that "homosexual relations between consenting adults should . . . be legal," compared to 43% in 1977. See Frank Newport, *In Depth Analyses: Homosexuality*, GALLUP POLL NEWS, Sept. 2002. In another 2002 survey, 77% of respondents said that sexual orientation should not affect job opportunities and 50% favored the inclusion of sexual orientation in written non-discrimination policies. See Press Release, CBS Market Watch, *Survey: 40% of Gays Report Bias in the Workplace* (Sept. 12, 2002).

Chapter 6

1. ALEXIS DE TOCQUEVILLE, DEMOCRACY IN AMERICA 513 (George Lawrence trans., New York: Harper Perennial 1988).

2. *Id.* at 515.

3. *Id.* at 513–17, 523.

4. Robert D. Putnam, Bowling Alone: The Collapse and Revival of American Community 22 (New York: Simon & Schuster 2000) [hereinafter Putnam, Bowling Alone].

5. *Id.* at 23.

6. Tocqueville, *supra* note 1, at 515.

7. On the republican idea of "free labor," its schizophrenic evolution during the nineteenth century, and its legal significance, *see* William Forbath, *The Ambiguities of Free Labor: Labor and the Law in the Gilded Age*, 1985 Wis. L. Rev. 767 [hereinafter Forbath, *Ambiguities*].

8. I rely heavily in this section on two wonderful books by Albert Hirschman: Albert Hirschman, The Passions and the Interests: Political Arguments for Capitalism before Its Triumph (Princeton, N.J.: Princeton U.P. 1977) [hereinafter Hirschman, Passions]; Albert Hirschman, Rival Views of Market Society (New York: Viking 1986) [hereinafter Hirschman, Rival Views].

9. Montesquieu, De L'esprit des Lois 8, *quoted in* Hirschman, Rival Views, *supra* note 8, at 107.

10. Thomas Paine, The Rights of Man 215, *quoted in* Hirschman, Rival Views, *supra* note 8, at 108.

11. He feared that the untamed pursuit of material comfort would lead citizens to "find it a tiresome inconvenience to exercise political rights which distract them from industry" and the pursuit of wealth. Tocqueville, *supra* note 1, at 540.

12. *Id.* at 554–59.

13. Karl Marx, *Critique of the Gotha Programme, in* Basic Writings on Politics and Philosophy 119 (Lewis S. Feuer ed., Garden City, N.J.: Doubleday 1959).

14. Émile Durkheim, The Division of Labor in Society (W. D. Halls trans., New York: Free Press 1984) [hereinafter Durkheim, Division of Labor]; Émile Durkheim, Suicide: A Study in Sociology 378–82 (George Simpson ed., John A. Spaulding & George Simpson trans., Glencoe, Ill.: Free Press 1951).

15. Durkheim, Division of Labor, *supra* note 14, at 332–33.

16. *Id.* at 333.

17. *Id.* at 164. *See also id.* at 173.

18. *Id.* at 173.

19. *Id.* at 306.

20. *Id.* at 307.

21. *Id.* at 307–08.

22. Durkheim observed, presciently, that "[t]he economists would not have left this essential characteristic of the division of labour unclarified and as a result would not have lain it open to this undeserved reproach, if they had not reduced it to being only a way of increasing the efficiency of the social forces, but had seen it above all as a source of solidarity." *Id.* at 308.

23. *Id.* at liv.

24. *See id.* at liv–lv.

25. Durkheim thought that labor unions "represent[ed] the beginnings of an organisation by occupation," though "still in a rudimentary and amorphous form." *Id.* at xxxvi.

26. *Id.* at xxxv. The corporatist elements of Dorkheim's analysis entered the book in a later preface to the second edition.

27. John Dewey, The Public and Its Problems 212–13 (New York: H. Holt & Co. 1927) (emphasis added).

28. Some of Dewey's contemporaries were more forthcoming about the importance of "industrial democracy." *See, e.g.*, HERBERT CROLY, PROGRESSIVE DEMOCRACY (New York: Macmillan 1914). But Dewey is especially interesting for his parallel focus on the social integration and the importance of face-to-face interaction; the interest for me lies as much in what he did not say (about the link between social integration and workplace interaction) as in what he did.

29. DEWEY, *supra* note 27, at 211, 218.

30. *Id.* at 213.

31. *See* Roderick M. Hills, Jr., *Romancing the Town: Why We (Still) Need a Democratic Defense of City Power*, 113 HARV. L. REV. 2009 (2000) (reviewing GERALD E. FRUG, CITY MAKING: BUILDING COMMUNITIES WITHOUT BUILDING WALLS (Princeton, N.J.: Princeton U.P. 1999)).

32. Dewey's scattered writings on industrial democracy are reviewed in ROBERT B. WESTBROOK, JOHN DEWEY AND AMERICAN DEMOCRACY 49–50, 176–79, 192, 224–26 (Ithaca, N.Y.: Cornell U.P. 1991); and in Robert B. Westbrook, *Schools for Industrial Democrats: The Social Origins of John Dewey's Philosophy of Education*, 100 AM. J. OF EDUC. 401 (1992) [hereinafter Westbrook, *Schools for Industrial Democrats*]. Westbrook adduces ample evidence—much of it unpublished—that Dewey held radically anti-capitalist views that required, in place of the capitalist order, "a genuinely cooperative society where workers are in control of industry and finance as directly as possible." *Id.* at 415. When such views became seen as dangerously dissident, even within the academy, in the 1890s, he turned to educational philosophy and practice, and to the establishment of the Laboratory School at the University of Chicago, as a relatively safe place in which to develop and test out his ideas. *Id.* at 409–412. According to Westbrook, "[t]he Dewey school was above all an experiment in education for industrial democracy." *Id.* at 412.

33. *See generally* LIZABETH COHEN, MAKING A NEW DEAL: INDUSTRIAL WORKERS IN CHICAGO, 1919–1939 202–09 (New York: Cambridge U.P. 1990).

34. See especially the writings of William Forbath, *Ambiguities, supra* note 7; WILLIAM E. FORBATH, , LAW AND THE SHAPING OF THE AMERICAN LABOR MOVEMENT (Cambridge, Mass. : Harvard U.P. 1991); William Forbath, *Caste, Class, and Equal Citizenship*, 98 MICH. L. REV. 1 (1999).

35. *See* Mark Barenberg, *The Political Economy of the Wagner Act: Power, Symbol, and Workplace Cooperation*, 106 HARV. L. REV. 1379, 1410–14 (1993).

36. Barenberg shows, however, that Wagner himself viewed his labor legislation as part of a more ambitious "cooperationist" reconstruction of society. *Id.*

37. PUTNAM, BOWLING ALONE, *supra* note 4, at 19. Putnam finds that the term "social capital" has been "independently invented at least six times over the twentieth century, each time to call attention to the ways in which our lives are made more productive by social ties." *Id. See also* JAMES S. COLEMAN, FOUNDATIONS OF SOCIAL THEORY 300–21 (Cambridge, Mass.: Belknap Press 1990); Glenn Loury, *A Dynamic Theory of Racial Income Differences, in* WOMEN, MINORITIES, AND EMPLOYMENT DISCRIMINATION (Phyllis Ann Wallace & Annette A. LaMond eds., Lexington, Mass.: Lexington Books 1977).

38. Indeed, Putnam and like-minded contemporaries have been described as "neo-Durkheimian" in their emphasis on "the socialization of individuals into shared norms and cooperative societal action." Theda Skocpol & Morris P. Fiorina, *Making Sense of the Civic Engagement Debate, in* CIVIC ENGAGEMENT IN AMERICAN DEMOCRACY 13 (Theda Skocpol & Morris P. Fiorina eds., Washington, D.C.: Brookings 1999).

39. PUTNAM, BOWLING ALONE, *supra* note 4, at 171.

40. *Id.* at 182–83.

41. *Id.* at 296–349.

42. *Id.* at 31–147. Some commentators questioned Putnam's initial empirical case for "America's declining social capital," pointing especially to its neglect of volunteer activity, advocacy organizations, and connections on the Internet. *See, e.g.,* Everett C. Ladd, *The Data Just Don't Show Erosion of America's 'Social Capital',* Pub. Perspective, June/July 1996, at 1; Michael Schudson, *What If Civic Life Didn't Die?,* Am. Prospect, March/April 1996, at 17–20. In his book, Putnam casts a wider net and makes a persuasive case that many aspects of formal and informal associational life, as well as generalized social trust, have declined in the past few decades.

43. Putnam, Bowling Alone, *supra* note 4, at 92.

44. *Id.* at 87.

45. *Id.* at 362. *See also id.* at 407.

46. Verba et al. found that the workplace was a significant site for developing civic skills and a sense of political efficacy, especially for managerial and professional workers. *See* Sidney Verba et al., Voice and Equality: Civic Voluntarism in American Politics 312–13 (Cambridge, Mass.: Harvard U.P. 1993). *See also* Carole Pateman, Participation and Democratic Theory (Cambridge: Cambridge U.P. 1970). Recent evidence suggests that blue-collar workers cultivate civic skills in increasingly collaborative and communicative work processes. *See* Vicki Smith, Crossing the Great Divide: Worker Risk and Opportunity in the New Economy 69–72 (Ithaca, N.Y.: ILR Press 2001).

47. That it is not more central in Putnam's account in *Bowling Alone* appears to stem partly from the fact that "of all the domains of social and community connectedness surveyed . . . , systematic long-term evidence on workplace-based connections has proven the most difficult to find." Putnam, Bowling Alone, *supra* note 4, at 87. That fact alone tends to marginalize the subject of workplace ties in a study whose greatest strength is its careful analysis of "systematic long-term evidence" on social connections.

48. In the rise and fall of union membership in the last century, Putnam observes a striking parallel to the trajectory of organizational membership in other spheres. Putnam, Bowling Alone, *supra* note 4, at 80–81. But the dramatic rise of unionization began immediately after the enactment of the National Labor Relations Act, which sought to promote unionization, and its decline began soon after the enactment of the Taft-Hartley Act in 1947, which sought to curb the power and growth of unions.

49. Alejandro Portes & Patricia Landolt, *The Downside of Social Capital,* Am. Prospect, May–June 1996, at 18, 94.

50. Skepticism largely predominates in Putnam's fullest account of his thesis. See Bowling Alone, *supra* note 4, at 87–92. More recent work by Putnam and his collaborators is more sanguine about the potential contribution of workplace ties to the rebuilding of social capital. *See Better Together: Report of the Saguaro Seminar: Civic Engagement in America* (Kennedy School of Government, Harvard Univ. 2001).

51. Putnam, Bowling Alone, *supra* note 4, at 87, 319–21; Mark S. Granovetter, *The Strength of Weak Ties,* 78 Am. J. Soc. 1360–80 (1978).

52. Putnam, Bowling Alone, *supra* note 4, at 87, 92. *See also* Alan Wolfe, *Developing Civil Society: Can the Workplace Replace Bowling?,* 8 The Responsive Community 41, 45 (1998).

53. Putnam, Bowling Alone, *supra* note 4, at 92.

54. *See, e.g.,* Jürgen Habermas, Between Facts and Norms (Cambridge: Polity Press 1996), and the essays collected in two recent volumes, Deliberative Politics: Essays on Democracy and Disagreement (Stephen Macedo ed., New York: Oxford U.P. 1999) (hereinafter Deliberative Politics), and Deliberative Democracy: Essays on Reason and

POLITICS (James Bohman & William Rehg eds., Cambridge, Mass.: MIT Press 1997) (hereinafter DELIBERATIVE DEMOCRACY). The link between civil society and public discourse is discussed in HABERMAS, *supra*, at 366–73. For an "agnostic" view of the value of discourse, *see* Frederick Schauer, *Discourse and its Discontents*, 72 NOTRE DAME L. REV. 1309 (1997).

55. *See, e.g.*, Joshua Cohen, *Deliberation and Democratic Legitimacy, in* DELIBERATIVE DEMOCRACY, *supra* note 54, at 67–91 [hereinafter Cohen, *Deliberation*]; David Estlund, *Beyond Fairness and Deliberation: The Epistemic Dimension of Democratic Authority, in* DELIBERATIVE DEMOCRACY, *supra* note 54, at 173–204.

56. *See* James Bohman, *Deliberative Democracy and Effective Social Freedom: Capabilities, Resources, and Opportunities, in* DELIBERATIVE DEMOCRACY, *supra* note 54, at 321–47; Joshua Cohen, *Procedure and Substance in Deliberative Democracy, in* DELIBERATIVE DEMOCRACY, *supra* note 54, at 407–37 [hereinafter Cohen, *Procedure and Substance*]; Jack Knight and James Johnson, *What Sort of Equality Does Deliberative Democracy Require?, in* DELIBERATIVE DEMOCRACY, *supra* note 54, at 279–319.

57. *See* Jane Mansbridge, *Everyday Talk in the Deliberative System, in* DELIBERATIVE POLITICS, *supra* note 54, at 211.

58. *See* Robert Huckfeldt et al., *Political Environments, Cohesive Social Groups, and the Communication of Public Opinion*, 39 AM. J. POL. SCI. 1025, 1031–32 (1995); Bruce C. Straits, *Bringing Strong Ties Back In: Interpersonal Gateways to Political Information and Influence*, 55 PUBL. OP. Q. 432, 446 (1991).

59. I take here a conventional view of "politics" as consisting of the formal institutions of governance and activities designed to influence the election of representatives or the decisions of governmental actors. For a broader view of "politics" that includes citizens' direct efforts to improve public life and public spaces through "public work," *see* HARRY BOYTE & NANCY KARI, BUILDING AMERICA: THE DEMOCRATIC PROMISE OF PUBLIC WORK (Philadelphia: Temple U.P. 1996).

60. Voter turnout in presidential elections—the highest-drawing elections—has declined from about 60% to just about 50% since 1960. See PUTNAM, BOWLING ALONE, *supra* note 4, at 31–32. Other forms of political participation are downright exceptional. Since 1970, the percentage of voters—already a subset of citizens—who had attended a political meeting ranged from under 10% to under 6%, and the percentage who said they had worked for a political party ranged from about 7% to under 3%; both trends were downward. *Id.* at 39.

61. This claim is most central to those who hold to an "epistemic" conception of democracy: the view that democratic procedures are justified, at least in part, by their tendency to reach more just or true outcomes. *See, e.g.*, David Estlund, *supra* note 55; Iris Marion Young, *Difference as a Resource for Democratic Communication, in* DELIBERATIVE DEMOCRACY, *supra* note 54, at 400. But even pluralists may recognize that the free exchange of views produces outcomes that better reflect actual preferences. That is one of the fundamental premises of free speech theory. Its empirical accuracy is of course debatable. *See* Schauer, *supra* note 54, at 1316–24.

62. Iris Marion Young, *supra* note 61, at 385.

63. This point is emphasized by Huckfeldt et al., *supra* note 58: "When social communication occurs through weak ties, beyond the boundaries of cohesive groups, public opinion becomes more fully public," *id.* at 1028–29, and "more than the sum of its parts," *id.* at 1035.

64. Robert C. Post, *Racist Speech, Democracy, and the First Amendment*, 32 WM. & MARY L. REV. 267, 289 (1991). Post argues that, if workplace speech is to be protected by the First Amendment at all, "it will be on the basis of constitutional values other than democratic self-governance." *Id.* at 289 n. 113. *See also* Rodney A. Smolla, *Rethinking First Amendment Assumptions about Racist and Sexist Speech*, 47 WASH. & LEE L. REV. 171, 207 (1990).

65. See HABERMAS, *supra* note 54, at 299, 304–06.

66. Habermas himself is characteristically elusive on this point. In the main, public discourse takes place in civil society, which is "quite distinct from both state and economy alike." *Id.* at 301. Yet he disavows a spatial definition of these distinct spheres, and he recognizes that citizens experience needs and grievances chiefly in their roles as "employees and consumers, insured persons and patients, taxpayers and clients of bureaucracies . . ." *Id.* at 365–66.

> The communication channels of the public sphere are linked to private spheres—to the thick networks of interaction found in families and circles of friends as well as to the looser contacts with neighbors, work colleagues, acquaintances, and so on. . . . The threshold separating the private sphere from the public is not marked by a fixed set of issues or relationships but by *different conditions of communication.* [These differences] do not seal off the private from the public but only channel the flow of topics from the one sphere into the other. For the public sphere draws its impulses from the private handling of social problems that resonate in life histories.

Id. A fair reading of Habermas suggests that workplace and other economic relations have a "hard-wired" instrumental logic and are properly insulated from democracy-enhancing reforms. *See* William E. Forbath, *Habermas's Constitution: A History, Guide, and Critique,* 23 LAW & SOC. INQUIRY 969, 996–1007 (1998).

67. New York Times v. Sullivan, 376 U.S. 254, 270 (1964).

68. POST, *supra* note 64, at 147.

69. *Id.*; *see also id.* at 134–50.

70. *See* Frederick Schauer, *Talking as a Decision Procedure, in* DELIBERATIVE POLITICS, *supra* note 54, at 24.

Chapter 7

1. *See* Mark Tushnet, *The Constitution of Civil Society,* 75 CHI.-KENT L. REV. 379, 379–80 (2000).

2. *See id.* at 382–86. For a good introduction to the complications and paradoxes surrounding the concept of freedom of association, see Amy Gutmann, *Freedom of Association: An Introductory Essay, in* FREEDOM OF ASSOCIATION (Amy Gutmann, ed., Princeton, N.J.: Princeton U. Press 1998).

3. *See* Title VII, Civil Rights Act of 1964, 42 U.S.C. § 2000e (1994) (equal employment); Title VI, 42 U.S.C. § 2000d (education); Title II, 42 U.S.C. § 2000a (fair housing); Title VIII, 42 U.S.C. § 3604 (fair housing).

4. *See* Heart of Atlanta Motel, Inc. v. United States, 379 U.S. 241, 244 (1964). *But see* RICHARD A. EPSTEIN, FORBIDDEN GROUNDS: THE CASE AGAINST EMPLOYMENT DISCRIMINATION LAWS 11–12 (Cambridge, Mass.: Harvard U.P. 1992).

5. Already in 1972, 97% of white respondents said that they believed blacks should have equal opportunities in employment. *See* STEPHAN THERNSTROM & ABIGAIL M. THERNSTROM, AMERICA IN BLACK AND WHITE: ONE NATION, INDIVISIBLE (New York: Simon & Schuster 1997).

6. 468 U.S. 609, 617–18 (1984).

7. 530 U.S. 640 (2000).

8. Roberts, 468 U.S. at 628.

9. *Id.* at 618–19 (citations omitted).

10. *Id.* at 620.

11. *Id.* The Jaycees, by virtue of their size and lack of selectivity, were too close to the workplace end of the spectrum to claim the freedom of intimate association.

12. *Id.* at 622.

13. *Id.* at 623–24. Some commentators have criticized *Roberts* as giving too little weight to the intrinsic liberty interest in choosing one's associates. *See, e.g.,* George Kateb, *The Value of Association, in* FREEDOM OF ASSOCIATION, *supra* note 2 at 35, 41–42, 59; Nancy L. Rosenblum, *Compelled Association: Public Standing, Self-Respect, and the Dynamic of Exclusion, in* FREEDOM OF ASSOCIATION, *supra* note 2, at 76, 86–88.

14. *Roberts,* 468 U.S. at 656–57. The typical state or local "public accommodation" provisions tend to reach commercially oriented clubs. *See* New York State Club Ass'n, Inc. v. City of New York, 487 U.S. 1 (1988); Board of Dirs. of Rotary Int'l v. Rotary Club of Duarte, 481 U.S. 537 (1987).

15. *See* NANCY L. ROSENBLUM, MEMBERSHIP AND MORALS 86, 103 (Princeton, N.J.: Princeton U.P. 1998).

16. *See* United Steelworkers v. Weber, 443 U.S. 193, 202 (1979) (reviewing the legislative history of Title VII).

17. Paul A. Jargowsky, *Take the Money and Run: Economic Segregation in U.S. Metropolitan Areas,* 61 AM. SOC. REV. 984 (1996).

18. *See* San Antonio Indep. Sch. Dist. v. Rodriguez, 411 U.S. 1 (1973).

19. ROBERT D. PUTNAM, BOWLING ALONE: THE COLLAPSE AND REVIVAL OF AMERICAN COMMUNITY 92 (New York: Simon & Schuster 2000) [hereinafter PUTNAM, BOWLING ALONE].

20. *See* Robert C. Post, *Racist Speech, Democracy, and the First Amendment,* 32 WM. & MARY L. REV. 267, 289 (1991).

21. JÜRGEN HABERMAS, BETWEEN FACTS AND NORMS 366–67 (Cambridge: Polity Press 1996).

22. *See* MILTON DERBER, THE AMERICAN IDEA OF INDUSTRIAL DEMOCRACY 1865–1965 (Urbana: U. Ill. Press 1970); Mark Barenberg, *The Political Economy of the Wagner Act: Power, Symbol, and Workplace Cooperation,* 106 HARV. L. REV. 1379, 1412–30 (1993).

23. 2 NATIONAL LABOR RELATIONS BOARD, LEGISLATIVE HISTORY OF THE NATIONAL LABOR RELATIONS ACT, 1935, at 2321–22 (Washington, D.C.: U.S. Gov't Printing Office 1949) [hereinafter LEG. HIST. OF NLRA] (statement of Sen. Wagner); *id.* at 3132 (statement of Rep. Withrow); *id.* at 2257, 2271 (statement of William Leiserson).

24. *See* JAMES B. ATLESON, VALUES AND ASSUMPTIONS IN AMERICAN LABOR LAW (Amherst: U. Mass. Press 1983); Karl E. Klare, *Judicial Deradicalization of the Wagner Act and the Origins of Modern Legal Consciousness, 1937–1941,* 62 MINN. L. REV. 265 (1978); Katherine Van Wezel Stone, *The Post-War Paradigm in American Labor Law,* 90 YALE L.J. 1509 (1981); Paul C. Weiler, *Striking a New Balance: Freedom of Contract and the Prospects for Union Representation,* 98 HARV. L. REV. 351 (1984); Paul C. Weiler, *Promises to Keep: Securing Workers' Rights to Self-Organization under the NRLA,* 96 HARV. L. REV. 1769, 1771 n. 4 (1983) [hereinafter Weiler, *Promises to Keep*].

25. 29 U.S.C. § 157(a) (2000).

26. These activities must generally be "concerted"—engaged in by two or more workers or by one with an eye toward engaging others—in order to be protected. *See, e.g.,* Meyers Industries, 268 NLRB 493, 497 (1984), *remanded sub nom.* Prill v. NLRB, 755 F.2d 941 (D.C. Cir. 1987), *on remand,* Meyers Industries, 281 NLRB 882 (1986), *aff'd sub nom.,* Prill v. NLRB, 835 F.2d 1481 (D.C. Cir.).

27. *See* Republic Aviation Corp. v. NLRB, 324 U.S. 793 (1945); Eastex, Inc. v. NLRB, 437 U.S. 556 (1978); Beth Israel Hosp. v. NLRB, 437 U.S. 483 (1978).

28. It is noteworthy that early public forum cases involved union activity on public property. *See* Hague v. CIO, 307 U.S. 496, 515–16 (1939). Indeed, when the Supreme Court extended the public forum doctrine to the privately owned sidewalks of a "company town" in *Marsh v. Alabama,* 326 U.S. 501 (1946), it cited *Republic Aviation Corp. v. NLRB,* 324 U.S.

793 (1945), as precedent for the idea that "[t]he more an owner, for his advantage, opens up his property for use by the public in general, the more do his rights become circumscribed by the statutory and constitutional rights of those who use it."

29. *See generally* Clyde W. Summers, *The Privatization of Personal Freedoms and Enrichment of Democracy: Some Lessons from Labor Law*, 1986 U. ILL. L. REV. 689.

30. Section 7 is now only one part of a patchwork of speech protections in the private sector workplace. *See* Cynthia L. Estlund, *Free Speech and Due Process in the Workplace*, 71 IND. L.J. 101, 116–19 (1995).

31. Recent decisions limit *Congress'* power in some respects: First, sovereign immunity bars certain actions by individual state employees against their employer. *See* Alden v. Maine, 527 U.S. 706 (1999); Kimel v. Florida Bd. of Regents, 528 U.S. 62 (2000); Board of Trustees v. Garrett, 531 U.S. 356 (2001). But sovereign immunity does not extend to private (or municipal) employment. Second, the Court has limited Congress' power under the Commerce Clause and the 14th Amendment. *See* United States v. Lopez, 514 U.S. 549 (1995); City of Boerne v. Flores, 521 U.S. 507 (1997); United States v. Morrison, 120 S. Ct. 1740 (2000). But nothing in these decisions limits Congress' power to regulate private sector employment, which still falls squarely within the core of "commerce." Nor, of course, do those decisions affect the power of state courts or legislatures, from which most modern "employment law" emanates.

32. *See* CAROLE PATEMAN, PARTICIPATION AND DEMOCRATIC THEORY 35, 45 (Cambridge: Cambridge U.P. 1970).

33. *Id.* at 45.

34. *See, e.g.*, Kathleen M. Sullivan, *Defining Democracy Down*, AM. PROSPECT, Nov.–Dec. 1998, at 91.

35. *See* ROSENBLUM, *supra* note 15.

36. *See* MILTON FRIEDMAN, CAPITALISM AND FREEDOM (Chicago: U. Chicago Press 1962).

Part III

1. Susan Bisom-Rapp, *An Ounce of Prevention Is a Poor Substitute for a Pound of Cure: Confronting the Developing Jurisprudence of Education and Prevention in Employment Discrimination Law*, 22 BERKELEY J. EMP. & LAB. L. 1, 29–44 (2001) [hereinafter Bisom-Rapp, *Ounce of Prevention*]; Susan Sturm, *Second Generation Employment Discrimination: A Structural Approach*, 101 COLUM. L. REV. 458, 548 n. 332 (2001).

2. *See* Sturm, *supra* note 1, at 547, 564–65.

3. The heterogeneity of individuals' and firms' motivational schemes, and the prevalence of "good citizenship" behavior that cannot be explained strictly in terms of economic incentives, lies at the foundation of the concept of "responsive regulation" to which I make further reference in chapter 9 below. *See* IAN AYRES & JOHN BRAITHWAITE, RESPONSIVE REGULATION: TRANSCENDING THE DEREGULATION DEBATE (New York: Oxford U.P. 1992).

Chapter 8

1. See Vicki Schultz, *The Sanitized Workplace*, 112 Yale L.J.—(2003) [hereinafter Schultz, *Sanitized Workplace*]; Michael Yelnosky, The Prevention Justification for Affirmative Action (2002) (unpublished manuscript, on file with author).

2. See Noah D. Zatz, *Beyond the Zero-Sum Game: Toward Title VII Protection for Intergroup Solidarity*, 77 IND. L.J. 63 (2002).

3. *Id.* at 63 (discussing Childress v. City of Richmond, 907 F. Supp. 934, 938 (E.D. Va. 1995), *claims dismissed*, 919 F. Supp. 216 (E.D. Va. 1996), *vacated and remanded*, 120 F.3d

476 (4th Cir. 1997) (panel opinion), *panel opinion vacated and judgment below aff'd en banc,* 134 F.3d 1205 (4th Cir. 1998) (per curiam)).

4. A fuller elaboration of the implications of "working together" for affirmative action appears in Cynthia L. Estlund, *Working Together: The Workplace, Civil Society, and the Law,* 89 GEO. L.J. 1 (2000) [hereinafter Estlund, *Working Together*].

5. For another recent exposition of the importance of integration as a justification for affirmative action, see Elizabeth Anderson, *Integation, Affirmative Action, and Strict Scrutiny,* 77 N.Y.U. L. REV. 1195 (2002).

6. JOHN J. HELDRICH CENTER FOR WORKFORCE DEVELOPMENT, A WORKPLACE DIVIDED: HOW AMERICANS VIEW DISCRIMINATION AND RACE ON THE JOB 17, 18–20, 33 (New Brunswick, N.J.: Rutgers U. 2002), *available at* http://www.heldrich.rutgers.edu/whatsnew/ A_Workplace_Divided_How_Americans_View_ Discrimination_and_Race_PDF.pdf.

7. The strong opposition to racial "preferences," even among whites expressing liberal racial attitudes, is thoroughly explored in PAUL M. SNIDERMAN & EDWARD G. CARMINES, REACHING BEYOND RACE (Cambridge, Mass.: Harvard U.P. 1997).

8. For a thorough study of the meaning of "diversity" in America, its positive valuation, and its prescriptive implications, *see* PETER H. SCHUCK, DIVERSITY IN AMERICA: KEEPING GOVERNMENT AT A SAFE DISTANCE (Cambridge, Mass.: Harvard U.P. 2003)

9. Indeed, though Justice Powell's concurrence in *Bakke* is often cited for the permissibility of seeking diversity, both Powell's and Brennan's opinions made a pro-integration argument for "bring[ing] the races together" into "an integrated student body." Regents of the Univ. of Cal. v. Bakke, 438 U.S. 265, 326 n. 1 (1978) (Brennan, White, Marshall, & Blackmun, JJ., concurring in part, dissenting in part). *See generally* Akhil Reed Amar & Neil Katyal, *Bakke's Fate,* 43 UCLA L. REV. 1745, 1753 (1996).

10. Yelnosky, *supra* note 1.

11. "Reverse discrimination" cases comprised 5.6% of employment discrimination cases in 1985–87. *See* John J. Donohue III & Peter Siegelman, *The Changing Nature of Employment Discrimination Litigation,* 43 STAN. L. REV. 983, 997 n. 53 (1991).

12. See chapter 4, supra.

13. See Donohue & Siegelman, *supra* note 11, at 1028 & n. 140; Alfred W. Blumrosen, *The Duty of Fair Recruitment under the Civil Rights Act of 1964,* 22 RUTGERS L. REV. 465 (1968).

14. Donohue & Siegelman, *supra* note 11, at 983–84, 1015–16. Harassment cases have also increased; as only employees, not applicants, can sue for harassment, their impact may parallel in many ways that of discharge claims.

15. *Id.* at 1027.

16. Data on EEOC claims through 1999 show a slightly greater predominance of discharge cases. If one adds retaliation and harassment claims, which similarly arise only posthiring and which have both multiplied since 1989, the proportion of claims challenging hiring decisions has fallen significantly. Unpublished data supplied by John Donohue & Peter Siegelman; on file with author.

17. One reason stems directly from Title VII's early successes: Many exclusionary hiring practices were dismantled by the first wave of Title VII litigation. Donohue & Siegelman, *supra* note 11, at 1010–13. The discriminatory hiring practices that remain are more subtle and harder to challenge, but are also less exclusionary. As a result, more minorities occupy good jobs, where they have a greater stake in challenging an allegedly unfair discharge. *Id.* at 1006–11.

18. *See id.* at 1011–12; Samuel Issacharoff, *Contracting for Employment: The Limited Return of the Common Law,* 74 TEX. L. REV. 1783 (1996); Linda H. Krieger, *Civil Rights Perestroika: Intergroup Relations after Affirmative Action,* 86 CAL. L. REV. 1251, 1319 (1998).

19. The opposite dynamic—lack of bias at hiring but bias in terminations—is entirely possible: Faced with a relatively abstract choice among applicants, the decisionmaker may

choose a minority applicant to meet "diversity" goals or to show a lack of bias. But once the applicant begins work, information may be filtered through unconscious biases. The resulting evaluations may then lead to adverse decisions without the decision maker being aware of the influence of bias. The empirical evidence suggests that bias is more likely with less information and contact, but that is not invariably true.

20. I focus on "disparate treatment" claims, which make up the bulk of Title VII litigation, and leave aside the theory of "disparate impact," under which facially neutral criteria or practices can be challenged, and employers required to justify them, if they have a significant disparate impact on minorities. See Griggs v. Duke Power Co., 401 U.S. 424 (1971). Disparate impact theory was enormously important in the first decades of Title VII litigation; its use has waned since then. See Donohue & Siegelman, *supra* note 11, at 998. The reinvigoration of disparate impact doctrine would be an important part of a reform strategy. In this short and nontechnical overview, however, I will leave aside further inquiry into that doctrine.

21. In a disparate treatment suit, it is not necessarily enough even to show that the employer's proffered reason for the decision was fabricated. See St. Mary's Honor Center v. Hicks 509 U.S. 502 (1993). In its subsequent decision in *Reeves v. Sanderson Plumbing Products, Inc.*, 530 U.S. 133 (2000), the Court explained that a plaintiff's proof that the employer's explanation is false, while it does not compel a finding of discrimination, may support such a jury's (or judge's) finding discriminatory motive.

22. Employment lawyers and consultants advise employers to carry out performance reviews with an eye to litigation, and to "sanitize" their personnel files—"to make sure that . . . potentially misleading or harmful documents are weeded out," and to "eliminate unneccessary references to sex, age, race, etc." See Susan Bisom-Rapp, *Bulletproofing the Workplace: Symbol and Substance in Employment Discrimination Law Practice*, 26 FLA. ST. U. L. REV. 959, 988–1017 (1999) [hereinafter Bisom-Rapp, *Bulletproofing*].

23. A 1974 study found that only about 1% of respondents who believed they had experienced job discrimination had even consulted a lawyer about the problem. BARBARA A. CURRAN, THE LEGAL NEEDS OF THE PUBLIC: THE FINAL REPORT OF A NATIONAL SURVEY 136 (1977), *cited in* Donohue & Siegelman, *supra* note 11, at 1004. A more recent study suggests a somewhat greater willingness to sue over job discrimination. Randall Samborn, *Many Americans Find Bias at Work*, NAT'L L.J., July 16, 1990, at 1, *cited in* Donohue & Siegelman, *supra* note 11, at 1004 n. 76. That has not, however, produced more hiring claims, even in absolute terms.

24. This is apparently not understood by employees, who overwhelmingly state a belief that it is illegal to fire an employee based on personal dislike or even in order to hire another willing to do the same job for a lower wage. See Pauline Kim, *Norms, Learning, and Law: Exploring the Influences on Workers' Legal Knowledge*, 1999 U. ILL. L. REV. 447; Pauline Kim, *Bargaining with Imperfect Information: A Study of Worker Perceptions of Legal Protection in an At-Will World*, 83 CORNELL L. REV. 105 (1997).

25. See Bisom-Rapp, *Bulletproofing*, *supra* note 22, at 993.

26. See Stuart Romm, *Layoffs: Principles and Practices*, *in* LOCAL JUSTICE IN AMERICA 153, 197–98, 200–01, 210–11, 213–14 (Jon Elster ed., New York: Russell Sage Foundation 1995).

27. See Linda H. Krieger, *The Content of Our Categories: A Cognitive Bias Approach to Discrimination and Equal Employment Opportunity*, 47 STAN. L. REV. 1161, 1211–41 (1995); Susan Sturm, *Second Generation Employment Discrimination: A Structural Approach*, 101 COLUM. L. REV. 458, 485–89 (2001).

28. Donohue & Siegelman, *supra* note 11, at 1024.

29. *Id. Cf.* Ian Ayres & Peter Siegelman, *The Q-Word as Red Herring: Why Disparate Impact Liability Does Not Induce Hiring Quotas*, 74 TEX. L. REV. 1487, 1489–91 (1996).

30. *See, e.g.*, Sniderman & Carmines, *supra* note 7, at 15–58 (1997).

31. See, for example, the glossy magazine, Diversity Inc, and the eponymous website, *www.diversityinc.com*, which are filled with articles and advertisements touting the diversity initiatives of hundreds of companies and their successes and urging their expansion.

32. So, for example, the fact of an integrated workforce should be relevant evidence for the defense of a suit charging exit discrimination. This suggestion in some ways resembles the "bottom line" defense that was rejected in *Connecticut v. Teal*, 457 U.S. 440, 449 n. 10 (1983). *See* David Charny & G. Mitu Gulati, *Efficiency-Wages, Tournaments and Discrimination: A Theory of Employment Discrimination Law for "High-Level" Jobs*, 33 Harv. C.R.-C.L. L. Rev. 57, 94 (1998); Ayres & Siegelman, *supra* note 29, at 1517. If employers got "credit" for hiring more minorities in a suit claiming discrimination in discharge, it would help counteract the skewed incentives discussed above.

33. Perversely, the EEOC tends instead to focus its efforts on relatively routine individual discharge cases. See Michael Selmi, *Public vs. Private Enforcement of Civil Rights: The Case of Housing and Employment*, 45 UCLA L. Rev. 1401, 1404 (1998). Professor Selmi advocates a wholesale shift by the government away from individual discrimination claims and toward large class action cases.

34. *See* Ayres & Siegelman, *supra* note 29, at 1520; James J. Heckman & Peter Siegelman, *The Urban Institute Audit Studies: Their Methods and Findings*, in Clear and Convincing Evidence: Measurement of Discrimination in America 187 (Michael Fix & Raymond Struyk eds., Washington, D.C.: Urban Institute Press 1993) (on strengths and weaknesses of such auditing studies).

35. See Ayres & Siegelman, *supra* note 29, at 1520. That is why there is a probationary period in any just cause or civil service regime.

36. For a particularly lucid account of a regulatory framework that relies partly on "regulated self-regulation," *see* Ian Ayres & John Braithwaite, Responsive Regulation: Transcending the Deregulation Debate (New York: Oxford U.P. 1992). I will have more to say about regulated self-regulation and its cousin, "responsive regulation" below in chapter 9.

37. Some of these issues, especially the doctrinal components, are explored at greater length in Cynthia L. Estlund, *Freedom of Expression in the Workplace and the Problem of Discriminatory Harassment*, 75 Tex. L. Rev. 687 (1997).

38. Schultz, *Sanitized Workplace*, *supra* note 1.

39. *See id.*; Eugene Volokh, *How Harassment Law Restricts Free Speech*, 47 Rutgers L.J. 561 (1995).

40. Harris v. Forklift Sys., Inc., 510 U.S. 17, 21 (1993).

41. Professor Schultz provides numerous examples of cases in which interactions that appeared to be genuinely mutual, consensual, and friendly ended up being turned against the male participant, sometimes on pain of termination. Schultz, *Sanitized Workplace*, *supra* note 1.

42. See Miranda Oshige, Note, *What's Sex Got to Do with It?*, 47 Stan. L. Rev. 565, 589–90 (1995); Mary Becker, *How Free Is Speech at Work?*, 29 U.C. Davis L. Rev. 815, 859 (1996); Juan F. Perea, *Strange Fruit: Harassment and the First Amendment*, 29 U.C. Davis L. Rev. 875, 884–86 (1996).

43. Peter T. Kilborn, *Men Say Worry about Harassment Leads Them to Tone Down Conduct*, N.Y. Times, Nov. 7, 1991, at A-20.

44. See Barbara Lindemann & David D. Kadue, Sexual Harassment in Employment Law 421–23 (Washington, D.C.: BNA Books 1992); Steve Ulfelder, *Cupid Hits Cubeland: Employers Don't Encourage It, but Office Dating Gains Acceptance*, Boston Globe,

Feb. 11, 2001, at H1; Kathleen Kelleher, *Birds & Bees: Co-Workers Who Take a Chance on Romance*, L.A. TIMES, July 8, 2002, at B-2; *Compliance: Most Think Cubicle Romance Is Dangerous but Don't Restrict It*, HR REPORTER, Aug. 16, 2002; Stuart Silverstein, *New Rules of Office Romance*, L.A. TIMES, Sept. 23, 1998, at A1. For a recent investigation into the origins, shape, and incidence of "anti-fraternization" and similar policies, see Schultz, *Sanitized Workplace, supra* note 1.

45. Cynthia Fuchs Epstein, Robert Saute, Bonnie Oglensky, & Martha Gever, *Glass Ceilings and Open Doors: Women's Advancement in the Legal Profession: A Report to the Committee on Women in the Profession, The Association of the Bar of the City of New York*, 64 FORDHAM L. REV. 291, 376 (1995). *See also id.* at 355–56.

46. *See* Schultz, *Sanitized Workplace, supra* note 1; Vicki Schultz, *Reconceptualizing Sexual Harassment*, 107 YALE L.J. 1683 (1998).

47. By this I mean efforts not merely to shape firms' incentives to prevent discrimination and harassment but more direct engagement with firms' "internal" preventive practices. The picture includes internal grievance procedures and arbitration schemes, but bears further scrutiny through a broader lens. This project is outlined in Sturm, *supra* note 27, and has its firmest legal footing in the Supreme Court's decisions in *Faragher v. City of Boca Raton*, 524 U.S. 775 (1998); and *Burlington Industries v. Ellerth*, 524 U.S. 742 (1998).

48. *See* Samuel Issacharoff & Elyse Rosenblum, *Women and the Workplace: Accommodating the Demands of Pregnancy*, 91 COLUM. L. REV. 2154 (1994).

49. For an ambitious effort to ground a duty to accommodate child-related responsibilities in existing antidiscrimination law and to minimize the identification of those accommodation requirements with women, *see* JOAN WILLIAMS, UNBENDING GENDER: WHY FAMILY AND WORK CONFLICT AND WHAT TO DO ABOUT IT (Oxford: Oxford U.P. 2000).

50. *See, e.g.,* ELAINE SORENSEN, COMPARABLE WORTH: IS IT A WORTHY POLICY? (Princeton, N.J.: Princeton U.P. 1994); RICHARD PERLMAN & MAUREEN PIKE, SEX DISCRIMINATION IN THE LABOUR MARKET: THE CASE FOR COMPARABLE WORTH (New York: Manchester U.P. 1994); PAULA ENGLAND, COMPARABLE WORTH: THEORIES AND EVIDENCE (New York: Aldine de Gruyter 1992). For a lucid comparison of comparable worth theory to conventional theories of nondiscrimination in employment, see Mark Seidenfeld, *Some Jurisprudential Perspectives on Employment Sex Discrimination Law*, 21 RUTGERS L. REV. 269 (1990).

51. *See, e.g.,* ELLEN FRANKEL PAUL, EQUITY AND GENDER: THE COMPARABLE WORTH DEBATE (New Brunswick, N.J.: Transaction 1989).

52. As one commentator puts it, "[i]f occupational segregation is the problem, then the theory of comparable worth is not the solution"; indeed, "it might help to perpetuate the problem." George Rutherglen, *The Theory of Comparable Worth as a Remedy for Discrimination*, 82 GEO. L.J. 135 (1993).

53. *See* Francine D. Blau, Patricia Simpson & Deborah Anderson, *Continuing Progress? Trends in the Occupational Segregation in the United States over the 1970s and 1980s*, 4 FEMINIST ECON. 29 (1998).

Chapter 9

1. The original case for a "right to privacy" in American law responded to the perceived intrusiveness of the popular press into the social life of Boston's elite. *See* Samuel D. Warren & Louis D. Brandeis, *The Right to Privacy*, 4 HARV. L. REV. 193 (1890). The constitutional right of privacy protects the relationship between a woman and her doctor, as well as intimate sexual relationships, from state intrusion. *See, e.g.,* Griswold v. Connecticut, 381 U.S. 479 (1965); Eisenstadt v. Baird, 405 U.S. 438 (1972); Roe v. Wade, 410 U.S. 113 (1973). Some

commentators describe this aspect of the right of privacy as a freedom of "intimate association." *See* Kenneth Karst, *The Freedom of Intimate Association*, 89 YALE L.J. 624 (1980).

2. A few courts have afforded protection to employees' off-duty relationships. *See* Rulon-Miller v. Int'l Bus. Mach. Corp., 208 Cal. Rptr. 524 (1984); Pasch v. Katz Media Corp., 1995 U.S. Dist. LEXIS 11153 (S.D.N.Y.). But most have declined to do so. *See, e.g.*, State v. Wal-Mart Stores, Inc., 621 N.Y.S.2d 158 (1995); Patton v. J. C. Penney Co., 719 P.2d 854 (Or. 1986); Trumbauer v. Group Health Coop., 635 F. Supp. 543 (W.D. Wash.). Common law privacy arguments for the protection of communication *within* the workplace have largely failed. *See, e.g.*, Smyth v. Pillsbury Co., 914 F. Supp. 97 (E.D. Pa. 1996).

3. *See* Republic Aviation Corp. v. NLRB, 324 U.S. 793 (1945).

4. *See* Consolidated Edison Co. v. NLRB, 305 U.S. 197 (1938) (surveillance of employees in nonwork areas held unlawful under NLRA); Jeannette Corp. v. NLRB, 532 F.2d 916, 919 (3rd Cir. 1976) (pay secrecy rules held unlawful under the NLRA).

5. National Labor Relations Act, 29 U.S.C. § 8(a)(2) (2000).

6. It has indeed provoked a closer look, much of it critical, in the legal academic literature. For a sampling, *see* Mark Barenberg, *Democracy and Domination in the Law of Workplace Cooperation: From Bureaucratic to Flexible Production*, 94 COLUM. L. REV. 753 (1994); Charles B. Craver, *The National Labor Relations Act Must Be Revised to Preserve Industrial Democracy*, 34 ARIZ. L. REV. 397 (1992); Samuel Estreicher, *Employee Involvement and the "Company Union" Prohibition: The Case for Partial Repeal of Section 8(a)(2) of the NLRA*, 69 N.Y.U. L. REV. 125 (1994); Michael Gottesman, *In Despair, Starting Over: Imagining a Labor Law for Unorganized Workers*, 69 CHI.-KENT L. REV. 59, 86 (1993); Clyde W. Summers, *A Structured Exception to Section 8(a)(2)*, 69 CHI.-KENT L. REV. 129 (1993).

7. On the role of unions in the enforcement of workplace standards, *see* Robert J. Rabin, *The Role of Unions in the Rights-Based Workplace*, 25 U.S.F. L. REV. 169 (1991).

8. *See* 535 U.S. 137 (2002). The decision, which bars backpay or reinstatement, should not apply to undocumented workers who are hired knowingly; nor should it apply to backpay claims for minimum wage and overtime violations under the Fair Labor Standards Act, where the backpay is not for "years of work not performed," as the Supreme Court described the remedy in *Hoffman Plastics*, but rather "for hours an employee has actually worked." *See* Flores v. Alberton's, Inc., 2002 WL 1163623 (C.D. Cal. 2002); Liu v. Donna Karan Int'l, Inc., 207 F. Supp.2d 191 (S.D.N.Y. 2002).

9. Union involvement enhances enforcement; evidence as to whether nonunion forms of employee representation do so is more mixed but still encouraging. *See* Gregory R. Watchman, *Safe and Sound: The Case for Safety and Health Committees under OSHA and the NLRA*, 4 CORNELL J.L. & PUB. POL'Y 65, 82–89 (1994); Randy S. Rabinowitz & Mark M. Hager, *Designing Health and Safety: Workplace Hazard Regulation in the United States and Canada*, 33 CORNELL INT'L L.J. 373, 431 (2000). *Cf.* Mark Seidenfeld, *Empowering Stakeholders: Limits on Collaboration as the Basis for Flexible Regulation*, 41 WM. & MARY L. REV. 411, 497–98 (2000) (recognizing success of employee safety committees in reducing accident rates at California construction sites, but concluding that effectiveness in other contexts "remains an open question").

10. Steven Greenhouse, *Senate Votes to Repeal Rules Clinton Set on Work Injuries*, N.Y. TIMES, Mar. 7, 2001, at A1; Steven Greenhouse, *Bush Plan to Avert Work Injuries Seeks Voluntary Steps by Industry*, N.Y. TIMES, Apr. 6, 2002, at A1.

11. *Compare, e.g.*, Richard A. Epstein, *In Defense of the Contract at Will*, 51 U. CHI. L. REV. 947 (1984), *with* Lawrence E. Blades, *Employment at Will v. Individual Freedom: On Limiting the Abusive Exercise of Employer Power*, 67 COLUM. L. REV. 1404 (1967).

12. *See, e.g.*, *Symposium on the Regulatory Future of Contingent Employment*, 52 WASH. & LEE L. REV. 723 (1995).

13. I borrow the term "hydraulics" from Samuel Issacharoff & Pamela S. Karlan, *The Hydraulics of Campaign Finance Reform*, 77 TEX. L. REV. 1705 (1999), who use it to describe the analogous manner in which legal constraints on one avenue for campaign contributions drives money into other less regulated channels.

14. *See* Maria O'Brien Hylton, *The Case Against Regulating the Market for Contingent Employment*, 52 WASH. & LEE L. REV. 849, 851 (1995); Sharon Dietrich et al., *Work Reform: The Other Side of Welfare Reform*, 9 STAN. L. & POL'Y REV. 53, 58–59 (1998).

15. *See* Hylton, *supra* note 14, at 857–58, 861–62. In Europe, unjust dismissal laws have tended to increase the use of "temporary" workers, who are not covered by the laws. Law-makers have responded by regulating temporary employment, e.g., by limiting its duration. Some studies suggest that such regulations have contributed (along with higher wage and benefit costs) to chronically higher unemployment rates in Western Europe as compared to the United States. Bob Hepple, *Flexibility and Security of Employment*, *in* COMPARATIVE LABOUR LAW AND INDUSTRIAL RELATIONS IN INDUSTRIALIZED MARKET ECONOMIES 287–89 (6th ed., Roger Blanpain & Chris Engels eds., Boston: Kluwer Law Int'l 1998).

16. *See* International Labor Organization (ILO) Declaration on Fundamental Principles and Rights at Work (1998), *available at* http://www.ilo.org/public/English/standards/decl/declaration/text/index.htm; International Covenant on Civil and Political Rights, art. 22, 999 U.N.T.S. 171 (Dec. 16, 1966).

17. *See* DANIEL YERGIN, THE COMMANDING HEIGHTS: THE BATTLE FOR THE WORLD ECONOMY (New York: Simon & Schuster 2002).

18. More precisely, the employee can file a charge, on which the NLRB's General Counsel might, in its sole discretion, decide to issue a complaint, which the NLRB might uphold and order a remedy, which might be enforced by the federal appellate courts if the employer fails to comply. This is the sole avenue for relief on a claim of antiunion discrimination. Delay and uncertainty is endemic to this process. Paul Weiler, *Promises to Keep: Securing Workers' Rights to Self-Organization under the NLRA*, 96 HARV. L. REV. 1769, 1769–70 (1983).

19. *See* Cynthia L. Estlund, *Wrongful Discharge Protections in an At-Will World*, 74 TEX. L. REV. 1655, 1674–78 (1996).

20. Such a proposal would fit neatly within the model of "responsive regulation" out-lined in IAN AYRES & JOHN BRAITHWAITE, RESPONSIVE REGULATION: TRANSCENDING THE DEREGULATION DEBATE (New York: Oxford U.P. 1992).

21. United States Census Bureau, Public Employment and Payroll Data, *available at* http://www.census.gov/govs/www/apes.html; Press Release, Bureau of Labor Statistics, United States Department of Labor, The Employment Situation: March 2001, *available at* ftp://ftp.bls.gov/pub/news.release/History/empsit.04062001.news.

22. The federal workforce employs 30.4% minority workers as compared to 27.6% in the private sector. U.S. OFFICE OF PERSONNEL MANAGEMENT, THE FACT BOOK: FEDERAL CIVILIAN WORKFORCE STATISTICS 48 (Washington: Office of Personnel Management 2001), *available at* http://www.opm.gov/feddata/01factbk.pdf. Within white-collar occupations, 29.6% of workers in the federal executive branch are minorities, as compared to 22% in the private sector. U.S. OFFICE OF PERSONNEL MANAGEMENT, FEDERAL CIVILIAN WORKFORCE STATISTICS: DEMOGRAPHIC PROFILE OF THE FEDERAL WORKFORCE AS OF SEPTEMBER 30, 2000, at tbl.3 (Washington: Office of Personnel Management 2001), *available at* http://www.opm.gov/feddata/demograp/00demogr.pdf; U.S. Equal Employment Opportunity Commission, Occupational Employment in Private Industry by Race/Ethnic Group/Sex, and by Industry, United States (2000) *available at* http://www.eeoc.gov/stats/jobpat/2000/national.html ("white collar" being the combination of "Officials and Managers," "Professionals," "Technicians," and "Office and Clerical Workers" categories).

23. *See* http://stats.bls.gov/news.release/union2.nr0.htm. Some observers have pointed

to the contrasting trends in public and private sector unionization as evidence that employer opposition—which is generally muted in the public sector—accounts for much of the private sector decline. But the comparative lack of employer opposition may itself have a great deal to do with the lack of competitive pressures on most government agencies. *See, e.g.,* Samuel Estreicher, *Labor Law Reform in a World of Competitive Product Markets,* 69 CHI.-KENT L. REV. 3, 4–6 (1993); Richard B. Freeman, *Contraction and Expansion: The Divergence of Private Sector and Public Sector Unionism in the United States, in* RICHARD FREEMAN, LABOR MARKETS IN ACTION: ESSAYS IN EMPIRICAL ECONOMICS 221 (New York: Harvester Wheatsheaf 1989); Richard B. Freeman & Morris M. Kleiner, *Employer Behavior in the Face of Union Organizing Drives,* 43 INDUS. & LAB. REL. REV. 351 (1990); Weiler, *supra* note 18.

24. *See* Connick v. Myers, 461 U.S. 138 (1983); Elrod v. Burns, 427 U.S.347 (1976); O'Connor v. Ortega, 480 U.S. 709 (1987).

25. Public employees who have a right under statute, regulation, or contract not to be fired except for some kind of cause have a "property" interest in their jobs and are entitled to constitutionally prescribed minimum standards of due process. *See* Cleveland Board of Education v. Loudermill, 470 U.S. 532 (1985).

26. *See, e.g.,* Adarand Constructors, Inc. v. Pena, 515 U.S. 200 (1995).

27. Craig Becker, *With Whose Hands: Privatization, Public Employment and Democracy,* 6 YALE L. & POL'Y REV. 88 (1988).

28. *See* Gillian Metzger, *Privatization as Delegation,* 103 COLUM. L. REV. (forthcoming 2003).

29. HERMAN BELZ, EQUALITY TRANSFORMED: A QUARTER CENTURY OF AFFIRMATIVE ACTION 250–56 (New Brunswick, N.J.: Transaction Publishers 1991); William L. Kandel, *Affirmative Action and the Glass Ceiling: Contract Compliance and Litigation Avoidance,* EMPLOYEE RELATIONS L.J., Autumn 1995, 109, 109–18.

30. *See* Building & Constr. Trades Council of the Metro. Dist. v. Assoc. Builders & Contractors of Mass./R.I., Inc., 507 U.S. 218 (1993).

31. *See* Chamber of Commerce v. Reich, 74 F.2d 1322, *petition for reh'g denied,* 83 F.3d 439 (D.C. Cir. 1996); Wisconsin Dep't of Industry, Labor & Human Relations v. Gould, 475 U.S. 282 (1986). It would similarly preclude government contracts from being conditioned on the establishment of employee representation committees that fell afoul of the NLRA's broad ban on "company unions."

32. It might be a seed of "democratic experimentalism," as elucidated by Professors Dorf and Sabel. *See* Michael C. Dorf & Charles F. Sabel, *A Constitution of Democratic Experimentalism,* 98 COLUM. L. REV. 267 (1998).

Chapter 10

1. ALEXIS DE TOCQUEVILLE, DEMOCRACY IN AMERICA 515 (George Lawrence trans., New York: Harper Perennial 1988).

2. Putnam rejects that hypothesis partly because "[t]he decline in group membership is essentially identical among whites who favor segregation, whites who oppose segregation, and blacks." ROBERT D. PUTNAM, BOWLING ALONE: THE COLLAPSE AND REVIVAL OF AMERICAN COMMUNITY 280 (New York: Simon & Schuster 2000) [hereinafter PUTNAM, BOWLING ALONE]. But that does not contradict the hypothesis that greater diversity may corrode trust and civic engagement without regard to conscious racial attitudes. Putnam also rejects the contrary hypothesis that "social capital" is in tension with greater tolerance; he cites evidence that citizens of higher social capital states express greater tolerance of racial and gen-

der equality and of civil liberties. *Id.* at 356. But the fact that citizens profess more abstract racial tolerance in an overwhelmingly white social environment unfortunately does not contradict the hypothesis that greater heterogeneity is associated with less community involvement and generalized social trust.

3. *Id.* at 352–54.

4. In Putnam's words, that civic generation "came of age in the first half of the century, when American society was objectively more segregated and subjectively more racist than in the 1960s and 1970s." *Id.* at 280. For him that contradicts the claim that "civic disengagement represent[s] white flight from integrated community life after the civil rights revolution." *Id.* But I am suggesting not that invidious segregation and racism fostered social trust, but that sameness and familiarity within one's social environment—brought about in part by invidious segregation—may have done so.

5. *Id.* at 293.

6. *See Saguaro Seminar on Civic Engagement in America, Social Capital Community Benchmark Survey, Executive Summary* 5–6 (Kennedy School of Government, Harvard U. 2001), *available at* http://www.ksg.harvard.edu/saguaro/communitysurvey/results.html; Alberto Alesina & Eliana La Ferrara, Participation in Heterogeneous Communities, National Bureau of Econ. Research Working Paper No. 7155 (1999).

7. The decline of membership in these and other organizations is charted in PUTNAM, BOWLING ALONE, *supra* note 2, at 438–44.

8. In Putnam's words, "[s]ome kinds of bonding social capital may discourage the formation of bridging social capital and vice versa." *Id.* at 362.

REFERENCES

Abrams, Kathryn, *Gender Discrimination and the Transformation of Workplace Norms*, 42 VAND. L. REV. 1183 (1989).

Adams, Jerome, Robert W. Rice & Debra Instone, *Follower Attitudes toward Women and Judgments Concerning Performance by Female and Male Leaders*, 27 ACAD. OF MGMT. J. 636 (1984).

Akerlof, George A., *Labor Contracts as Partial Gift Exchange*, 97 Q. J. ECON. 543 (1982).

Alderfer, C. P., *An Intergroup Perspective on Group Dynamics*, in HANDBOOK OF ORGANIZATIONAL BEHAVIOR (Jay William Lorsch ed., Englewood Cliffs, N.J.: Prentice-Hall, 1987).

Aleinikoff, T. Alexander, *The Constitution in Context: The Continuing Significance of Racism*, 63 U. COLO. L. REV. 325 (1992).

Alesina, Alberto & Eliana La Ferrara, Participation in Heterogeneous Communities, National Bureau of Econ. Research Working Paper No. 7155 (1999).

ALLPORT, GORDON W., THE NATURE OF PREJUDICE (2d ed., Garden City, N.Y.: Doubleday 1958).

Amar, Akhil Reed & Neil Katyal, *Bakke's Fate*, 43 UCLA L. REV. 1745 (1996).

Anderson, Elizabeth, *Integration, Affirmative Action, and Strict Scrutiny*, 77 N.Y.U. L. REV. 1195 (2002).

Arriola, Elvia R., *"What's the Big Deal?" Women in the New York City Construction Industry and Sexual Harassment Law, 1970–85*, 22 COLUM. HUM. RTS. L. REV. 21 (1990).

ATLESON, JAMES B., VALUES AND ASSUMPTIONS IN AMERICAN LABOR LAW (Amherst: U. Mass. Press 1983).

Austin, Regina, *"Bad for Business": Contextual Analysis, Race Discrimination, and Fast Food*, 34 J. MARSHALL L. REV. 207 (2000).

Austin, Regina, *"Not Just for the Fun of It": Governmental Restraints on Black Leisure, Social Inequality, and the Privatization of Public Space*, 71 S. CAL. L. REV. 667 (1998).

Ayres, Ian & Peter Siegelman, *The Q-Work as Red Herring: Why Disparate Impact Liability Does Not Induce Hiring Quotas*, 74 TEX. L. REV. 1487 (1996).

AYRES, IAN & JOHN BRAITHWAITE, RESPONSIVE REGULATION: TRANSCENDING THE DEREGULATION DEBATE (New York: Oxford U.P. 1992).

BARBER, BENJAMIN R., JIHAD VS. MCWORLD (New York: Times Books 1995).

Barber, Jeremy S., *Re-orienting Sexual Harassment: Why Federal Legislation is Needed to Cure Same-Sex Sexual Harassment Law*, 52 AM. U. L. REV. (2002).

Barenberg, Mark, *Democracy and Domination in the Law of Workplace Cooperation: From Bureaucratic to Flexible Production*, 94 COLUM. L. REV. 753 (1994).

Barenberg, Mark, *The Political Economy of the Wagner Act: Power, Symbol, and Workplace Cooperation*, 106 HARV. L. REV. 1379 (1993).

Barnard, Thomas H. & Timothy J. Downing, *Emerging Law on Sexual Orientation and Employment*, 29 U. MEM. L. REV. 555 (1999).

Becker, Craig, *With Whose Hands: Privatization, Public Employment and Democracy*, 6 YALE L. & POL'Y REV. 88 (1988).

Becker, Mary, *How Free Is Speech at Work?*, 29 U.C. DAVIS L. REV. 815 (1996).

Bell, Abraham & Gideon Parchomovsky, *The Integration Game*, 100 COLUM. L. REV. 1965 (2000).

Bell, Derrick, *Serving Two Masters: Integration Ideals & Client Interests in School Desegregation Litigation*, 85 YALE L.J. 470 (1976).

Belous, Richard S., *The Rise of the Contingent Work Force: The Key Challenges and Opportunities*, 52 WASH. & LEE L. REV. 863 (1995).

BELZ, HERMAN, EQUALITY TRANSFORMED: A QUARTER CENTURY OF AFFIRMATIVE ACTION 250–56 (New Brunswick, N.J.: Transaction Publishers. 1991).

Bertrand, Marianne & Sendhil Mullainathan, *Are Emily and Brendan More Employable than Lakisha and Jamal? A Field Experiment on Labor Market Discrimination* (Working Paper, Nov. 18, 2002, on file with author).

Bettencourt, B. Ann et al., *Cooperation and the Reduction of Intergroup Bias: The Role of Reward Structure and Social Orientation*, 28 J. EXPERIM. SOC. PSYCH. 301 (1992).

Better Together: Report of the Saguaro Seminar: Civic Engagement in America (Kennedy School of Government, Harvard Univ. 2001).

BEWLEY, TRUMAN, WHY WAGES DON'T FALL DURING A RECESSION (Cambridge, Mass.: Harvard U.P. 1999).

Bhatnagar, Deepti & Ranjini Swamy, *Attitudes toward Women as Managers: Does Interaction Make a Difference?*, 48 HUM. RELA. 1285 (1995).

Bisom-Rapp, Susan, *An Ounce of Prevention Is a Poor Substitute for a Pound of Cure: Confronting the Developing Jurisprudence of Education and Prevention in Employment Discrimination Law*, 22 BERKELEY J. EMP. & LAB. L. 1 (2001).

Bisom-Rapp, Susan, *Bulletproofing the Workplace: Symbol and Substance in Employment Discrimination Law Practice*, 26 FLA. ST. U. L. REV. 959 (1999).

Blades, Lawrence E., *Employment at Will vs. Individual Freedom: Limiting the Abusive Exercise of Employer Power*, 67 COLUM. L. REV. 1404 (1967).

Blair, Irene, *The Maleability of Automatic Stereotypes and Prejudice*, 6 PERS. SOC. PSYCH. REV. 242 (2002).

Blair, Margaret M. & Lynn A. Stout, *Trust, Trustworthiness, and the Behavioral Foundations of Corporate Law*, 149 U. PA. L. REV. 1735 (2001).

Blasi, Gary, *Advocacy against the Stereotype: Lessons from Cognitive Social Psychology*, 49 UCLA L. REV. 1241 (2002).

Blau, Francine, Trends in the Well-Being of American Women, 1970–1995, National Bureau of Economic Research Working Paper No. 6206 (1995).

BLAU, FRANCINE D. & MARIANNE A. FERBER, THE ECONOMICS OF WOMEN, MEN AND WORK (Englewood Cliffs, N.J.: Prentice-Hall 1986).

Blau, Francine D., Patricia Simpson, & Deborah Anderson, *Continuing Progress? Trends in Occupational Segregation in the United States over the 1970s and 1980s*, 4 FEMINIST ECON. 29 (1998).

Blumrosen, Alfred W., *The Law Transmission System and the Southern Jurisprudence of Employment Discrimination*, 6 INDUS. REL. L.J. 313 (1984).

Blumrosen, Alfred W., *The Duty of Fair Recruitment under the Civil Rights Act of 1964*, 22 Rutgers L. Rev. 465 (1968).

Bohman, James & William Rehg, eds., Deliberative Democracy: Essays on Reason and Politics (Cambridge, Mass.: MIT Press 1997).

Bonacich, Edna & Richard P. Appelbaum, Behind the Label: Inequality in the Los Angeles Apparel Industry (Berkeley: U. of Cal. Press 2000).

Bond, James T. et al., The 1997 National Study of the Changing Workforce (New York: Families & Work Inst. 1997).

Boss, Shira J., *Face-to-Face Won't Soon Bow to Technology*, Christian Science Monitor (Dec. 20, 1999).

Bowen, William G. & Derek Bok, The Shape of the River: Long-Term Consequences of Considering Race in College and University Admissions (Princeton, N.J.: Princeton U.P. 1998).

Bowles, Samuel, *Endogenous Preferences: The Cultural Consequences of Markets and Other Economic Institutions*, 36 J. Econ. Lit. 75 (1998).

Boyte, Harry C., *Off the Playground of Civil Society*, 9 The Good Society No. 2 (1999).

Boyte, Harry & Nancy Kari, Building America: The Democratic Promise of Public Work (Philadelphia: Temple U.P. 1996).

Brewer, Marilynn B., *Managing Diversity: The Role of Social Identities*, *in* Diversity in Work Teams: Research Paradigms for a Changing Workplace 47 (Susan E. Jackson & Marian N. Rudman eds., Wash., D.C.: American Psych. Ass'n 1995).

Briggs, Xavier de Souza, Social Capital and Segregation: Race, Connections, and Inequality in America, John F. Kennedy School of Government, Harvard University, Faculty Research Working Paper Series, RWP02-011 (2002).

Brooks, Roy L., Integration or Separation? A Strategy for Racial Equality (Cambridge, Mass.: Harvard U.P. 1996).

Brown, Rupert, Prejudice: Its Social Psychology (Cambridge, Mass.: Blackwell 1995).

Burns, Nancy, Kay Lehman Schlozman & Sidney Verba, *The Public Consequences of Private Inequality: Family Life and Citizen Participation*, 91 Am. Pol. Sci. Rev. 373 (1997).

Calmore, John O., *Race/ism Lost and Found: The Fair Housing Act at Thirty*, 52 U. Miami L. Rev. 1067 (1998).

Calmore, John O., *Random Notes of an Integration Warrior*, 81 Minn. L. Rev. 1441 (1997).

Cappelli, Peter, *Career Jobs Are Dead*, 42 Cal. Mgmt. Rev. 146 (1999).

Cappelli, Peter, *A Market-Driven Approach to Retaining Talent*, Harv. Bus. Rev., Jan.–Feb. 2000, at 108.

Cappelli, Peter, The New Deal at Work: Managing the Market-Driven Workforce (Boston: Harvard Business School Press 1999).

Cappelli, Peter & Nikolai Rogovsky, *Employee Involvement and Organizational Citizenship: Implications for Labor Law Reform and "Lean Production,"* 51 Indus. & Lab. Rel. Rev. 633 (1998).

Carbado, Devon W. & Mitu Gulati, *Conversations at Work*, 79 Or. L. Rev. 103 (2000).

Carbado, Devon W. & Mitu Gulati, *Working Identity*, 85 Cornell L. Rev. 1259 (2000).

Carter, Stephen L., Civility: Manners, Morals, and the Etiquette of Democracy (New York: Basic Books 1998).

Cashin, Sheryll D., *Middle-Class Black Suburbs and the State of Integration: A Post-Integrationist Vision for Metropolitan America*, 86 Cornell L. Rev. 729 (2001).

Chambliss, Elizabeth, *Organizational Determinants of Law Firm Integration*, 46 Am. U. L. Rev. 669 (1997).

Chambliss, Elizabeth & Christopher Uggen, *Men and Women of Elite Law Firms: Reevaluating Kanter's Legacy*, 25 LAW & SOC. INQUIRY 41 (2000).

Charny, David & G. Mitu Gulati, *Efficiency-Wages, Tournaments and Discrimination: A Theory of Employment Discrimination Law for "High-Level" Jobs*, 33 HARV. C.R.-C.L. L. REV. 57 (1998).

COHEN, DON & LAURENCE PRUSAK, IN GOOD COMPANY: HOW SOCIAL CAPITAL MAKES ORGANIZATIONS WORK (Boston: Harvard Bus. School Press 2001).

COHEN, JEAN L. & ANDREW ARATO, CIVIL SOCIETY AND POLITICAL THEORY (Cambridge, Mass.: MIT Press 1992).

COHEN, LIZABETH, MAKING A NEW DEAL: INDUSTRIAL WORKERS IN CHICAGO, 1919–1939 (New York: Cambridge U.P. 1990).

COLEMAN, JAMES S., FOUNDATIONS OF SOCIAL THEORY (Cambridge, Mass.: Belknap Press 1990).

Coleman, James S., *Social Capital in the Creation of Human Capital*, 94 AM. J. SOC. 95 (1988).

Collins, Patricia Hill, *African-American Women and Economic Justice: A Preliminary Analysis of Wealth, Family, and African-American Social Class*, 65 U. CIN. L. REV. 825 (1997).

Cook, S. W., *Cooperative Interaction in Multiethnic Contexts, in* GROUPS IN CONTACT: THE PSYCHOLOGY OF DESEGREGATION (Norman Miller & Marilynn Brewer eds., Orlando: Academic Press 1984).

Cordery, John L. et al., *Attitudinal and Behavioral Effects of Autonomous Group Working*, 34 ACAD. OF MGMT. J. 464 (1991).

COSE, ELLIS, THE RAGE OF A PRIVILEGED CLASS (New York: Harper Collins 1993).

Crain, Marion, *Colorblind Unionism*, 49 UCLA L. REV. 1313 (2002).

Crain, Marion, *Whitewashed Labor Law, Skinwalking Unions*, 23 BERKELEY J. EMP. & LAB. L. 211 (2002).

Crain, Marion, *Women, Labor Unions, and Hostile Work Environment Sexual Harassment: The Untold Story*, 4 TEX. J. WOMEN & L. 9 (1995).

Craver, Charles B., *The National Labor Relations Act Must Be Revised to Preserve Industrial Democracy*, 34 ARIZ. L. REV. 397 (1992).

CROLY, HERBERT, PROGRESSIVE DEMOCRACY (New York: Macmillan 1914).

CRUSE, HAROLD, THE CRISIS OF THE NEGRO INTELLECTUAL (New York: Morrow 1967).

Cummings, Scott L., *Community Economic Development as a Progressive Politics: Toward a Grassroots Movement for Economic Justice*, 54 STAN. L. REV. 399 (2001).

DEAUX, KAY, THE BEHAVIOR OF WOMEN AND MEN (Monterey, Cal.: Brooks/Cole Pub. Co. 1976).

Dietrich, Sharon et al., *Work Reform: The Other Side of Welfare Reform*, 9 STAN. L. 6 POL'Y REV. 53 (1998).

Denton, Nancy A., *The Persistence of Segregation: Links between Residential Segregation and School Segregation*, 80 MINN. L. REV. 795 (1996).

DERBER, MILTON, THE AMERICAN IDEA OF INDUSTRIAL DEMOCRACY 1865–1965 (Urbana: U. Ill. Press 1970).

DEWEY, JOHN, THE PUBLIC AND ITS PROBLEMS (New York: H. Holt & Co. 1927).

Dietrich, Sharon et al., *Work Reform: The Other Side of Welfare Reform*, 9 STAN. L. & POL'Y REV. 53 (1998).

Donohue, John J., III & James J. Heckman, *Continuous Versus Episodic Change: The Impact of Civil Rights Policy on the Economic Status of Blacks*, 29 J. ECON. LITERATURE 1603 (1991).

Donohue, John J., III & James J. Heckman, *The Law and Economics of Racial Discrimination in Employment: Re-Evaluating Federal Civil Rights Policy*, 79 GEO. L.J. 1713 (1991).

Donohue, John J., III & Peter Siegelman, *The Changing Nature of Employment Discrimination Litigation*, 43 STAN. L. REV. 983 (1991).

Dorf, Michael C. & Charles F. Sabel, *A Constitution of Democratic Experimentalism*, 98 COLUM. L. REV. 267 (1998).

Douglas, Davison M., *The End of Busing?*, 95 MICH. L. REV. 1715 (1997).

Drago, Robert, *New Systems of Work and New Workers*, *in* CONTINGENT WORK: AMERICAN EMPLOYMENT RELATIONS IN TRANSITION 144 (Kathleen Barker & Kathleen Christensen eds., Ithaca, N.Y.: ILR Press 1998).

Drew, Josia N., Note, *Caught between the Scylla and Charybdis: Ameliorating the Course of Sexual Orientation Anti-discrimination Rights and Religious Free Exercise Rights in the Workplace*, 16 BYU J. PUB. L. 287 (2002).

DURKHEIM, ÉMILE, THE DIVISION OF LABOR IN SOCIETY (W. D. Halls trans., New York: Free Press 1984).

DURKHEIM, EMILE, SUICIDE: A STUDY IN SOCIOLOGY (George Simpson ed., John A. Spaulding & George Simpson trans., Glencoe, Ill.: Free Press 1951).

Edelman, Lauren B., *Legal Environments and Organizational Governance: The Expansion of Due Process in the American Workplace*, 95 AM. J. OF SOC. 1401 (1990).

EHRENBERG, JOHN, CIVIL SOCIETY: THE CRITICAL HISTORY OF AN IDEA (New York: NYU Press 1999).

EHRENREICH, BARBARA, NICKEL AND DIMED: ON (NOT) GETTING BY IN AMERICA (New York: Henry Holt & Co. 2001).

EISENBERG, SUSAN, WE'LL CALL YOU IF WE NEED YOU: EXPERIENCES OF WOMEN WORKING CONSTRUCTION (Ithaca, N.Y.: ILR Press 1998).

Ellison, Christopher G. & Daniel A. Powers, *The Contact Hypothesis and Racial Attitudes among Black Americans*, 75 SOC. SCI. Q. 385 (1994).

ELSTER, JON, THE CEMENT OF SOCIETY: A STUDY OF SOCIAL ORDER (New York: Cambridge U.P. 1989).

ENGLAND, PAULA, COMPARABLE WORTH: THEORIES AND EVIDENCE (New York: Aldine de Gruyter 1992).

Engle, Karen, *The Persistence of Neutrality: The Failure of the Religious Accommodation Provision to Redeem Title VII*, 76 TEX. L. REV. 317 (1997).

Epstein, Cynthia Fuchs, Robert Saute, Bonnie Oglensky, & Martha Gever, *Glass Ceilings and Open Doors: Women's Advancement in the Legal Profession: A Report to the Committee on Women in the Profession, The Association of the Bar of the City of New York*, 64 FORDHAM L. REV. 291 (1995).

EPSTEIN, RICHARD A., FORBIDDEN GROUNDS: THE CASE AGAINST EMPLOYMENT DISCRIMINATION LAWS (Cambridge, Mass.: Harvard U.P. 1992).

Epstein, Richard A., *In Defense of the Contract at Will*, 51 U. CHI. L. REV. 947 (1984).

Estlund, Cynthia L., *The Changing Workplace as a Locus of Integration in a Diverse Society*, 2000 COLUM. BUS. L. REV. 331 (2000).

Estlund, Cynthia L., *Freedom of Expression in the Workplace and the Problem of Discriminatory Harassment*, 75 TEX. L. REV. 687 (1997).

Estlund, Cynthia L., *Free Speech and Due Process in the Workplace*, 71 IND. L.J. 101 (1995).

Estlund, Cynthia L., *Work and Family: How Women's Progress at Work (and Employment Discrimination Law) May Be Transforming the Family*, 21 COMP. LAB. L. & POL'Y J. 467 (2000).

Estlund, Cynthia L., *Working Together: The Workplace, Civil Society, and the Law*, 89 GEO. L.J. 1 (2000).

Estlund, Cynthia L., *The Workplace in a Racially Diverse Society: Preliminary Thoughts on the Role of Labor and Employment Law*, 1 U. PA. J. LAB. & EMP. L. 49 (1998).

Estlund, Cynthia L., *Wrongful Discharge Protections in an At-Will World*, 74 TEX. L. REV. 1655 (1996).

Estreicher, Samuel, *Employee Involvement and the "Company Union" Prohibition: The Case for Partial Repeal of Section 8(a)(2) of the NLRA*, 69 N.Y.U. L. REV. 125 (1994).

Estreicher, Samuel, *Labor Law Reform in a World of Competitive Product Markets*, 69 CHI.-KENT L. REV. 3 (1993).

FANTASIA, RICK, CULTURES OF SOLIDARITY: CONSCIOUSNESS, ACTION, AND CONTEMPORARY AMERICAN WORKERS (Berkeley: U. Cal. Press 1988).

Farley, Reynolds & William H. Frey, *Changes in the Segregation of Whites from Blacks during the 1980s: Small Steps toward a More Integrated Society*, 59 AM. SOC. REV. 23 (1994).

FEDERAL GLASS CEILING COMM'N, U.S. DEP'T OF LABOR, GOOD FOR BUSINESS: MAKING FULL USE OF THE NATION'S HUMAN CAPITAL (1995).

Fineman, Martha, *Masking Dependency: The Political Role of Family Rhetoric*, 81 VA. L. REV. 2181 (1998).

Forbath, William E., *The Ambiguities of Free Labor: Labor and the Law in the Gilded Age*, 1985 WIS. L. REV. 767.

Forbath, William E., *Caste, Class, and Equal Citizenship*, 98 MICH. L. REV. 1 (1999).

Forbath, William E., *Habermas's Constitution: A History, Guide, and Critique*, 23 LAW & SOC. INQUIRY 969 (1998).

FORBATH, WILLIAM E., LAW AND THE SHAPING OF THE AMERICAN LABOR MOVEMENT (Cambridge, Mass.: Harvard U.P. 1991).

FORBES, H. D., ETHNIC CONFLICT: COMMERCE, CULTURE, AND THE CONTACT HYPOTHESIS (New Haven: Yale U.P. 1997).

FOX , ALAN, BEYOND CONTRACT: WORK, POWER, AND TRUST RELATIONS (London: Faber 1974).

Franke, Katherine M., *The Central Mistake of Sex Discrimination Law: The Disaggregation of Sex from Gender*, 144 U. PA. L. REV. 1 (1995).

Freeman, Richard B., *Contraction and Expansion: The Divergence of Private Sector and Public Sector Unionism in the United States*, in RICHARD FREEMAN, LABOR MARKETS IN ACTION: ESSAYS IN EMPIRICAL ECONOMICS 221 (Cambridge, Mass.: Harvard U.P. 1989).

Freeman, Richard B. & Morris M. Kleiner, *Employer Behavior in the Face of Union Organizing Drives*, 43 INDUS. & LAB. REL. REV. 351 (1990).

FREEMAN, RICHARD B. & JAMES MEDOFF, WHAT DO UNIONS DO? (New York: Basic Books 1984).

FREEMAN, RICHARD B. & JOEL ROGERS, WHAT WORKERS WANT (Ithaca, N.Y.: Cornell U.P. 1999).

FRIEDMAN, MILTON, CAPITALISM AND FREEDOM (Chicago: U. Chicago Press 1962).

Friesen, Jane, *Alternative Economic Perspectives on the Use of Labor Market Policies to Redress the Gender Gap in Compensation*, 82 GEO. L.J. 31 (1994).

FUCINI, JOSEPH & SUZY FUCINI, WORKING FOR THE JAPANESE: INSIDE MAZDA'S AMERICAN AUTO PLANT (New York: Free Press 1990).

FUKUYAMA, FRANCIS, TRUST: THE SOCIAL VIRTUES AND THE CREATION OF PROSPERITY (New York: Free Press 1995).

FULLWOOD, SAM III, WAKING FROM THE DREAM: MY LIFE IN THE BLACK MIDDLE CLASS (New York: Anchor 1996).

Gaertner, Samuel L. & John F. Dovidio, *The Aversive Form of Racism*, in PREJUDICE, DISCRIMINATION, AND RACISM 61 (John F. Dovidio & Samuel L. Gaertner eds., Orlando: Academic Press 1986).

Gallup Poll Social Audit on Black/White Relations in the United States, Executive Summary (1999), *available at* http://www.gallup.com/poll/socialaudits/sa970610.asp.

GEAGIN, JOE R. & MELVIN P. SIKES, LIVING WITH RACISM: THE BLACK MIDDLE-CLASS EXPERIENCE (Boston: Beacon Press 1994).

GELLNER, ERNEST, CONDITIONS OF LIBERTY: CIVIL SOCIETY AND ITS RIVALS (London: Hamish Hamilton 1992).

GETMAN, JULIUS, THE BETRAYAL OF LOCAL 14: PAPERWORKERS, POLITICS, AND PERMANENT REPLACEMENTS (Ithaca, N.Y.: Cornell U.P. 1998).

Gilson, Ronald & Mark Roe, *Lifetime Employment and the Evolution of Japanese Corporate Governance*, 99 COLUM. L. REV. 508 (1999).

GINZBERG, ELI, THE UNEMPLOYED (New York: Harper & Bros. 1943).

Godard, John, *High Performance and the Transformation of Work: The Implications of Alternative Work Practices for the Experience and Outcomes of Work*, 54 INDUS. & LAB. REL. REV. 776 (2001).

Goldin, Claudia, *Monitoring Costs and Occupational Segregation by Sex: A Historical Analysis*, 4 J. LAB. ECON. 1 (1986).

Gottesman, Michael, *In Despair, Starting Over: Imagining a Labor Law for Unorganized Workers*, 69 CHI.-KENT L. REV. 59 (1993).

Granovetter, Mark S., *The Strength of Weak Ties*, 78 AM. J. SOC. 1360 (1978).

Greeley, Andrew, *The Other Civic America: Religion and Social Capital*, 32 AM. PROSPECT 68 (1997).

Greenawalt, Kent, *Title VII and Religious Liberty*, 33 LOY. U. CHI. L.J. 1 (2001).

GREENBERG, EDWARD S., WORKPLACE DEMOCRACY: THE POLITICAL EFFECTS OF PARTICIPATION (Ithaca, N.Y.: Cornell U.P. 1986).

Greene, Jay P., *A Meta-analysis of the Rossell and Baker Review of Bilingual Education Research*, 21 BILINGUAL RESEARCH JOURNAL (1997), *available at* http://brj.asu.edu/archives/23v21/articles/art1.html.

Gruber, James E., *The Impact of Male Work Environments and Organizational Policies on Women's Experiences of Sexual Harassment*, 12 GENDER & SOC'Y 301 (1998).

GUINIER, LANI & GERALD TORRES, THE MINER'S CANARY: ENLISTING RACE, RESISTING POWER, TRANSFORMING DEMOCRACY (Cambridge, Mass.: Harvard U.P. 2002).

GUTEK, BARBARA, SEX AND THE WORKPLACE: THE IMPACT OF SEXUAL BEHAVIOR AND HARASSMENT ON WOMEN, MEN AND ORGANIZATIONS (San Francisco: Jossey Bass 1985).

Gutmann, Amy, *Freedom of Association: An Introductory Essay*, in FREEDOM OF ASSOCIATION (Amy Gutmann, ed., Princeton, N.J.: Princeton U. Press 1998).

HABERMAS, JÜRGEN, BETWEEN FACTS AND NORMS (Cambridge: Polity Press 1996).

HACKER, ANDREW, TWO NATIONS: BLACK AND WHITE, SEPARATE, HOSTILE, UNEQUAL (New York: Scribner's 1992).

Hagen, Randi L. & Arnold Kahn, *Discrimination against Competent Women*, 5 J. APP. SOC. PSYCH. 362 (1975).

Hamilton, D., *Some Thoughts on the Cognitive Approach*, in COGNITIVE PROCESSES IN STEREOTYPING AND INTERGROUP BEHAVIOR 333 (D. Hamilton ed., Hillsdale, N.J.: L. Erlbaum Associates 1981).

Heckman, James J. & J. Hoult Verkerke, *Racial Disparity and Employment Discrimination Law: An Economic Perspective*, 8 YALE L. & POL'Y REV. 276 (1990).

Henrich, Joseph et al., *In Search of Homo Economicus: Behavioral Experiments in 15 Small-Scale Societies*, 91 AMER. ECON. REV. 73 (2001).

Herek, Gregory M. & John P. Capitanio, *Some of My Best Friends: Intergroup Contact, Con-*

cealable Stigma, and Heterosexuals' Attitudes toward Gay Men and Lesbians, 22 PER-SONALITY & SOC. PSYCHOL. BULL. 412 (1996).

Herek, Gregory M. & Eric K. Glunt, *Interpersonal Contact and Heterosexuals' Attitudes toward Gay Men: Results from a National Survey*, 30 J. SEX RES. 239 (1993).

Hills, Roderick M., Jr., *Romancing the Town: Why We (Still) Need a Democratic Defense of City Power*, 113 HARV. L. REV. 2009 (2000).

HIRSCHMAN, ALBERT, EXIT, VOICE, AND LOYALTY (Cambridge, Mass.: Harvard U.P. 1970).

HIRSCHMAN, ALBERT, THE PASSIONS AND THE INTERESTS: POLITICAL ARGUMENTS FOR CAPITALISM BEFORE ITS TRIUMPH (Princeton, N.J.: Princeton U.P. 1977).

HIRSCHMAN, ALBERT, RIVAL VIEWS OF MARKET SOCIETY (New York: Viking 1986).

HOCHSCHILD, ARLIE RUSSELL, THE TIME BIND: WHEN WORK BECOMES HOME AND HOME BECOMES WORK (New York: Metropolitan Books 1997).

Holmes, Steven A., *Which Man's Army*, in THE NEW YORK TIMES, HOW RACE IS LIVED IN AMERICA 41 (New York: Times Books 2001).

Huckfeldt, Robert et al., *Political Environments, Cohesive Social Groups, and the Communication of Public Opinion*, 39 AM. J. POL. SCI. 1025 (1995).

Hyde, Alan, *Employee Caucus: A Key Institution in the Emerging System of Employment Law*, 69 CHI.-KENT L. REV. 149 (1993).

HYDE, ALAN, WORKING IN SILICON VALLEY (Armonk, N.Y.: M. E. Sharpe 2003).

Hylton, Maria O'Brien, *The Case against Regulating the Market for Contingent Employment*, 52 WASH. & LEE L. REV. 849 (1995).

Ingber, Stanley, *Rediscovering the Communal Worth of Individual Rights: The First Amendment in Institutional Contexts*, 69 TEX. L. REV. 1 (1990).

Issacharoff, Samuel, *Contracting for Employment: The Limited Return of the Common Law*, 74 TEX. L. REV. 1783 (1996).

Issacharoff, Samuel & Elyse Rosenblum, *Women and the Workplace: Accommodating the Demands of Pregnancy*, 91 COLUM. L. REV. 2154 (1994).

JACKMAN, MARY R., THE VELVET GLOVE: PATERNALISM AND CONFLICT IN GENDER, CLASS, AND RACE RELATIONS (Berkeley: U. Cal. Press 1994).

Jackman, Mary R. & Marie Crane, *"Some of My Best Friends Are Black . . .": Interracial Friendship and Whites' Racial Attitudes*, 50 PUB. OPINION Q. 459 (1986).

Jacoby, Sanford, *Are Career Jobs Headed for Extinction?*, 42 CAL. MGMT. REV. 123 (1999).

Jacoby, Sanford, *Current Prospects for Employee Representation in the U.S.: Old Wine in New Bottles?*, 16 J. LAB. RES. 387 (1995).

Jacoby, Sanford M., *Melting into Air? Downsizing, Job Stability, and the Future of Work*, 76 CHI.-KENT L. REV. 1195 (2000).

Jacoby, Sanford M., *Reply: Premature Reports of Demise*, 42 CAL. MGMT. REV. 168 (1999).

JAHODA, MARIE, PAUL LAZARSFELD & HANS ZEISEL, MARIENTHAL: THE SOCIOGRAPHY OF AN UNEMPLOYED COMMUNITY (Chicago: Aldine-Atherton, 1933 [1971]).

Jargowsky, Paul A., *Take the Money and Run: Economic Segregation in U.S. Metropolitan Areas*, 61 AM. SOC. REV. 984 (1996).

Jehn, Karen A., *Managing Workteam Diversity, Conflict, and Productivity: A New Form of Organizing in the Twenty-first Century Workplace*, 1 U. PA. J. LAB. & EMPL. L. 473 (1998).

JOHN J. HELDRICH CENTER FOR WORKFORCE DEVELOPMENT, A WORKPLACE DIVIDED: HOW AMERICANS VIEW DISCRIMINATION AND RACE ON THE JOB (New Brunswick, N.J.: Rutgers U.P. 2002).

Johnson, Alex M., Bid Whist, Tonk, *and* United States v. Fordice*: Why Integrationism Fails African-Americans Again*, 81 CAL. L. REV. 1401 (1993).

Johnson, Alex M., Jr., *The Underrepresentation of Minorities in the Legal Profession: A Critical Race Theorist's Perspective*, 95 MICH. L. REV. 1005 (1997).

Jolls, Christine, *Is There a Glass Ceiling?*, 25 HARV. WOMEN'S L.J. 1 (2002).

Kamiat, Walter, *Strikers and Replacements: A Labor Union Perspective*, in PROCEEDINGS OF NEW YORK UNIVERSITY 43RD ANNUAL NATIONAL CONFERENCE ON LABOR 34 (Bruno Stein ed., 1990).

Kandel, William L., *Affirmative Action and the Glass Ceiling: Contract Compliance and Litigation Avoidance*, EMPLOYEE RELATIONS L.J., Autumn 1995, 109.

KANTOR, ROSABETH MOSS, MEN AND WOMEN OF THE CORPORATION (2d ed., New York: Basic Books 1993).

Karst, Kenneth L., *The Coming Crisis of Work in Constitutional Perspective*, 82 CORNELL L. REV. 523 (1997).

Karst, Kenneth L., *Private Discrimination and Public Responsibility:* Patterson *in Context*, 1989 SUP. CT. REV. 1.

Karst, Kenneth L., *The Pursuit of Manhood and the Desegregation of the Armed Forces*, 38 UCLA L. REV. 499 (1991).

Karst, Kenneth, *The Freedom of Intimate Association*, 89 YALE L.J. 624 (1980).

Kateb, George, *The Value of Association*, in FREEDOM OF ASSOCIATION 35 (Amy Gutmann ed., Princeton, N.J.: Princeton U.P. 1998).

KATZ, HARRY C. & OWEN DARBISHIRE, CONVERGING DIVERGENCES: WORLDWIDE CHANGES IN EMPLOYMENT SYSTEMS (Ithaca, N.Y.: ILR Press 2000).

KENNEDY, RANDALL, INTERRACIAL INTIMACIES: SEX, MARRIAGE, IDENTITY, AND ADOPTION (New York: Pantheon 2003).

Kim, Pauline, *Bargaining with Imperfect Information: A Study of Worker Perceptions of Legal Protection in an At-Will World*, 83 CORNELL L. REV. 105 (1997).

Kim, Pauline, *Norms, Learning, and Law: Exploring the Influences on Workers' Legal Knowledge*, 1999 U. ILL. L. REV. 447.

Klare, Karl E., *Judicial Deradicalization of the Wagner Act and the Origins of Modern Legal Consciousness, 1937–1941*, 62 MINN. L. REV. 265 (1978).

KOCHAN, THOMAS & PAUL OSTERMAN, THE MUTUAL GAINS ENTERPRISE (Boston: Harvard Bus. School Press 1994).

KOCHAN, THOMAS A., HARRY C. KATZ, & ROBERT B. MCKERSIE, THE TRANSFORMATION OF AMERICAN INDUSTRIAL RELATIONS (New York: Basic Books 1986).

Kohler, Thomas C., *Civic Virtue at Work: Unions as Seedbeds of the Civic Virtues*, 36 B.C. L. REV. 279 (1995).

Kohler, Thomas C., *Individualism and Communitarianism at Work*, 1993 BYU L. REV. 727.

KORNBLUM, WILLIAM, BLUE COLLAR COMMUNITY (Chicago: U. of Chicago Press 1974).

Kornhauser, Lewis A. & Richard L. Revesz, *Legal Education and Entry into the Legal Profession: The Role of Race, Gender, and Educational Debt*, 70 N.Y.U. L. REV. 829 (1995).

Krieger, Linda H., *Civil Rights Perestroika: Intergroup Relations after Affirmative Action*, 86 CAL. L. REV. 1251 (1998).

Krieger, Linda H., *The Content of Our Categories: A Cognitive Bias Approach to Discrimination and Equal Employment Opportunity*, 47 STAN. L. REV. 1161 (1995).

LANE, ROBERT, THE MARKET EXPERIENCE (Cambridge: Cambridge U.P. 1991).

Lawrence, Charles R., III, *The Id, the Ego, and Equal Protection: Reckoning with Unconscious Racism*, 39 STAN. L. REV. 317 (1987).

Leduff, Charlie, *At a Slaughterhouse, Some Things Never Die*, in NEW YORK TIMES, HOW RACE IS LIVED IN AMERICA 97 (New York: Times Books 2001).

Lester, Gillian, *Careers and Contingency*, 51 STAN. L. REV. 73 (1998).

LINDEMANN, BARBARA & DAVID D. KADUE, SEXUAL HARASSMENT IN EMPLOYMENT LAW (Washington, D.C.: BNA Books 1992).

Llewellyn, Karl, *What Law Cannot Do for Inter-Racial Peace*, 3 VILL. L. REV. 30 (1957).

Loury, Glenn, *A Dynamic Theory of Racial Income Differences, in* WOMEN, MINORITIES, AND EMPLOYMENT DISCRIMINATION (Phyllis Ann Wallace & Annette A. LaMond eds., Lexington, Mass.: Lexington Books 1977).

MacCormick, Neil, *Institutions and Laws Again*, 77 TEX. L. REV. 1429 (1999).

Macedo, Stephen, ed., DELIBERATIVE POLITICS: ESSAYS ON *DEMOCRACY AND DISAGREEMENT* (New York: Oxford U.P. 1999).

MACKINNON, CATHARINE, SEXUAL HARASSMENT OF WORKING WOMEN: A CASE OF SEX DISCRIMINATION (San Francisco: Jossey-Bass 1979).

Mahoney, Martha, The Anti-Transformation Cases, September 16, 1999 (unpublished manuscript on file with author).

Malamud, Deborah C., *Engineering the Middle Classes: Class Line-Drawing in New Deal Hours Legislation*, 96 MICH. L. REV. 2212 (1998).

Malin, Martin H., *Protecting the Whistleblower from Retaliatory Discharge*, 16 U. MICH. J.L. REFORM 277 (1983).

Marcus-Newhall, Amy et al., *Cross-cutting Category Membership with Role Assignment: A Means of Reducing Intergroup Bias*, 32 BRIT. J. OF SOC. PSYCH. 125 (1993).

Marks, Stephen R., *Intimacy in the Public Realm: The Case of Co-workers*, 72 SOCIAL FORCES 843 (1994).

MARSHALL, F. RAY, THE NEGRO AND ORGANIZED LABOR (New York: Wiley 1965).

Marshall, F. Ray, *The Negro in Southern Unions, in* THE NEGRO AND THE AMERICAN LABOR MOVEMENT 128 (Julius Jacobson ed., Garden City, N.Y.: Anchor Books 1968).

Marx, Karl, *Critique of the Gotha Programme, in* BASIC WRITINGS ON POLITICS AND PHILOSOPHY 119 (Lewis S. Feuer ed., Garden City, N.Y.: Doubleday 1959).

MASSEY, DOUGLAS S. & NANCY A. DENTON, AMERICAN APARTHEID: SEGREGATION AND THE MAKING OF THE UNDERCLASS (Cambridge, Mass.: Harvard U.P. 1993).

McCue, Kristin & Manuelita Ureta, *Women in the Workplace: Recent Economic Trends*, 4 TEX. J. OF WOMEN & L. 125 (1995).

McUsic, Molly S. & Michael Selmi, *Postmodern Unions: Identity Politics in the Workplace (An Essay)*, 82 IOWA L. REV. 1339 (1997).

Miller, Katherine I. and Peter R. Monge, *Participation, Satisfaction, and Productivity: A Meta-analytic Review*, 29 ACAD. OF MGMT. J. 727 (1986).

Miller, Norman & Marilynn B. Brewer, eds., GROUPS IN CONTACT: THE PSYCHOLOGY OF DESEGREGATION (Orlando: Academic Press 1984).

MOODY, KIM, WORKERS IN A LEAN WORLD: UNIONS IN THE INTERNATIONAL ECONOMY (New York: Verso 1997).

MOSKOS, CHARLES C. & JOHN SIBLEY BUTLER, ALL THAT WE CAN BE: BLACK LEADERSHIP AND RACIAL INTEGRATION THE ARMY WAY (New York: Basic Books 1996).

MYRDAL, GUNNAR, AN AMERICAN DILEMMA: THE NEGRO PROBLEM AND MODERN DEMOCRACY (New York: Harper & Brothers 1944).

NEUMARK, DAVID, ED., ON THE JOB: IS LONG-TERM EMPLOYMENT A THING OF THE PAST? (New York: Russell Sage Foundation 2000).

Neumark, David & Wendy A. Stock, The Effects of Race and Sex Discrimination Laws, NBER Working Paper Series, Working Paper 8215 (2001), *available at* http://www.nber.org/papers/w8215.

ORFIELD, GARY ET AL., DISMANTLING DESEGREGATION: THE QUIET REVERSAL OF *BROWN v. BOARD OF EDUCATION* (New York: New Press 1996).

Osborn, Richard N. & William M. Vickers, *Sex Stereotypes: An Artifact in Leader Behavior and Subordinate Satisfaction Analyses*, 19 ACAD. OF MGMT. J. 439 (1976).

Oshige, Miranda, Note, *What's Sex Got to Do with It?*, 47 STAN. L. REV. 565 (1995).

Oster, Sharon M., *Is There a Policy Problem?: The Gender Wage Gap*, 82 GEO. L.J. 109 (1994).

Osterman, Paul, *Work Reorganization in an Era of Restructuring: Trends in Diffusion and Effects on Employee Welfare*, 53 INDUS. & LAB. REL. REV. 179 (2000).

Palmer, Helen T. & Jo Ann Lee, *Female Workers' Acceptance in Traditionally Male-Dominated Blue-Collar Jobs*, 22 SEX ROLES 607 (1990).

Parker, Mike & Jane Slaughter, *Unions and Management by Stress, in* LEAN WORK: EMPOWERMENT AND EXPLOITATION IN THE GLOBAL AUTO INDUSTRY (Steve Babson ed., Detroit: Wayne State U.P. 1995).

PATEMAN, CAROLE, PARTICIPATION AND DEMOCRATIC THEORY (Cambridge: Cambridge U.P. 1970).

PATTERSON, ORLANDO, THE ORDEAL OF INTEGRATION: PROGRESS AND RESENTMENT IN AMERICA'S "RACIAL" CRISIS (Washington, D.C.: Civitas/Counterpoint 1997).

PAUL, ELLEN FRANKEL, EQUITY AND GENDER: THE COMPARABLE WORTH DEBATE (New Brunswick, N.J.: Transaction 1989).

Perea, Juan F. Perea, *Strange Fruit: Harassment and the First Amendment*, 29 U.C. DAVIS L. REV. 875 (1996).

PERLMAN, RICHARD & MAUREEN PIKE, SEX DISCRIMINATION IN THE LABOUR MARKET: THE CASE FOR COMPARABLE WORTH (New York: Manchester U.P. 1994).

Pettigrew, Thomas F., *Intergroup Contact Theory*, 49 ANN. REV. PSYCH. 65 (1998).

PETTIGREW, THOMAS F., RACIALLY SEPARATE OR TOGETHER? (New York: McGraw-Hill 1971)

PINKNEY, ALPHONSO, THE MYTH OF BLACK PROGRESS (New York: Cambridge U.P. 1984).

PIORE, MICHAEL & CHARLES SABEL, THE SECOND INDUSTRIAL DIVIDE: POSSIBILITIES FOR PROSPERITY (New York: Basic Books 1984).

Poarch, Maria T., *Ties that Bind: US Suburban Residents on the Social and Civic Dimensions of Work*, 1 COMMUNITY, WORK, & FAMILY 125 (1998).

Portes, Alejandro & Patricia Landolt, *The Downside of Social Capital*, 26 AM. PROSPECT 18 (1996).

PORTES, ALEJANDRO & RUBÉN G. RUMBAUT, LEGACIES: THE STORY OF THE IMMIGRANT SECOND GENERATION (Berkeley: U. Cal. Press 2001).

Post, Robert C., *Racist Speech, Democracy, and the First Amendment*, 32 WM. & MARY L. REV. 267 (1991).

Powell, John A., *Living and Learning: Linking Housing and Education*, 80 MINN. L. REV. 749 (1996).

Powers, Daniel A. & Christopher G. Ellison, *Interracial Contact and Black Racial Attitudes: The Contact Hypothesis and Selectivity Bias*, 74 SOC. FORCES 205 (1995).

Putnam, Robert D., *Bowling Alone: America's Declining Social Capital*, 6 J. DEMOCRACY 65 (1995).

PUTNAM, ROBERT D., BOWLING ALONE: THE COLLAPSE AND REVIVAL OF AMERICAN COMMUNITY (New York: Simon & Schuster 2000).

PUTNAM, ROBERT D., MAKING DEMOCRACY WORK: CIVIC TRADITIONS IN MODERN ITALY (Princeton, N.J.: Princeton U.P. 1993).

Putnam, Robert D., *The Strange Disappearance of Civic America*, 24 AM. PROSPECT 34 (1996).

Rabin, Robert J., *The Role of Unions in the Rights-Based Workplace*, 25 U.S.F. L. REV. 169 (1991).

Rabinowitz, Randy S. & Mark M. Hager, *Designing Health and Safety: Workplace Hazard Regulation in the United States and Canada*, 33 CORNELL INT'L L.J. 373 (2000).

Rhode, Deborah L., *Occupational Inequality*, 1988 DUKE L.J. 1207.

RIFKIN, JEREMY, THE END OF WORK: THE DECLINE OF THE GLOBAL LABOR FORCE AND THE DAWN OF THE POST-MARKET ERA (New York: G.P. Putnam's Sons 1995).

RINEHART, JAMES, CHRIS HUXLEY, & DAVID ROBERTSON, JUST ANOTHER CAR FACTORY? LEAN PRODUCTION AND ITS DISCONTENTS (Ithaca, N.Y.: ILR Press 1997).

ROBINSON, JOHN P. & GEOFFREY GODBEY, TIME FOR LIFE: THE SURPRISING WAYS AMERICANS USE THEIR TIME (University Park: Penn. State U.P. 1997).

Romm, Stuart, *Layoffs: Principles and Practices*, in LOCAL JUSTICE IN AMERICA 153 (Jon Elster, ed., New York: Russell Sage Foundation 1995).

Rosenblum, Nancy L., *Compelled Association: Public Standing, Self-Respect, and the Dynamic of Exclusion*, in FREEDOM OF ASSOCIATION 76 (Amy Gutmann ed., Princeton, N.J.: Princeton U.P. 1998).

ROSENBLUM, NANCY L., MEMBERSHIP AND MORALS (Princeton, N.J.: Princeton U.P. 1998).

Rosenthal, Patrice, *Gender and Managers' Causal Attributions for Subordinate Performance: A Field Story*, 34 SEX ROLES 1 (1996).

Rossell, Christine H. & Keith Baker, *The Educational Effectiveness of Bilingual Education*, RESEARCH IN THE TEACHING OF ENGLISH 30 (1996).

Rutherglen, George, *The Theory of Comparable Worth as a Remedy for Discrimination*, 82 GEO. L. J. 135 (1993).

Sabel, Charles F., *Constitutional Ordering in Historical Context*, in GAMES IN HIERARCHIES AND NETWORKS 114 (Fritz Scharpf ed., Boulder, Colo.: Westview Press 1993).

Sabel, Charles, *Flexible Specialization and the Re-Emergence of Regional Economies*, in REVERSING INDUSTRIAL DECLINE? INDUSTRIAL STRUCTURE AND POLICY IN BRITAIN AND HER COMPETITORS 17 (Paul Hirst & Jonathan Zeitlin eds., New York: St. Martin's Press 1989).

Saguaro Seminar on Civic Engagement in America, Social Capital Community Benchmark Survey (Cambridge, Mass.: John F. Kennedy School of Government, Harvard U. 2001), *available at* http://www.cfsv.org/communitysurvey/results3.html.

Sander, Richard H., Comment, *Individual Rights and Demographic Realities: The Problem of Fair Housing*, 82 Nw. U. L. REV. 874 (1988).

Schauer, Frederick, *Discourse and its Discontents*, 72 NOTRE DAME L. REV. 1309 (1997).

SCHLOSSER, ERIC, FAST FOOD NATION: THE DARK SIDE OF THE ALL-AMERICAN MEAL (Boston: Houghton Mifflin 2001).

SCHOR, JULIET B., THE OVERWORKED AMERICAN: THE UNEXPECTED DECLINE OF LEISURE (New York: Basic Books 1991).

SCHUCK, PETER, DIVERSITY IN AMERICA: KEEPING GOVERNMENT AT A SAFE DISTANCE (Cambridge, Mass.: Harvard U.P. 2003).

Schudson, Michael, *What If Civic Life Didn't Die?*, AM. PROSPECT, March/April 1996.

Schultz, Vicki, *Reconceptualizing Sexual Harassment*, 107 YALE L.J. 1683 (1998).

Schultz, Vicki, *The Sanitized Workplace*, 112 YALE L.J.—(forthcoming 2003).

Schultz, Vicki, *Telling Stories about Women and Work: Judicial Interpretations of Sex Segregation in the Workplace in Title VII Cases Raising the Lack of Interest Argument*, 103 HARV. L. REV. 1750 (1990).

Schwab, Stewart, *The Diversity of Contingent Workers and the Need for Nuanced Policy*, 52 WASH. & LEE L. REV. 915 (1995).

Schwab, Stewart, *Life-Cycle Justice: Accommodating Just Cause and Employment at Will*, 92 U. MICH. L. REV. 8 (1993).

Schweizer, Steven L., *Participation, Workplace Democracy, and the Problem of Representative Government*, 27 POLITY 359 (1995).

Seidenfeld, Mark, *Empowering Stakeholders: Limits on Collaboration as the Basis for Flexible Regulation*, 41 WM. & MARY L. REV. 411 (2000).

Seidenfeld, Mark, *Some Jurisprudential Perspectives on Employment Sex Discrimination Law,* 21 RUTGERS L. REV. 269 (1990).

Selmi, Michael, *Family Leave and the Gender Wage Gap,* 78 N. CAR. L. REV. 707 (2000).

Selmi, Michael, *Public vs. Private Enforcement of Civil Rights: The Case of Housing and Employment,* 45 UCLA L. REV. 1401 (1998).

SHELLENBARGER, SUE, WORK AND FAMILY: ESSAYS FROM THE "WORK AND FAMILY" COLUMN OF THE WALL STREET JOURNAL (New York: Ballentine 1999).

Sigelman, Lee & Susan Welch, *The Contact Hypothesis Revisited: Black–White Interaction and Positive Racial Attitudes,* 71 SOC. FORCES 781 (1993).

Sigelman, Lee et al., *Making Contact? Black–White Social Interaction in an Urban Setting,* 101 AM. J. SOC. 1306 (1996).

Skocpol, Theda, *Unravelling from Above,* 25 AM. PROSPECT 20 (1996).

Skocpol, Theda & Morris P. Fiorina, *Making Sense of the Civic Engagement Debate, in* CIVIC ENGAGEMENT IN AMERICAN DEMOCRACY 13 (Theda Skocpol & Morris P. Fiorina eds., Washington, D.C: Brookings 1999).

SMITH, VICKI, CROSSING THE GREAT DIVIDE: WORKER RISK AND OPPORTUNITY IN THE NEW ECONOMY (Ithaca, N.Y.: ILR Press 2001).

Smolla, Rodney A., *Rethinking First Amendment Assumptions about Racist and Sexist Speech,* 47 WASH. & LEE L. REV. 171 (1990).

SNIDERMAN, PAUL M. & EDWARD G. CARMINES, REACHING BEYOND RACE (Cambridge, Mass.: Harvard U.P. 1997).

SORENSEN, ELAINE, COMPARABLE WORTH: IS IT A WORTHY POLICY? (Princeton, N.J.: Princeton U. Press 1994).

Soskice, David, *Divergent Production Regimes; Coordinated and Uncoordinated Market Economies, in* CONTINUITY AND CHANGE IN CONTEMPORARY CAPITALISM (H. Kitscheldt, P. Lange & G. Marks eds., New York: Cambridge U.P. 1999).

Stone, Katherine Van Wezel, *The New Psychological Contract: Implications of the Changing Workplace for Labor and Employment Law,* 48 UCLA L. REV. 519 (2001).

Stone, Katherine Van Wezel, *The Post-War Paradigm in American Labor Law,* 90 YALE L.J. 1509 (1981).

Straits, Bruce C., *Bringing Strong Ties Back In: Interpersonal Gateways to Political Information and Influence,* 55 PUBL. OP. Q. 432 (1991).

Sturm, Susan, *Second Generation Employment Discrimination: A Structural Approach,* 101 COLUM. L. REV. 458 (2001).

Sturm, Susan, *Race, Gender, and the Law in the Twenty-first Century Workplace: Some Preliminary Observations,* 1 U. PA. J. OF LAB. & EMPL. L. 639 (1998).

Sullivan, Kathleen M., *Defining Democracy Down,* 33 AM. PROSPECT 91(1998).

Summers, Clyde W., *A Structured Exception to Section 8(a)(2),* 69 CHI-KENT L. REV. 129 (1993).

Summers, Clyde W., *Individual Protection against Unjust Dismissal: Time for a Statute,* 62 VA. L. REV. 481 (1976).

Summers, Clyde W., *The Privatization of Personal Freedoms and Enrichment of Democracy: Some Lessons from Labor Law,* 1986 U. ILL. L. REV. 689.

Tajfel, Henri et al., *Social Categorization and Intergroup Behaviour,* 1 EUR. J. SOC. PSYCHOL. 149 (1971).

Tallichet, Suzanne E., *Gendered Relations in the Mines and the Division of Labor Underground,* 9 GENDER & SOC. 697 (1995).

THERNSTROM, STEPHAN & ABIGAIL M. THERNSTROM, AMERICA IN BLACK AND WHITE: ONE NATION, INDIVISIBLE (New York: Simon & Schuster 1997).

Thomas, David A. & Robin D. Ely, *Cultural Diversity at Work: The Effects of Diversity Perspectives on Work Group Processes and Outcomes,* 46 ADMIN. SCI. Q. 229 (2001).

Thomas, David A. & Robin D. Ely, *Making Differences Matter: A New Paradigm for Managing Diversity*, HARV. BUS. REV. 79 (1996).

TOCQUEVILLE, ALEXIS DE, DEMOCRACY IN AMERICA (George Lawrence trans., New York: Harper Perennial 1988).

TURNER, MARGERY A. ET AL., OPPORTUNITIES DENIED, OPPORTUNITIES DIMINISHED: RACIAL DISCRIMINATION IN HIRING (Washington, D.C.: Urban Institute Press 1991).

Tushnet, Mark, *The Constitution of Civil Society*, 75 CHI.-KENT L. REV. 379 (2000).

U.S. DEP'T OF LABOR, GOOD FOR BUSINESS: MAKING FULL USE OF THE NATION'S HUMAN CAPITAL: A FACT-FINDING REPORT OF THE FEDERAL GLASS CEILING COMMISSION, DAILY LAB. REP., Mar. 17, 1995 (Special Supp. DLR No. 52).

Verba, Sidney et al., *The Big Tilt: Participatory Inequality in America*, 32 AM. PROSPECT 74 (1997).

VERBA, SIDNEY ET AL., VOICE AND EQUALITY: CIVIC VOLUNTARISM IN AMERICAN POLITICS (Cambridge, Mass.: Harvard U.P. 1993).

Volokh, Eugene, *How Harassment Law Restricts Free Speech*, 47 RUTGERS L.J. 561 (1995).

Wachter, Michael L. & George M. Cohen, *The Law and Economics of Collective Bargaining: An Introduction and Application to the Problems of Subcontracting, Partial Closure, and Relocation*, 136 U. PA. L. REV. 1349 (1988).

Wall, Toby D. et al., *Outcomes of Autonomous Workgroups: A Long-Term Field Experiment*, 29 ACAD. OF MGMT. J. 280 (1986).

WALSHOK , MARY L., BLUE-COLLAR WOMEN: PIONEERS ON THE MALE FRONTIER (Garden City, N.Y.: Anchor Books 1981).

Warren, Samuel D. & Louis D. Brandeis, *The Right to Privacy*, 4 HARV. L. REV. 193 (1890).

Watchman, Gregory R., *Safe and Sound: The Case for Safety and Health Committees under OSHA and the NLRA*, 4 CORNELL J.L. & PUB. POL'Y 65 (1994).

Wax, Amy L., *Discrimination as Accident*, 74 IND. L.J. 1129 (1999).

WEILER, PAUL C., GOVERNING THE WORKPLACE (Cambridge, Mass.: Harvard U.P. 1990).

Weiler, Paul C., *A Principled Reshaping of Labor Law for the Twenty-first Century*, 3 U. PA. J. LAB. & EMP. L. 177 (2001).

Weiler, Paul C., *Promises to Keep: Securing Workers' Rights to Self-Organization under the NRLA*, 96 HARV. L. REV. 1769 (1983).

Weiler, Paul C., *Striking a New Balance: Freedom of Contract and the Prospects for Union Representation*, 98 HARV. L. REV. 351 (1984).

WESTBROOK, ROBERT B., JOHN DEWEY AND AMERICAN DEMOCRACY (Ithaca, N.Y.: Cornell U.P. 1991).

Westbrook, Robert B., *Schools for Industrial Democrats: The Social Origins of John Dewey's Philosophy of Education*, 100 AM. J. OF EDUC. 401 (1992).

WHYTE ,WILLIAM H., JR., THE ORGANIZATION MAN (New York: Simon & Schuster 1956).

Wilkins, David B. & G. Mitu Gulati, *Reconceiving the Tournament of Lawyers: Tracking, Seeding, and Information Control in the Internal Labor Markets of Elite Law Firms*, 84 VA. L. REV. 1581 (1998).

WILLBORN, STEVEN L., STEWART J. SCHWAB & JOHN F. BURTON, JR., EMPLOYMENT LAW: CASES & MATERIALS (2d ed., Charlottesville, Va.: Lexis 1998).

Williams, Katherine Y. & Charles A. O'Reilly III, *Demography and Diversity in Organizations: A Review of 40 Years of Research*, 20 RESEARCH IN ORG. BEHAVIOR 77 (1998).

WILSON, WILLIAM JULIUS, THE BRIDGE OVER THE RACIAL DIVIDE: RISING INEQUALITY AND COALITION POLITICS (Berkeley: U. Cal. Press 1999).

WILSON, WILLIAM JULIUS, WHEN WORK DISAPPEARS: THE WORLD OF THE NEW URBAN POOR (New York: Alfred A. Knopf 1996).

Winkler, Anne E., *Earnings of Husbands and Wives in Dual-Earner Families*, 121 MONTHLY LAB. REV., Apr. 1998.

Wolfe, Alan, *Developing Civil Society: Can the Workplace Replace Bowling?*, 8 THE RESPONSIVE COMMUNITY 41 (1998).

WOLFE, ALAN, WHOSE KEEPER? SOCIAL SCIENCE AND MORAL OBLIGATION (Berkeley: U. of Cal. Press 1989).

Yelnosky, Michael J., *Title VII, Mediation, and Collective Action*, 1999 U. ILL. L. REV. 583 (1999).

YERGIN, DANIEL, THE COMMANDING HEIGHTS: THE BATTLE FOR THE WORLD ECONOMY (New York: Simon & Schuster 2002).

Yoshino, Kenji, *Covering*, 111 YALE L. J. 769 (2002).

Yoshino, Kenji, *Assimilationist Bias in Equal Protection: The Visibility Presumption and the Case of "Don't Ask, Don't Tell,"* 108 YALE L.J. 485 (1998).

Zatz, Noah D., *Beyond the Zero-Sum Game: Toward Title VII Protection for Intergroup Solidarity*, 77 IND. L. J. 63 (2002).

INDEX

Affirmative action, 16, 147–49, 175
African Americans. *See also*
  Employment discrimination; Racial
  integration; Racial segregation
  attitudes toward integration, 67–68,
  81–83
  discrimination against. *See*
  Employment discrimination
  economic status of, 63–64, 129
  interactions with whites. *See* Race
  relations at work
  occupational distribution, 63–64
  segregation. *See* Racial segregation
Alternative work practices. *See*
  Organization of work
Antidiscrimination law. *See*
  Employment, discrimination;
  Housing, discrimination
Army. *See* Military
Associational rights. *See* Freedom of
  association
Associations. *See also* Freedom of
  association; Social capital
  bonding associations, 107, 180
  bridging associations, 107–8, 180–81
  compelled association, 126–29
  Durkheim and, 111
  linking functions of, 13, 106
  secondary associations, 111
  "sword and shield" functions, 13, 106,
  126
  Tocqueville and, 105–09

value of, 105–08, 137, 177
voluntary associations, 8–9, 26, 106,
  127–29, 180–81
workplace associations. *See*
  Cooperation; Freedom of
  association; Sociability; Unions

Belonging, 6–7, 21, 28. *See also*
  Connectedness
Bias and stereotyping. *See also*
  Intergroup relations
  aversive racism, 77
  effects within organizations, 79–81,
  141–44
  gender bias, 85–87, 92–94
  litigation avoidance and, 152
  social psychology of, 77–83
  unconscious bias, 81–82
Bilingual education, 97
Black employees. *See* African Americans
Black-white interactions. *See* Race
  relations at work
Blue-collar workers. *See also* Low-wage
  workplace
  gender lines, interaction across, 89–
  90
  "lifetime employment" model, 41
  racial integration among, 11, 70–72
  unions. *See* Unions
Bonding associations. *See* Associations
Bowling Alone. See Putnam, Robert
Boy Scouts of America v. Dale, 127–28